Cloning Noah

A Novel by
Cheri Barton Ross

Copyright © 2015 Cheri Barton Ross
All rights reserved.

ISBN: 1508401373
ISBN 13: 9781508401377
Library of Congress Control Number: 2015909090
CreateSpace Independent Publishing Platform
North Charleston, South Carolina

For Carol Abrams

Who taught me that reinvention is a wonderful thing and led by an awe inspiring example.
I was blessed to know you.
Thank you for lighting the way ~

Santa Rosa, California
McDonald Avenue
Sunrise, Friday Morning

The weathered looking man hurries across the street to his parked Chevy truck. He hopes the John Deer cap pulled down low just above his steely blue eyes will do a good job of hiding his face in this upscale historic neighborhood. Unfortunately, going unseen isn't in the cards for him today. He looks up just in time to see a young teen girl peddling her bike quickly past him. She appears to not pay much attention to him but he can't be certain. As he turns to watch her he sees that she's focused on steering her bike, which is weighted down by a satchel of newspapers anchored to the handlebars of the orange cruiser. Her blonde braids fly out from under her matching bike helmet as she approaches the house that is known in Santa Rosa as the 'Hitchcock House' because it was used to film *Shadow of a Doubt*. The irony of this house being the one owned by the people the man hates isn't lost on him. The man turns his back towards his truck, swings open the door and climbs up into the cab. *What the hell is a kid doing delivering newspapers at this early hour? Didn't that job go to adults driving cars?* He questions and pulls the cab door shut. He steals a glance out of the rearview mirror and sees that the girl is clutching a folded newspaper in her right hand and gripping the handlebars with her left. His heart skips a beat as he watches the papergirl steer around the dirty black BMW parked in the street in front of the 'Hitchcock house.' *Shit, this is gonna be close.*

The BMW explodes knocking the girl off her bike sending her skidding across the pavement. Her limp body comes to a stop halfway down the street. The man jams the truck key into its ignition and glances into the mirror again. He sees pajama-clad neighbors appearing in windows and doorways of the Victorian houses lining the street. One by one the neighbors tentatively venture outside to get a better look at the rising flames and smoke.

Starting the ignition the man realizes he needs to get the hell out of there before anyone sees him and associates him with the car bomb he had set. For a brief moment he considers turning around and driving past the girl to make certain she's not dead. His view of the girl is now masked by smoke. He quickly decides that it's too risky to go to her. He's accomplished what he's come to do. *Besides, it's outta of my hands - it's all part of God's plan*, he thinks as he speeds out of the neighborhood.

The papergirl is helped to a sitting position by a portly man who has come to her aide. "Are you all right?" he asks. The girl responds with a cry. With a grunt, the portly man hoists her into his arms and carries her to his wife, who's quickly walking down the driveway of their home and clutching her bathrobe around her small frame. The portly man sets the girl down on his driveway. Emergency vehicles roll down the street and come to a stop in front of the wreckage. Men and women in uniforms climb out of the vehicles and go to work. The neighbors watch as a jet spray of water coming from the fire truck hose quenches the cars thirsty flames. The BMW symbol on the hood of the burning vehicle is still intact, although the rest of the car has become a burned shell of a wreck. Two EMT's attend the paper girl who is being comforted by the portly man's wife.

"Does anyone know who owns this Beemer?" a policeman inquires as he approaches the portly man and his wife. The portly man moves past the EMT's and the small group of anxious neighbors who surround them to address the officer.

"Belongs to Elliot Gaynor."

"Is he home?"

"No."

The portly man and the rest of the neighbors know that the Gaynors disappeared a while ago, soon after the stories and speculation began. No one knows if they are coming back. No one, that is, except for the scientist who cloned their son, Noah. It's now apparent, to all concerned, that they didn't leave because of the hateful accusations hurled against them or the frequent drive-by sightseers who wanted a glimpse of the boy. They left because someone wants them dead.

Santa Rosa, California
Monday Evening
Two Years Earlier

The wipers on Susan and Elliot's three-year-old shiny black BMW are turned on high to keep pace with the sheets of rain that slam the windshield. Susan thinks that the rain is uncharacteristic for this time of year in Northern California. Yet somehow it seems appropriate, even welcome, after today's meeting with the geneticist. It was if the skies were crying with them. As Elliot concentrates on his driving, Susan reaches back from the passenger's seat into the back seat where their two-year-old son sleeps safely strapped into his tan padded car seat. As Susan carefully checks car seat straps that hold her sleeping toddler she sees that he is dreaming. When Noah dreams his little body twitches and his full pink lips pursed, as though he were drinking from a bottle. All of a sudden it strikes Susan as to how trusting and innocent he is. Her heart shatters a bit more each time she thinks about what will come. Noah has done nothing to deserve his fate. She knows she'll do anything to take away the pain her son might soon feel. The tears well up again in her already puffy eyes as she tucks the blanket securely around his body and turns back in her seat. "Please slow down, Elliot," Susan demands as she refastens her seat belt.

"I'm doing the best that I can," Elliot reminds her pulling his shoulders back in an effort to sit up straight.

The best that I can. These words ring in her head over and over again until they fall into cadence with the wipers. Susan has come to hate these words. She wants to yell at her husband, at the rain, at the world, and at God. But she doesn't. She keeps it all contained. She knows that to give in to her anger will be like giving up. Susan feels that in order to not give up, she—they—must believe. They must believe that what the geneticist had told them was a mistake. If it wasn't, well then, there was *something* they could and would do, for Noah, and by God it wouldn't be just *the best that they can.*

Elliot reaches over and strokes Susan's soft blonde hair. "We're almost home "She recoils from his touch. She's too angry to be comforted.

"Susan, what if. " Elliot attempts to ask her, but she cuts him off.

"Can you please keep both of your hands on the wheel?"

"Do you want to drive, Susan? Because if you do, I'll be happy to pull over and let you have at it."

For a moment Elliot's words make her want to lash out at him even more. She pauses and then forgives Elliot's aggression as she realizes it's only in response to her own. Elliot's a safe, convenient target. It's been a hard day for both of them. Her thoughts drift back to the place they've just come from, the office of Dr. Ronald Barron and replay the meeting in her head.

Santa Rosa, California
Earlier That Same Day, Late Afternoon

"I have some difficult news," Dr. Barron states with a compassionate sigh. "The test results confirm that Noah has X-linked adrenoleukodystrophy, or ALD."

Once out of his mouth, the words seem to pierce the air. Susan watches Dr. Barron's heavy gray eyebrows knit together in an expression of concern, perhaps empathy. Dr. Barron had kept talking, but she had stopped listening. Susan knew all about ALD. Her nephew Josh had been diagnosed, a year ago, at age five. She knew the worst of the prognosis. The neuropathy associated with the disease eventually robbed a child of his ability to function on the most basic human level. Most children didn't live past the age of nine. In the past year, Josh had deteriorated noticeably. His cognitive abilities suffered. He could no longer attend school. Now even home schooling was out of the question. There seemed to be no point as it just seemed to frustrate him. While her sister Kim and husband Jake had been hopeful that they would find a cure, most of their hope had vanished with the unrelenting progression of the disease. Two weeks ago a caregiver had started to assist Kim with Josh's daily needs. Watching Joshua deteriorating so quickly had terrified Susan. Blindness and deafness would soon follow, further robbing Josh of the ability to communicate and draw comfort from seeing his family and hearing their soothing words. Kim and Jake had been told by doctors that it was just a matter of time before Josh would die. But they had one last option to try to save him: a bone marrow transplant treatment. There is a small chance that it could provide Josh with more time.

When Susan tunes back in to what the doctor is saying, she feels as if she is choking on the lump that has swelled in her throat.

"It's a progressive degenerative myelin disorder, meaning that myelin, the insulation around nerves, breaks down over time. Without myelin, some nerves can't function normally, or at all. Unfortunately, the body can't grow replacement myelin, so the disorder gets worse with time," Barron says.

This part of the conversation reminds Susan of the similarities between ALD and MS, multiple sclerosis, a disease her college roommate had. It was a disease that was difficult to treat, with little hope of a cure.

The doctor has gone through all the facts. Most of them she and Elliot already know, but both of them listen to it all again.

"The disorder leaves the body unable to break down large fat molecules. The fat molecules build up and clog up cells, and hurt nerve cells in the brain and spinal cord. It's a rare disease affecting about one in twenty thousand males."

It's a rare disease, Susan thinks, but one that has attacked two little boys in the same family. It seems so unlikely, so unfair and completely wrong. Susan has to watch her nephew succumb to the disease. She doesn't want to watch her son's health slip away too.

Dr. Barron carries on with his explanation. He speaks dispassionately, as if he is reciting medical texts. "The clinical range of severities of X-linked ALD is classified into several categories. The most common form is childhood. It includes approximately thirty percent of all patients with X-ALD. It often occurs between the ages of two and ten. Development is normal until the onset of the disease. The symptoms most commonly noted are difficulty in school, behavioral problems, and impaired vision and hearing."

Susan recalls these problems in Joshua. Before receiving a diagnosis there had been little question marks, notable behavioral changes that Kim, Susan's sister, had inquired about to Josh's pediatrician. No one ever expected that their concerns would lead to such a horrific diagnosis. It had been a punch in the gut that was still tender to all of them.

"After these initial neurological symptoms appear," Dr. Barron continues, "the patient's health often deteriorates rapidly. In addition to these symptoms, other symptoms may include dementia, poor coordination, seizures, hyperactivity, difficulty with speech, and headaches. Ultimately, the patient will succumb to a vegetative state and die within approximately two years."

Susan feels her chest tighten and silently reminds herself to breathe. As she swallows the acid bile rising in her throat Susan sends up a prayer that she won't vomit. Looking over at Elliot she realizes that he must be feeling sick too, as his face has turned as pale as the white shade that covers the only window in the room.

"Yes, Dr. Barron, we are familiar with childhood X-linked ALD. Our nephew is dying from it," Elliot replies.

Dr. Barron clears his throat. "Of course. We'll move onto other types of the disease. There is a later onset that will present between the ages of eleven and twenty-one. The progression of the disease is often somewhat slower. The symptoms are similar to those of childhood cerebral ALD, though."

Listening to this makes Susan feel as if she is having an out-of-body experience. She is somehow floating above the words and willing them to move away from her family.

"Mr. and Mrs. Gaynor, would you like a bottle of water?"

"No, no thank you," they reply almost in unison.

"Noah may have a type of the disease that is delayed in its onset. The form of the disease that doesn't attack until the early twenties is adrenomyeloneuropathy or AMN and comprises approximately forty percent of all X-ALD patients."

A beam of hope flashes through Susan's mind. There are two numbers Dr. Barron just mentioned that she clings to—forty percent and twenty-one years. They could work with this. There is hope for Noah if he has this form of the disease.

Dr. Barron takes a deep breath and plows through the final part of the discussion. "Generally, initial symptoms include stiffness/clumsiness in the legs, weight loss, nausea..."

Susan has heard enough. *Shut up, shut up!* She screams inside her head.

"I realize how difficult this diagnosis is for you to hear."

Through a dry mouth and strangled throat, Susan asks, "May I have that water now?"

"Certainly," Dr. Barron replies. He turns in his chair toward the small refrigerator directly behind his desk and takes out three chilled water bottles and places them on his desk.

Susan picks up one of the bottles and twists off the cap, mirroring Dr. Barron. Both of them take long pulls of the cool water.

Elliot reaches for the third bottle just as Susan asks, "Did I pass this disease on to our son?"

Stopping in mid-reach, Elliot turns to Susan and looks deeply into her cornflower-blue eyes that brim with tears.

"The genetic screening you recently completed, Susan, indicates that you are a carrier for the ABCD1 gene that is associated with ALD. Because of this fact, most male offspring will have a fifty percent chance of getting ALD."

What is left unsaid is the fact that trying to have another biological child would be out of the question. When Noah turned one she and Elliot discussed trying to get pregnant with a second child but decided to wait awhile. Looking back, it is now apparent that waiting had been a blessing since the disease is genetic.

"Susan, this isn't your fault. It's a genetic crap shoot," Elliot quickly explains.

"But it's *my* DNA. I gave this to our son," Susan states emphatically. *And it's my DNA that will prevent us from having more children,* she thinks.

"We cannot help our DNA and unfortunately it cannot be corrected. One day we will be able to do this but not now," Dr. Barron remarks.

"You said one day we will be able to correct our DNA? Really? How soon?" Susan inquires.

"Susan, right now that doesn't matter," Elliot soothes.

"But it does," Susan replies leaving unsaid her desire to someday have another child.

"There's a company in San Francisco that makes hardware systems for laser printing DNA. They currently are able to fix the mutations in our DNA, but the technology to get it into a person's body isn't safely available yet," Dr. Barron explains.

"Is there any current technology that might help our son?" Elliot inquires.

"There's gene therapy, along with therapeutic cloning and embryonic stem cell differentiation that can make tailored cellular therapies for genetic disorders."

"How far off into the future is all of this?" Elliot asks.

"New therapies are currently being tried in animals. Unfortunately, not in humans. We believe that they will be available to humans at some point-most likely within Noah's lifetime."

"But Noah may not have a lifetime," Susan says.

"There's also a chance that the disease won't strike until he's an adult," Dr. Barron reminds her.

Noah was only two. They had a ways to go before they could safely say he had escaped the childhood onset of the disease. Yes, that was it. Noah must escape. They would help Noah to escape. Even as this thought races through her mind, Susan knows the odds. However, she wants to hang on to this sliver of hope with all of her heart.

"The good news is that your son has no signs or symptoms of the disease."

"Yes, that's good, doctor," Susan agrees, looking to Elliot for confirmation.

"There's something else we should discuss. The MRI scan of Noah's brain yielded some abnormal results. The blood testing for the very long chain of fatty acids, VLCFA, revealed abnormal levels."

It's as if the doctor had taken a pin and popped her balloon of hope. Susan feels rung out—completely drained. In a short span of time she's experienced a roller coaster ride of emotions. Although Noah's disease isn't active, it is confirmed. She hasn't been able to shake the mental fatigue and the intrusive, repetitive thought that Noah will ultimately suffer like Josh and it is all her fault.

Dr. Barron runs his long, slender fingers through his curly gray hair and arches his back in a stretch that strains two of the buttons on his navy polo shirt, then relaxes his shoulders and drops his back into his leather chair. Taking a big breath and letting it out slowly, he says, "As you know, there's no cure; however, there is hope."

"Hope?" Elliot asks mockingly.

"Yes. Hope that scientific knowledge will advance while Noah's growing up, and that science will one day find a cure," Dr. Baron replies.

"Is there anything we can do now besides just waiting for symptoms?" Elliot asks.

"Feed Noah a diet low in very-long-chain fatty acids with foods such as skimmed milk, egg whites, chicken, white fish, fruit, vegetables, potatoes, pasta, low-fat yogurt, and cottage cheese. Taking special oils can lower the blood levels of very-long-chain fatty acids. I have a list here for you," Dr. Barron replies, sliding it across the table toward Elliot.

"This treatment's still being tested for X-linked adrenoleukodystrophy. It doesn't cure the disease and may not help all patients. Perhaps you've heard of it from the book or movie *Lorenzo's Oil*?

"I have. The oils are named after the son of the family who discovered the treatment," Elliot informs.

"I remember my sister telling me that she wished they had received a diagnosis for Josh much earlier, before he became symptomatic, because this was a treatment they could've tried," Susan says.

"Wasn't it first discovered in the nineteen eighties? I mean, that was a long time ago. Aren't there newer treatments?" Elliot asks.

"For now, this is your best shot. While it hasn't been approved by the FDA, I could get you into a clinical trial. The oil is manufactured in Great Britain and is made from olive and rapeseed oil. If started early in boys who have ALD but no symptoms, as in Noah's case, it's known to have some benefit in preventing the childhood cerebral form of ALD."

"Of course we'd like to have Noah included in the trials," Elliot responds and looks to Susan for confirmation.

"Is there anything else we can do?" Susan inquires, leaning forward in her chair and locking pleading eyes with Dr. Barron.

"Not at this stage. As you are probably aware, with your nephew's treatment, there's bone marrow or umbilical cord blood transplant treatment. The idea is to replace cells that have the defective ALD gene with cells that have a normal ALD gene and can break down fats. However, this is not a treatment we'd do while Noah is asymptomatic."

"Thank you Dr. Barron," Elliot says.

"I'll be in touch with Noah's pediatrician regarding clinical trials."

I couldn't go on without my son, please God don't let this happen, Susan sends up a silent plea.

Santa Rosa, California
Later That Night

Slipping out of her peach dress, Susan lets it drop into a puddle on her bedroom floor. Stepping over it, she has the strange sensation of feeling completely drained while at the same time her heart races wildly. She sits at the foot of the bed, kicks off her wedged sandals, and calms herself by taking slow, deep breaths, concentrating on her breathing as she wiggles her toes. Her focus is interrupted by the sound of the toilet flushing, the water running, and the click of the light as Elliot finishes in the bathroom. So predictable, stable, steady—all of the things she likes in a partner. She doesn't want the crazy, never-knowing-what-to-expect life she had lived with her parents. But at the same time, as he walks over to her, leans down, and kisses her bare shoulder before crawling under the bed covers, she resents the hell out him. Somehow this seemingly normal act of preparing for sleep makes her furious. She wants to smack him with his pillow, but instead clenches her jaw.

"Come sleep," he says softly as he reaches for her.

"I'm going to check on Noah first." With that said she's up, throwing on her robe as she quickly crosses their room and heads down the hall to the nursery.

Susan looks at her sleeping toddler lying in his crib. He sucks his thumb, a habit they have recently been trying to break, but one she will put aside for now. She strokes the curly blond locks that fall across his head. When he is up and running around, he's a tiny terror. But now, he's just a baby full of innocence. *How long of a life will he have?* Susan wonders. God, how she wishes Kim were here with her now. She needs her sister's understanding and love. She wonders how Kim can stand knowing that every day she has with Josh moves him one day closer to his impending death. Susan knows that she doesn't have the kind of courage that Kim possesses. Kim has told Susan that she's not courageous. She simply has no choice. Will Noah have a choice? Susan hopes he will. If either she or Kim had known that they were carriers of this terrible disease, would they have chosen to pursue a pregnancy? Would she have terminated her own pregnancy? Susan doesn't want to think about this anymore. Noah is here and she loves him with every fiber of her being. Besides, there is no use playing the "what if" game. Josh wasn't diagnosed until after Susan had given birth to Noah. It has taken a while to get a correct diagnosis for Josh, and even when they did get it, Kim and Susan hadn't been informed about the genetic component immediately.

Susan's thoughts seem to run from hot to cold. She finds them softening toward her husband. Maybe Elliot needs to follow his routine in order to cope. Men are taught to be strong and not to show emotion. How messed up is that? She wants to cry with someone who understands what she's facing, who loves Noah as much as she does. She knows Elliot won't allow himself to go there. She resigns herself to waiting. She will share all of these feelings with someone who walks in her shoes—her sister.

Susan remembers reading about the stages of grief in a long-ago college psychology textbook. She recalls what she learned: denial is considered to be one of the first stages, followed by anger, guilt, bargaining, sadness, and then acceptance or resolution. Can grief be so neatly outlined and experienced? She doubts it. Her heart feels as if it has been ripped from her chest and stomped on. A tear slips down her cheek and hits Noah squarely on the nose. He stirs as she wipes it away; she kisses his forehead and turns to leave the room.

How can this be happening to my beautiful boy?

Santa Rosa, California
Tuesday Morning

Sesame Street plays in the background as Elliot pours a second cup of coffee. Susan catches him making a silly face at Noah as she feeds him his Cheerios. He giggles at his daddy and squirms in the highchair, knocking over his sippy-cup.

"Uh-oh," Noah says as he looks to the fallen cup on the floor.

Elliot picks up the cup as Susan mops up the spilled milk with a dishtowel from the table.

"Can you fill his cup back up?" Susan asks taking the milk soaked dishtowel to the sink.

"Sure," Elliot replies.

Susan turns to see Elliot retrieving the carton of whole milk from the refrigerator.

"What're you doing?"

"Getting Noah's milk."

"That's not his milk. That's whole milk. Noah's milk is nonfat."

"What's the big deal?"

"What's the big deal? Are you kidding me? It's full fat! Noah is on a reduced-fat diet. You know this!" Susan replies visibly upset.

"It's not going to hurt him to have this one cup."

"It could, Elliot. You know what diet he's supposed to be on. I can't believe that you're his father and you're insisting on giving him the wrong milk."

"Geez Susan, lighten up," Elliot reprimands as he poured the cup of milk down the sink drain.

Susan sits down at the table next to Noah trying her best to calm her emotions. She notices the sun shining through the window, temporarily blinding her as she looks over to Elliot, who is now pouring the nonfat milk into Noah's cup. The halo of light around Elliot makes him look like an angel. Angel Elliot and devil Susan - Susan thinks. She's a devil for having passed this disease onto their only child. At times like these the guilt she feels seeps into her thoughts, even though intellectually she knows it isn't deserved. She wishes she could push it out of her head. The ringing phone diverts her attention as she responds by jumping a little in her chair. Susan watches as Elliot hands Noah his sippy-cup. The phone rings a second time. Elliot hurries over to the phone. Susan listens as he speaks. "Hello? - No, it isn't good news. Here, let me get Susan." Elliot hands the cordless phone to Susan and mouths the words, "It's your sister."

"Kim?" Susan asks into the phone.

"The diagnosis is confirmed. It's ALD . . . Okay."

"Kim's on her way over."

Noah offers Elliot the Cheerio he's holding tightly between his chubby finger and thumb. "Yum," Elliot says, bending down to allow Noah to place it into his mouth.

"Why are you leaving so early?" She inquires as she sets the phone down on the kitchen table.

"I've got some extra paperwork to do on a case that's going to trial soon," Elliot explains as he walks out the back door.

Susan leaves Noah to finish his breakfast and walks over to the sink. She runs the hot water and pours soap over the dirty dishes. She thinks about how it was just a week ago; they had been planning their Christmas vacation. They were deciding between Lake Tahoe to play in the snow or Hotel Del Coronado in San Diego. Susan had wanted to ski, and Elliot had wanted to relax on the beach. There would be no relaxing on a beach with a toddler, Susan had informed Elliot. Elliot then inquires as to how they would ski with Noah. She had explained that there was daycare and kids' camps at the ski lodge. Elliot had countered that the same services must be offered to parents at the hotel on the beach. A predictable argument had ensued. Up until now, this had been the biggest issue they faced. Within seven days, they had gone from that petty discussion to this ugly reality. Susan's eyes fill with tears as she turns off the water and dries her hands with a dishtowel. Seeing that Noah is finished eating, she scoops him up and holds him a little too tightly as she walks into the family room. "No mama," Noah says as he pulls away arching his back. She replies, "I'm sorry, honey," as she carefully sets him down in front of the TV where *Sesame Street* is still playing. "Monther!" Noah says pointing to the Cookie Monster.

"Yes, honey, that's right." She stands next to her son watching a sketch with Bert, Ernie and the Cookie Monster. Soon her tears are dammed and a smile crosses her lips. Noah is laughing. Hearing her son giggle makes Susan laugh also until the doorbell rings. Upon hearing the doorbell, Noah gets up and runs to the front door. Susan quickens her step to keep pace with him. She opens it and relief washes over her when she sees Kim. Noah reaches up to hug his aunt. "Look at this big boy!" Kim exclaims as she picks him up and gives him a kiss on the cheek. She sets Noah down and he grabs his aunt's hand, pulling her to the television.

Soon Noah was back in front of the television watching Bert and Ernie take a bath, and Kim and Susan were sitting next to each other on the sofa.

"I know you're not okay so I'm just going to say, how sorry I am, Susan."

"Why us? Why did this happen to our sons?"

"When Joshua was first diagnosed, my mother-in-law says to me, 'It's God's will, dear.' Although I realized she meant well, I wanted to take and shake her and scream that she was wrong. God would never will such a thing on a child."

"If someone says that to me, I just might have to hurt them, Kim."

Kim takes Susan's hand and squeezes it. "I know honey. I honestly don't know why this is happening to our boys."

"It's as if the doctors had discovered a tiny switch in Noah that can be turned on at any moment."

"Children should be exempt from life-threatening diseases, Susan."

"I wonder if we have the ability to find the switch before it's even turned on? Couldn't we learn how to keep it turned off—at least just long enough for our children to live a lifetime?"

Kim speaks gently to her sister. "Ideally. But as far as I know there isn't anyone who can help, and if there were — well it's too late for Josh but maybe not for Noah. We still don't know how his ALD will be expressed. He could have a lot more time than Josh does."

"I'm so sorry, Kim. Sorry for you, sorry for me, sorry for our sons. I don't even know how you stand this," Susan's voice brakes and the tears flow.

Kim sits with her sister until her tears stop. Taking both of her sister's hands in hers, Kim says, "Let your grief out and keep letting it out. But don't ever succumb to self-pity. It can be a dangerous thing. The reality is that it's not going to be easy; you know-you've experienced it with us with Joshua. The only advice I'm giving is to take care of yourself and take care of your family. It's easy to want to blame Elliot and to hate each other. Elliot needs you and you need him. Pull together for Noah's sake. Don't let this tear you apart."

Kim's words hang in the air like fresh laundry on the line. As the words gently sway in her mind, Susan realizes that Kim knows better than anyone else what she is facing. Susan has seen the cracks in her sister's marriage. The stress of living with a dying child takes its toll on the strongest of unions. However, just when things seem to be stretched to the breaking point, Kim and her husband always seem to retract and keep their family intact.

Standing up from the sofa and stretching, Kim says, "I need to go. I have some errands to run before Josh's caregiver leaves. Remember, I'm always here for you. I love you."

"I love you too," Susan replies as the two make their way to the door, embrace, and say goodbye.

Sonoma, California
Tuesday, Late Afternoon

Elliot does his best to concentrate during the meeting at his law firm of Greenspan, Howard, and Feldman, where he's a junior partner. His firm specializes in estate law. Not his first choice. Like Susan, Elliot had set out to be a trial lawyer. While still at Boalt Hall at U.C. Berkeley, Elliot had decided to change to estate law. His decision became painfully easy as he started experiencing panic attacks and was soon diagnosed with a generalized anxiety disorder. He had tried thinking himself out of his panic, which didn't work, and had discovered that anxiety brought him to his knees. He found a good therapist and was able to learn how to manage his anxiety cognitively and also with the aid of a little biopharmaceutical relief—Zoloft. He had discovered that a Xanax every now and then helped him to get a good night's sleep. It hadn't just been law school that caused him to feel this way. The root of his problem could be traced back to a chaotic childhood in which he had very little control. His parents had uprooted their family every couple of years;

his father had always kept an eye on climbing the corporate ladder. The result for his son had been a lack of stability and a mother who experienced emotional problems and wasn't available to her son. His father was a high functioning alcoholic. Elliot suspected that he too had anxiety, but chose to self-medicate with liquor. It had been a difficult life. His parents had divorced when he was in high school. When Elliot married Susan, he had made a couple of vows. He would buy a house and live there until he died. He would also be the kind of dad who had open arms and an open heart. He would manage his stress and never take on more than he could handle. Unfortunately, life had other plans for him.

Feelings of failure to protect his son bubble up inside of him. A sense of dread and foreboding that he hasn't experienced since his last panic attack, a couple of years ago, begin to smother him like a hot towel placed over his face after a barber's shave. "Concentrate on the meeting," he silently reminds himself. He shifts his attention to the immediate task. The owner of a big-name local winery recently died. His will is being contested by his second wife. Apparently, the winery owner had been more generous with the child from his first marriage, a son, who was also the winemaker, than he had been with his current wife. She had been expecting to get more than the ten percent of the estate (still a sizeable sum) she was being given and was furious.

As much as he tries, Elliot isn't able to control his thoughts and finds himself wandering in and out of a mental replay of the conversation with Dr. Barron. A wave of nausea rides up from his stomach into his throat. He tastes the sourness of his stomach acid as it burns the back of his esophagus. He feels hot. Shedding his suit coat onto the back of his chair, he loosens his tie, unbuttons the top two buttons of his blue dress shirt, and takes a deep breath. *Relax*, Elliot quietly reminds himself. *Shit, it's not working*; he thinks and feels as if he's choking. He reaches for the water bottle sitting in front of him and sees the room spin. Elliot stands up to excuse himself, and his legs buckle. He grabs the side of the conference table to steady himself.

"Are you okay?" one of his associates asks. But to Elliot the question sounds far away. Two other colleagues rush to his aid. His heart beats wildly and he breaks out into a cold sweat as his chest tightens. *Down, down, down the elevator shaft, I'm dying*.

Westchester, New York
Tuesday Evening
LAB

The genie is about to be let out of the bottle. After this there is no turning back. Dr. James Eastman, a tall and distinguished dark-haired man in his forties, graying at the temples, sips coffee and readies himself for the nationally televised press conference, looking confident. He glances out the window of his office. It's a beautiful day; the leaves on the trees are vibrant with yellows and reds. He loves autumn on the East Coast. Mentally pushing aside his pleasant thoughts Eastman focuses his attention to the statement is just above to give. He meticulously reviews his notes one last time and thinks; *impart the exciting news, but don't exaggerate the announcement.*

Prior to today, there had been a lengthy discussion with the other members of the LAB (Life Aided through Biotechnology); a privately owned company founded by Eastman, on whether or not to even publish this information. His three closest associates, Dr. Alan Anderson, a thirty-six-year-old veterinarian who studied at Purdue University and had success in cloning sheep; fifty-year-old Paul Zorvelli, a geneticist who spent the past two plus decades studying the way human hereditary qualities are transmitted; and Dr. Kathryn MacMurray, a thirty-six-year-old human embryologist who practiced as an infertility specialist before joining the LAB three years ago make up the core team. Eastman's team also includes an ethics advisory panel that provides oversight and guidance regarding the areas they are addressing and a variety of other scientists and assistants.

Many members of the team think that Eastman's announcement is premature. Eighty cells is not enough division to harvest the stem cells which is the goal of therapeutic cloning. A cell division of 160-200 was needed before the team could reasonably refer to the development of the blastocyst as a success. The majority of the team had hoped to wait to make the announcement until after they had reached that stage. Unfortunately, the cells stopped dividing after two days. If the cells would have progressed in develop for five days and reached a two hundred cell stage, the team wouldn't have any trepidation about making the announcement. They would have accomplished what they set out to do in order to develop a stem cell line that could be used to begin to cure disease.

However, Eastman had been afraid that they would miss the opportunity to announce this if they waited until they could try again. In order to try again they needed to keep the funding coming in.

The decision to announce has been a "beat the clock" consideration for Eastman. The LAB needs money, and lots of it, if this type of work is to progress. At the same time, politically, this is a hot issue, an issue riddled with misinformation and fear. One fear for Eastman is that the federal government might issue a ban on therapeutic human cloning, thus taking the power away from individual states that will want to pursue it. Eastman knows that if science is to progress in the field of therapeutic cloning, he needs to educate lawmakers before they made it illegal. Misconceptions about the differences between therapeutic cloning and reproductive cloning were fueling lawmakers opposed to any kind of cloning. Unlike reproductive cloning in which an animal or human being is fully created, therapeutic cloning involves the process of growing cells using the patient's own DNA. DNA is inserted into an unfertilized egg cell and used to create embryonic stem cells. These stem cells held the promise of making cells young again and could ultimately be used to repair damage brought on by both disease and age. It was the real-life "fountain of youth." Therapeutic cloning can be used to treat everything from spinal cord injury to burns, to disease such as cancer, Parkinson's, and even in organ replacement. The applications were seemingly endless.

Journalists and camera crews stand by, anxiously awaiting Dr. Eastman's announcement. Eastman knows that his announcement is about to change the world. This is a historic moment.

Washington, D.C.
Oval Office, Tuesday, 6:10 p.m.

President Kenneth Longran, former Republican governor of Texas, enters the Oval Office. A lanky man with dark brown, close-cropped hair, graying at the temples, and piercing green eyes, appears comfortable in khakis and navy blue polo shirt. He takes his seat behind his prominent desk where many other presidents have sat.

"Mr. President," Chief of Staff Candace Carter, fiftyish, prim, with gray hair pulled tautly away from her face in a bun, acknowledges him from the other side of his desk, "there's going to be an announcement on human cloning in twenty minutes. The announcement is to be made by Dr. James Eastman, CEO and president of the LAB. The announcement follows his publication in the science journal *Nature*," She says sliding the article toward him from across the desk.

One of his aides turns on the television as Longran reviews the article.

"Interesting."

Longran, pro-life politician has always taken issue with anything that smacks of abortion, including the morning-after pill. He supports the harvesting of fetal stem cells, taken from discarded frozen IVF fetuses for researching cures for disease though. Curious to learn more about this new advancement in regenerative medicine he turns his attention to the television.

Westchester, New York
Tuesday Evening

As Eastman sets down his notes on his desk and primps one last time before he's called to the podium, he realizes that although he is a committed scientist who wants to make a significant contribution and offer hope to millions of people who currently have no hope, a part of him—maybe a very small part of him—likes the attention. There's something exciting about making an astonishing announcement, even more exciting than the adrenaline rush he got in his college days when he participated in extreme sports. He had blazed ski trails that weren't on any map. He skydived and had had a brief stint with surfing. He lived for the sensation of pushing the envelope and the way he'd feeling being in the zone. He believes this is what has helped him to learn to focus on his work. Losing his mom at a young age had taught him a powerful lesson. Death could be unexpected and didn't just happen to the old. He chose to always live his life to the absolute fullest.

Eastman notices that his hands are shaking and his mouth feels dry. He takes a sip of water and justifies to himself that the announcement he's about to make is the right one at the right time. *Perhaps it is premature but it is based solidly on scientific data. I'll be damned if another research lab, in some other part of the world, will beat me to it, Eastman thinks.* Still, he knows that this moment that carries him forward also means no way back.

He thinks back to all that has brought him here. He's worked hard, especially the past ten years, to achieve this breakthrough. He's hung in there with every twist and turn, every setback and advancement, often working around the clock both inside and outside of the LAB. He's helped to raise funds to pay for the research. In addition, he's been willing to teach and share his findings. He feels a small sting in his heart. He, he, he -but this truly isn't only about glory for himself. It's about helping people in a way that no one had been able to help his mom. He takes a moment to reflect on the beautiful woman who had died on the cusp of middle age. A lump rises up in his throat. Would she have been proud of him? *This is for you Mom.*

"You're on, James," Dr. Anderson says as he stands in the doorway of Eastman's office.

"If you're going to take a risk, make it a big risk," Eastman's father's words pop into his head and he's unaware that he's spoken them to Anderson. *This is a big risk, Pops,* Eastman thinks as he walks past Anderson on his way to the podium.

Washington, D.C.
Same Evening, 6:15 p.m.

Senator Anne Wilcox Brice (D., CA) is pouring herself a martini in the den of her elegant brownstone and looks up to see her assistant, Myles Brennan, standing in the threshold of her entryway.

"Ma'am?" he inquires tentatively.

"Come in, Myles," Anne calls from the big easy chair where she sits.

Myles crosses the room and sees holding a drink in one hand. "I thought you should know that there's going to be a live press conference in fifteen minutes that you should watch."

"What's it about?"

"Stem cells, regenerative medicine, what's being referred to as a human cloning breakthrough at the LAB. Dr. Eastman is making the announcement. You met with him briefly last year and have spoken to him a few times since then," Myles reminds her.

"I do. Well, this is should be interesting," Anne remarks as she recalls the bill passed in the House that will seriously disable the efforts toward any type of scientific cloning. Soon the bill will be up for a vote in the Senate. It's one she adamantly opposes. She is supporting another bill that is in favor of regenerative medicine that she hopes will make it through the House and receive full support in the Senate. She clicks on the set.

"Sit down, Myles," she instructs as she stretches out her long, shapely legs.

"Thank you, ma'am," he says taking a seat on the sofa.

"So Eastman finally did it?" she remarks as a hint of a smile crosses her face.

South Carolina
Same Evening, 6:20 p.m.

Senator John Dukesbury (R., SC) spits a piece of fat into his cloth napkin. "Damn gristle," he mutters and continues his pretense of listening to his wife, Caroline, discuss the merits of a second set of braces for their daughter. He wraps his thick fingers, ones that matched his frame, around the crystal hi-ball glass of bourbon. A swig of the amber liquid washes the fatty taste from his mouth. The last thing he wants is to be bothered with this nonsense. Does it really require his approval? He questions. He has to contend with more pressing issues.

He's been informed by his advisors that there is a woman who claims to have had an affair with him and is now pregnant with his child. The truth is that he's a big flirt but has never cheated on Caroline. He is concerned that this might negatively hurt his chances for reelection. Things like this tend to get out of control. He fears that not only might his wife doubt his loyalty, but the voters might too. Voters have become jaded hearing politicians proclaim their innocence and then be proven liars. "I never had sex with that woman," once says an infamous President who almost got himself impeached over the lie he told to the American public. He didn't want his own chances of getting reelected seriously hobbled if the voters were to remember his being accused of infidelity and forget the fact that he never did the deed. It is all about getting reelected. If you aren't, you're out of a job and powerless.

"Get her the damn braces, Caroline," he states in his thick southern drawl, smoothly laced with bourbon.

"John, honey, please don't say "damn.""

John does nothing to mask the upward roll of his eyes just as his cell phone vibrates on the table.

"Hello?"

"Senator, this is Faith Barrigan in the Vice President's office. The Vice President asks me to inform you that there's an announcement that's going to be made and that he wants you to hear."

"Announcement about what?"

"The first human clone has been achieved, sir."

Santa Rosa, California
Same Day, Late Afternoon

Susan stands by Elliot's hospital bed in the emergency room of the Santa Rosa Memorial Hospital. She sees that he's hooked up to a heart monitor, and an oxygen monitor is clipped to his right index finger. The steady sound of the various machines all helping to support life are background noise for the rest of the ER, where the trauma team is working on a teenager who has gone into anaphylactic shock. Susan overhears something about a food he shouldn't have eaten and then the strangled cry that escapes from a woman she assumes must be his frightened mother. Susan recalls her coworker who had a life-threatening peanut allergy. She had learned from her that even trace amounts could cause her to experience anaphylaxis. Susan sends up a silent prayer that the patient next to them will make a full recovery. Elliot shifts in his bed, prompting Susan to refocus her attention. She looks over to her husband and offers him a bright smile. He appears to Susan to be fairly calm. The wild look in his eyes has been washed away by a shot of Valium.

"What do you need, honey?"

"The blanket feels hot. Mind pulling it down?"

"Of course." Susan pulls the blanket toward the end of the bed.

"Mrs. Gaynor?" Susan looks up to find a young doctor, about her age, with wavy brown hair and horned-rimmed glasses, wearing blue scrubs. He addresses her as he pushes back the curtain and enters their tiny space.

"I'm Doctor Fitzpatrick."

Susan nods an acknowledgment to the doctor as he moves closer to Elliot's bedside. "How are you feeling Mr. Gaynor?"

"Better."

"Good, good. Your vitals have improved. Please just continue to relax."

"What's wrong with Elliot? Is it his heart?"

"I can tell you that we are confident your husband did not have a heart attack. We believe it was a panic attack."

"A panic attack?" Elliot exclaims questionably.

"A panic attack's symptoms can mimic the symptoms of a heart attack. What you experienced, Mr. Gaynor, was very real and extremely frightening. Is there anything stressful currently going on in your lives?"

Susan slowly meets Dr. Fitzpatrick's gaze. "Our son was recently diagnosed with ALD."

Dr. Fitzpatrick stares blankly for a moment registering her words. The facts of the rare disease he learned about in medical school pop into his head.

"I'm sorry," he replies with the kind of empathy normally reserved for the families of patients who were being told their loved ones had died.

"I can only imagine the pressures that both of you are facing right now. Given the context, a panic attack makes complete sense."

"Can I go home now?"

"Your blood pressure is a bit higher than we'd like. The orderlies will be coming down to transport you to a room. I'd like to keep you overnight for observation and to do some blood work."

"Doctor, I thought you said Elliot had a panic attack. Why does he have to stay overnight?"

"We believe it was, but we want to run a few tests to rule out the possibility of anything else. Mrs. Gaynor, after your husband is comfortable, why don't you go home and get some rest? I can give you a prescription for Valium if you like."

"That won't be necessary," Susan icily replies thinking *I'm not the one who is falling apart here.*

"You'll be moved upstairs to a room. Take care, Mr. Gaynor," Dr. Fitzpatrick says as he moves past the two orderlies who approach Elliot's bed.

The orderlies unlock the wheels on the bed. "Ready to roll to your new digs?" asks the taller of the two whom looks to Susan more like a rock musician than a hospital employee.

"Go for it."

It's almost as if Elliot is enjoying this, Susan thinks as she follows them into the elevator which takes them to the fourth floor. It was only a little over two years earlier that she and Elliot had been riding the same elevator to the third floor, Labor and Delivery, where Noah was born. Susan longed to peek at the newborns. However, with new fears of infants being stolen, this was no longer possible. The viewing window now has the shades closed tight. Susan was so entranced by her memories of Noah's birth that she didn't remember walking to Elliot's new room. She steps aside as the orderlies get Elliot situated into his bed. She looked out the window, still lost in her thoughts. She notices the darkness falling like a stage curtain across the hospital lawn. Still, it seems too early for the twilight's descent. *Not quite night but the days are getting shorter,* Susan realizes as she toggles the window shade closed.

"Where's Noah?" Elliot asks after the orderlies left.

"He's with Kim," Susan replies, turning and walking toward the bed. "Can I get you anything?"

"I'm fine. I don't see why I have to stay. I feel like a stupid fool."

"You're not." *Just stressed* is what she thinks, but leaves it unsaid because she's stressed too. However, she isn't the one in a hospital bed playing with the television remote.

Elliot lands on CNN's teaser of "breaking news," and Susan's mouth drops as she reads the tag line: "Dr. James Eastman, Founder and CEO, the LAB clones the first human."

Just as quickly as she can read it Elliot clicks on ESPN.

"Click it back!" Susan cries out.

Elliot fumbles with the remote and pushes the buttons for CNN.

"That's the guy I've been reading about on the Internet today!"

"What guy?"

"He's a scientist who's working on regenerative medicine. He's making an important statement," Susan explains as she takes the remote from Elliot and pushes volume up.

Westchester, New York
Tuesday, 6:30 p.m.

Eastman's dark hair is slicked back off of his handsome face. He's wearing his best dark blue suit that almost matches his piercing blue eyes, making him an impressive figure. Everyone watches as he arrives at the podium. He arranges a small stack of papers he is carrying pulls the microphone closer to his face.

"This is a historic moment. I'm happy to announce that we have achieved a miracle of science. It's a miracle because the implications for continued research to find cures for a variety of diseases will be unveiled here, tonight, at the LAB: Life Aided through Biotechnology.

Eastman pauses, clears his throat and says, "I'm excited to announce that we've taken the first step in therapeutic cloning. We've cloned the first human."

Gasps and shuffling sounds erupt.

"To be precise, the cloned human cells have divided to an eighty cell stage. It's our hope to use this technology to cure diseases such as Parkinson's, Diabetes, Alzheimer's, and many others. We've taken a giant leap toward what we hope will be a whole new era of medicine: Therapeutic Regenerative Medicine."

South Carolina
Same Evening

The heavy burgundy drapes covered the floor-to-ceiling windows, keeping warmth in the room and any remaining light out. A big-screen TV stretches from the corner of the door to the stand alone bar and is tuned in to Dr. Eastman's conference as Senator Dukesbury and his wife watch.

"What the hell?" Dukesbury inquires, but says it as more of a comment to his wife, who is sitting next to him on the overstuffed sofa in the impressive room.

Dukesbury had heard about human cloning but didn't know much about how it was done. His ability to make sense of all that is being explained is blinded by his shear anger—anger that this is somehow an abomination. He believes that the good Lord never intended such a thing to occur. It is bad enough that scientists are fooling around with animals in this way, but now people too? He is certain his constituency won't support this one bit. He'll see to it.

Butlerville, Indiana
Same Evening

Joseph Smith (Joe) shared Senator Dukesbury's outrage, although the two had never met. The tall, steely-gray eyed, thin man sat in his grand-pappys' hardback chair with his rifle across his lap. He had been cleaning his gun when his wife turned on the television in the parlor room of their farmhouse. The farm was located in a county whose claim to fame was being the childhood home of President Richard M. Nixon's mother, Hannah. This was quite a big deal in their town, even though Joe wasn't a fan of the former President. It was the President's failure to end the war right after he was elected that cost Joe his draft. His experience had left him with what the VA referred to as PTSD, or post-traumatic stress disorder. It isn't in just having to live with PTSD that both Joe and Gwen find challenging, sometimes he saw and heard things that others didn't. Another doctor gave him a name for this and some medication. Joe didn't like the way the meds made in feel so he quit taking it. On the really scary days Joe had flashbacks to his war experiences. His wife, Gwen, called them his "moods."

"It's time for the news. Turn it up, Joe. I want to hear the weather report."

Joe presses the volume up button on the television controller just in time to see a banner across the bottom of the screen announcing breaking news.

They listen to the newscaster explain what is to be announced in a press conference given by Dr. James Eastman at the LAB.

"My word, did you ever think such a thing could happen?" Gwen asks him from her seat in the rocking chair. Joe doesn't respond. His jaw tightens as does his grip around the rifle barrel. This is news that makes his skin crawl. It's against the law of man, of everything God would want, he thinks. He makes a mental commitment to explore this more on the internet. Surely there are other like-minded souls like him who are vehemently opposed to this blasphemes outrage.

Washington, D.C.
Same Evening

"Eighty cells. Not much of a clone. But it's a significant start," Anne remarks to Myles.

"Yes, it is," Myles readily agrees.

"It's more important than ever to defeat the bill in the House. We need to step up pressure and call in favors. Schedule a meeting with the staff for tomorrow morning."

"I'm on it now," Myles replies as he begins texting the staff on his cell phone.

Santa Rosa, California
Same Evening

Susan turns away from the television in Elliot's hospital room and addresses him. "Do you know what this could mean for Noah?"

"You're thinking that they might find a cure for ALD? That's crazy, Susan."

"Not really. Just listen."

Westchester, New York
Same Evening

"To be precise, therapeutic cloning, involves the transfer of a person's somatic cell into an egg cell, thus forming a preimplantation embryo. From this embryo we would harvest stem cells and develop an embryonic stem cell line specific to that person in order to treat disease and regenerate organs and all types of tissues specific to the person they are derived from. I will now take questions from the press," Eastman continues.

Eastman acknowledges a balding, heavy set reporter in the front row, "Dr. Eastman, Duncan Mansfield, *Washington Post*, briefly tell us what exactly you have done? Why human cloning?"

"Therapeutic cloning involves creating cloned human blastocysts for the purpose of extracting stem cells. These are the building block cells that ultimately develop into all the specialized cells and tissues in our bodies. The idea is to do something we've never been able to do before. We want to eradicate diseases and provide replacement cells and tissues, even create organs, for people who need them"

"That's a lofty goal but is it a realistic one? It doesn't sound like you are very far along with the process. Also, can you provide us with an example on how exactly you would cure disease?" Mansfield follows up with a second question.

"It's very realistic. When considering disease, let's consider diabetes - what happens when you lose cells in the pancreas— the cells that produce insulin to control blood sugar? You develop diabetes. Unfortunately, there's no cure for the millions of people currently suffering from diabetes. We can help make it better with insulin. But what if the goal in medicine were to make replacement cells, or tissues, such as a new pancreas, in the case of diabetes, that could cure the disease? If it were, as I believe it should be, then you could say we've now taken the first steps toward doing this."

Eastman points to a tall woman with her hand raised high above her red hair.

"Julia Burton, reporter with *Newsweek*. When people hear the words 'human cloning' they get very nervous because they assume it's going to result in the cloning of fully formed human beings. But this isn't what you are talking about, is it?"

"That's correct. It's not our goal to create a fully formed human being. Let me emphasize this point. We're talking pre-fetal development," Eastman pauses, takes a quick look at his notes and says, "You know, I think it's parallel in some ways to in-vitro fertilization. Just some thirty-five years ago, when scientists said they wanted to help people who are infertile by making test-tube babies, it scared a lot of people. It reminded them of the novel *Brave New World*. People feared test tube babies. The truth is that there were no babies grown in a test-tube. They were started in a petri dish and then implanted in a woman's womb. We are growing cells in a petri dish that we can harvest stem cells from. But that's as far as we go with the process."

"But the cells could grow into a human being. Isn't that right?" Burton asks.

"That would be reproductive cloning. That's not what we're doing. Therapeutic cloning involves creating cloned human blastocysts for the purpose of extracting stem cells. To ensure that these cells don't develop into a fully formed human being they are never implanted into a womb."

Eastman points to a reporter standing next to Burton whom Eastman was familiar. The reporter with salt and pepper hair was known for being a pit bull when pursuing information. Eastman hopes he will refrain from sinking his teeth into him tonight.

"David Camm from the *New York Times*, please explain, for those who don't have a lot of science background, exactly how is this done, the cloning of human cells?"

"The technique used by the LAB's scientists is called somatic cell nuclear transfer, or SCNT, also referred to as human therapeutic cloning. You all remember Dolly the sheep cloned back in the 1990's? Well we used the Dolly technique or Somatic Cell Nuclear Transfer - SCNT. A cell from a patient's body, often a skin cell, is combined with an egg cell that has had its DNA removed. We take out the donated eggs DNA and we insert the donated skin cells DNA into the egg. This reprograms the body cell's DNA back to an embryonic state, and stem cells identical to the patients are produced."

Ignoring the raised hands of several reporters in the room, Eastman takes a quick sip of water and dives into the rest of the explanation, "These are extremely young cells, which make them different from using adult donor cells or even frozen fetal cells. They're much better to work with because they *are* youthful. They're undifferentiated and can morph into any cell or tissue in the human body such as liver cells, nerve cells and heart cells. While there's much work to be done in developing safe and effective stem cell treatments, we believe this is a significant step forward in developing the cells that could be used in ultimately curing disease."

Mansfield raises his hand and Eastman calls on him again. "Where did you get the eggs and the skin cells?"

"We used human egg donors and separate skin cell donors."

"How did you remove the DNA from the egg cell and place the DNA from the skin cell back into the egg's nucleus?" Mansfield further questions.

"Using a pipette. It's similar to a long needle in which we can suck out the egg's DNA and insert the DNA from the skin cell."

A compact man wearing jeans and sport coat doesn't wait for Eastman to call on him. "Tim Shockey, from the *Los Angeles Times*, Let me clarify. You've cloned a human embryo for the first time, is that what you're saying?"

"I'd correct the term embryo. What we really have is the *beginning* of the blastocyst stage. It is a pre-embryo stage because there is no separation of what might ultimately become the embryo and placenta.

"Okay so this ball of cells develops into a blastocyst. Please define and discuss what a blastocyst is," Shockey requests.

"A blastocyst is a structure formed in the early embryogenesis of mammals, after the formation of the morula." Interrupting, Burton inquires, "For us lay people a quick definition of a morula, Dr. Eastman"

"Once the biological entity has divided into 16 cells, it begins to resemble a mulberry, hence the name *morula* - the Greek word for mulberry. It's a specifically mammalian example of a blastula. It possesses an inner cell mass that forms the embryo, and an outer layer of cells, or trophoblast, which later forms the placenta. The trophoblast surrounds the inner cell mass and a fluid-filled blastocyst cavity known as the blastocoele or the blastocystic cavity. The human blastocyst is made up of seventy to one hundred cells. Blastocyst formation begins at day five after fertilization in humans. The blastocoele opens up in the morula - a process known as hatching."

"I think I speak for all of us when I say, 'Huh?'"

Shockey's remark elicits laughter. It's a refreshing moment of levity for the journalists in a heavily scientific-jargoned interview. It's a wake-up call for Eastman. He realizes similar to explaining the facts of life to a child he would do better to keep his explanations simple and concise.

Eastman light heartedly replies, "I hear you. Basically, we've created a new biological entity never before seen in nature."

He nods to a journalist at the back of the audience who is dressed in a black and gray suit and who has her hand raised. She speaks loudly in order to be heard. "Dr. Eastman, Allyson Meade of the *Minneapolis Tribune*. Please explain the therapeutic benefits of this type of medicine."

"Well, this is a whole new frontier in medicine we are working with here. Once this new biological entity divides to the blastocyst stage, we can create embryonic stem cells that have the same genetic blueprint as the person they come from, and that's key to successful treatments because they are identical to the person afflicted with disease. These stem cells can be genetically tailored to treat people suffering from all sorts of diseases and afflictions. Also, as I stated earlier, from this undifferentiated cellular life we can make almost anything— tissue, cells, and organs—all identical to the patient's."

"So the possibilities are numerous?" Meade asks.

"They are," Eastman points to an older journalist whose left hand is raised up high as his right hand strokes his graying beard.

"Frank Stone with the *New Jersey Star Ledger*, is this ethical? Is it moral?"

"Is it ethical or moral to treat disease and alleviate suffering? Why should we hold hostage a person's ability to overcome disease?" Eastman emphatically replies.

"Why clone at all when we have frozen fetal embryos we can harvest stem cells from?" Camm counters.

"The drawback for using stem cells harvested from frozen embryos, and it's a significant one for many people, is that anti-rejection drugs must be taken because the material is donor material. The side effects in using these anti-rejection medications can be very difficult for people seeking transplanted organs and stem cells. It limits the possibilities for success."

Camm persists, "So you are saying that by using the person's cloned stem cells you avoid this?"

"That's correct. A patient will not experience rejection using his or her own stem cells. That's huge."

"How do you go about treating diseases?" Stone asks.

"Somatic cell nuclear transfer, or SCNT, may have applications in the creation of embryonic stem cells, which can be used for the development of patient-specific and disease-specific cell-based therapies as well as the production of stem cells with specific disease characteristics for research purposes."

"In lay terms, please," Burton requests.

"Right on," a young male journalist in the back of the room shouts in support of Burton's request.

More laughter reverberates through the audience.

Eastman knows this is critical as well. It's his responsibility to provide the language with which people can talk about his work intelligently and without exaggeration.

"We will use these cell clones in order to cure Parkinson's, Alzheimer's, or diabetes and to help an individual who is paralyzed and even aid people in growing their own new organs. We can help patients who are fighting, ALS, ALD, eye diseases such as Stargardt's disease, macular degeneration; you name it the list goes on and on."

"Explain *exactly* how you achieve this?" Burton implores.

"With the help of genetic engineering, the host's, or patient's, own stem cells can be repaired and used for autologous transplantation. It's a procedure in which a person donates blood or tissue to themselves. Patients will no longer need organ, blood, or tissue donors. Therapeutic cloning can be to patients with spinal cord injuries what the invention of the wheel was to transportation," Eastman enthusiastically explains.

"The truth about all of this is that the success rate has been very poor. How did you succeed where many, many others have failed?" Camm asks.

"Persistence. That's the short answer. The longer answer is that we were able to succeed with SCNT and we will succeed with developing stem cell lines that will assist in curing disease."

"Be specific. How did you get the SCNT to work this time?" Meade inquires.

Eastman's eyes sparkle as he leans forward, excited to share the information - almost like how a chef might feel when revealing the special ingredient for an award winning dish. "The trick was how do we get the egg to act as if it had been fertilized? We discovered that the secret was to keep the eggs in a phase of its growth cycle called "metaphase."

Eastman notices that Camm is about to ask a question Eastman already anticipates. He raises a hand signaling patience, and then explains, "Metaphase is when the DNA aligns in the middle of the cell prior to the egg dividing. Another little secret I'm going to share is that we discovered we got the best results when we grew the egg in something many of you journalists couldn't make it through the day without," Eastman pauses and his smile broadens when he says, "Caffeine!"

"But how did you get the egg to successfully divide? Don't you need sperm to do that?" Burton inquires.

"In nature sperm is used to divide and egg. In cloning we don't use sperm - we us stimulating electric pulses to help 'activate' the egg so it starts dividing."

Meade shouts out, "But what's to stop someone else from using the technology, the breakthrough that you've come up with, to attempt to clone a human being and grow it into a fully formed person?

"Currently it's illegal to do so. In the United States, the Food and Drug Administration regulates human reproductive cloning. So if you want to go into a clinic and have yourself cloned, it'll never happen. The FDA will come in and stop that effort."

"But there wouldn't be any stopping of an effort outside of the United States, necessarily?" Stone presses Eastman.

Eastman lowers his chin slightly, looks directly ahead and acknowledges, "That's true."

The adrenalin Eastman initially felt is beginning to wane. Fatigue is now replacing the initial surge of energy. Eastman wants to sit down and rub his temples where a headache is creeping in. He shifts his weight ever so subtly from one foot to the other.

A short fire-plug of a man with a thick thatch of black hair not quite hiding his equally thick ears, is standing on his tip toes waving a pen in the air. Eastman points to him. Jim Flores, from the *Orlando Sentinel*, "From doing my research, I know that there are other scientists around the world working in the fields of both therapeutic and reproductive cloning. Isn't it reasonable to expect that a scientist somewhere in the world may one day create a cloned infant? And aren't you helping him to do it by publishing your results?"

"We may have accelerated the cloning of a human being for reproductive purposes by a few weeks or months. We may have made it so scientists in other countries who are pursuing reproductive cloning won't have to try this or that technique in order to succeed. But when we consider the potential benefit for saving human lives, and that people suffering from disease who will be cured using this technology -there's urgency to our work. We believe that it's imperative we publish the findings of therapeutic cloning to advance the cause, so scientists everywhere will have this data and begin working on cures for diseases."

Eastman steals a glance at his watch. He realizes he needs to wrap this conference up in order to watch the CNN interview with one of the LABS geneticists regarding this announcement. When he looks up he sees a tall, lanky man with long hair pulled back in a ponytail, wearing a green plaid flannel shirt and standing up. The man calls out to him, "Glenn Avery with the *Oregon County Register*. Do you believe that you will still be allowed to pursue your work, or do you think the federal government will try to stop it?"

"The U.S. Congress could decide to stop it. If federal law overrides state law, therapeutic cloning could be shut down in states that currently allow it. How and what they decide will have a significant impact on our work," Eastman replies and adds, "I will take one more question and then I'll have to call it an evening."

Against the wall on Eastman's right, a young woman wearing a red sweater, stands and waves her arms as if she were flagging down a motorist. She succeeds in catching Eastman's eye. He points to her. Without introducing herself, she excitedly asks, "How long is it going to take to be able to translate what you have done into some practical therapeutic benefit?"

This is more like it, Eastman thinks, and perks up a bit. In calling the press conference, he hopes to receive needed funding to keep operations going. He enthusiastically replies, "These are the first tentative steps toward this new area of medicine. We should not be under the illusion that next week, or next year, the people we care about most are going to be helped by this technology, even with the support of the U.S. Congress and the President. It's going to take some time. How much time? I can't say for certain. As I said before, once we get started we should be able to move through it expeditiously. This type of work does require both time and patience, but I do believe that we will find a cure for many, many diseases and it's certainly within our grasp."

Before Eastman has a chance to thank everyone for attending the conference Burton shouts out to him.

"What do you have to say to the people who are going to regard what you are doing as the beginning of life? They will contend that in many ways your blastocyst should be considered a human being."

There it is. If Eastman answers he is stepping into the right to life debate he hopes to avoid. He wishes he could make himself disappear. But he has no choice but to continue. To not answer would allow his critics to cry foul and crucify him and the LAB's work as something it isn't.

"They are fundamentally and biologically wrong. Again, we're talking about making human *cellular* life, not a whole human life. This is the fundamental difference between therapeutic cloning and reproductive cloning. I understand that some people, especially those in the pro-life community, may not see it this way," Eastman replies.

"So you aren't pro-life?" Burton clarifies.

"My own personal views are very much pro-life. If I weren't pro-life, I wouldn't be participating in this research."

"That's confusing. Explain what you mean by your statement Dr. Eastman," Avery directs.

"Human life begins later in development. Much later than what we are doing with our research. It's still just a ball of cells at this point. There is no separation of the placenta and what will ultimately become the fetus. It hasn't even decided whether it's going to be one person, fraternal or identical twins. Also, there is no implantation into the womb. This is the stage in which we harvest the cloned stem cells and it's a very early stage of development."

"Isn't that just semantics, Dr. Eastman? Aren't we talking about cells with a genetic code that is directing the material on how to evolve" Burton yells out.

"You can think of it as a tiny ball of cells no bigger than a period at the end of a sentence. When we compare this to what's being used now for harvesting stem cells—donated frozen embryos, many of which are left over from in vitro fertilization, or IVF— we see that they are at a much more advanced stage of development, a stage of development that I do consider as being human life."

Eastman feels the excitement in the air. There is so much discord and debate over this part of human existence it is one that most politicians often skillfully and expertly avoid. Eastman's stomach turns over as he realizes he is embarking on a discussion he hadn't anticipated but in retrospect should have. He immediately regrets using the phrase *beginning of life*. He had never intended to get into a "when does life begin?" discussion. But there it was, a question asked by Burton.

"Most pro-lifers believe that life begins at conception. When exactly do you believe life begins?"

"Life doesn't begin at conception. It begins at the primitive streak formation," Eastman emphatically states.

"What's that?" Avery inquires.

"It's what I was just discussing. It's when the ball of cells separate into what will become the placenta and embryo. I believe it's absolutely not a human being until what will become the fetus and what will become the placenta separate, and implantation occurs."

Eastman's forehead breaks out into little beads of sweat. He feels flushed as he envisions the headlines in his mind. Instead of breaking news in the advancement of therapeutic human cloning, the headlines might read, "Scientist announces when life begins."

"You've announced an 80 cell division of a cloned human. To get embryonic stem cells, you need to have a three-day-old embryo or blastocyst, as you refer to it that has *hundreds* of cells. Doesn't this make it a premature announcement? Why not wait?" Camm asks.

Eastman relaxes his shoulders. He's grateful to Camm for steering things in the direction in which he wants to wrap up the press conference. Checking the time again, Eastman says, "I thought I said 'last question' a few questions ago. I will answer your question and then I really must go. You are correct about the stage of embryonic development that needs to be reached in order to harvest stem cells. We chose to announce at this point because time is of the essence for people who are dying of life-threatening diseases. Our time schedule is based on a 'beat-the- clock' sort of effort. With ethical debate, proper oversight and consideration, we want to apply these technologies as fast as we can. We need to do this because there are people who cannot wait. They are running out of time."

"But isn't there a larger reason that you decided to publish your paper, your work, right now, at the 80 cell stage instead of waiting for the one hundred cell stage in which you can harvest the stem cells - due to the debate that's happening on Capitol Hill? Aren't you trying to influence legislation here in Washington and garner funding?" Burton asks.

"Funding and government support will go a long way in helping us to achieve our goals in a timely fashion," Eastman replies.

A distinguished man wearing a dark gray suit approaches Eastman at the podium and whispers something into his ear.

"I've been informed that we're out of time. Thank you all very much."

Reporters shout questions as Eastman steps away from the microphone and walks toward Dr. Paul Zorvelli, who is waiting around the corner. Zorvelli turns to Eastman and says, "It went well, but I can't help but wonder if we weren't too hasty in our announcement as the last reporter called you out on." Zorvelli runs a meaty hand through his thick, black hair before adding, "Maybe we should've waited until at least a 100 cell division with one of our eggs. Eighty is not a lot and we do need much more than that to create a stem cell line."

"I understand. But we're up against time, Paul. I truly believe we will achieve a greater cell division next time around. Besides we need funding and we need it badly. I'm painfully aware of what's happening on Capitol Hill and how that might affect us."

"And you think this announcement is going to change what's coming down from there?"

"No, I don't. That, my friend, may be too much to hope for. It can get us some more private funding, though. And who knows? Maybe we'll get through to one of the decision makers."

"Hell, let's hope you got through to the entire House and Senate."

That's a pipe dream, Eastman thinks as he and Zorvelli walk into his office, but he appreciates Zorvelli's optimism.

Washington, D.C.
Same Night

The news of the first human clone, although only to a blastocyst stage, reverberates throughout the Oval Office like a stone skipping across a pond sending ripples near and far. The advisors are meeting to discuss the statement the press secretary will make and to create a plan of action.

Viewing this as a threat to his own moral and ethical beliefs, the President addresses his closest advisors. "Cloning human beings is wrong. We shouldn't create life to destroy it."

"Is this what you'd like for me to reflect in your statement, Sir? We shouldn't create life to destroy it? I've got a concern about this, as you are in support of frozen, discarded embryos for stem cell research purposes," the press secretary says."

"Good point. We need to carefully consider this statement. We must also shut down this type of research."

"Yes, Sir," his top advisor replies in agreement and adds, "How would you like to start?"

"We've got to lean on the Senate. I want the bill that was passed by the House to be passed by the Senate; I want a full report on my desk from the advisory panel by the end of this week. Fucking get on it!"

Santa Rosa, California
Same Night

Sitting next to Elliot's hospital bed, Susan mutes the television monitor suspended from the corner of the hospital then turns to Elliot and says, "That's what I wanted to tell you. It's hopeful, and we have time."

"Time for what, Susan?"

"Time to find a cure for Noah!"

Elliot attempts to wrap his brain around her enthusiasm, his son's illness, and this announcement, and the fact that all of it had earned him an overnight stay in the hospital hooked up to heart monitors.

Susan is up on her feet.

"Don't you see, Elliot? Dr. Eastman said it all: We want these technologies as fast as we can get them; time is of the essence and there are people who cannot wait. He even mentioned ALD in his statement!"

Elliot leans back into his pillow and closes his eyes. The heart monitor wired to his chest reminds him of the fragility of life with each beep. A huge part of him wants to pretend none of this is happening. He doesn't want to be reminded of Noah's illness, and he especially doesn't want to collaborate with Susan on a war against it. Not now. Selfishly, but not without feeling a need for self-preservation, he wishes the nurse would come in and tell her to leave so he could rest. He thinks back to when he and Susan first met in law school and then married-,the time before Noah. Susan was so sweet and kind. No one really thought of her as anything else until they saw her in action. She had been a pit bull in the courtroom when she was a practicing prosecuting attorney working for the DA's office in Santa Rosa. She had graduated early and gotten hired on by the DA's office right out of law school. She fought with tenacity and passion. Elliot was the opposite. He had chosen a nice, quiet branch of the law, estate law, which usually didn't involve theatrics. Choosing to stay at home with Noah hadn't dulled her instincts—or her diligent, thorough research methods. She understood everything Eastman had been discussing. Now she wants him to not only agree with her but to get up out of this bed and fight with her for Noah's life. What kind of father would he be? What kind of husband? What kind of man if he refuses?

Elliot opens his eyes and asks Susan, "How, exactly, will this help Noah?"

Susan tells Elliot everything she's learned in the past few days about Noah's disease and how regenerative medicine, or therapeutic cloning, it would be the first big step in saving their son.

"We have time. Noah's only two years old."

"But he might start to show symptoms by age three. How does this give us time?" Elliot asks.

"I'm not looking at a year from now. I'm looking at eighteen years. There's a significant chance that Noah could remain asymptomatic until adulthood—that would buy us a lot of time."

Elliot sucks in a sharp breath. Turning away from Susan, he sadly replies, "Joshua is nine and at the end of his life. What makes you think it's going to be different for Noah?"

Susan swallows hard as the tears well up in her eyes. With all the courage and conviction she can muster, she replies flatly, "Because I have to believe."

Just then the nurse walked in with a tray holding a plastic cup of water and a small paper cup of pills. "I'm sorry, Mrs. Gaynor, but visiting hours are over. Your husband needs his rest." The nurse hands Elliot the cup with the pills and the one with water.

"What's this?"

"Something to help you sleep, Mr. Gaynor."

Elliot pops the pills into his mouth and chases them down with the water. He hopes they will work quickly.

Susan tenderly brushes Elliot's cheek with her lips. "Rest up. Noah needs you. I need you."

Westchester, New York
Late, Same Night

The LAB's ethicists, Dr. Gerald Brown, was about to be interviewed on CNN at any moment. The LAB's staff had gathered in the break room to watch it on the big screen TV. Eastman watches as Kathryn takes a seat next to him. She carefully balances a slice of veggie pizza on a flimsy paper plate on her lap and takes a sip of a bottle of Pacifico. She places the cold beer against her forehead. The office is stuffy and warm with so many people in it, Eastman thinks. He looks at her curiously and remarks, "You don't look like you're feeling well." Kathryn gives a tight smile and replies, "It's a bit warm in here. Eastman stands up and walks over to the window. He opens it wide and returns to his seat. "Thanks," she says, acknowledging the cool air streaming into the room.

Eastman looks up to see the interview has started. "Turn it up," Zorvelli commands from his seat next to Eastman. Eastman points the television controller at the set and increases the volume. "That's good," Anderson says from his seat on the other side of Kathryn.

Eastman listens as CNN reporters discuss the announcement, the interview, and the ethical ramifications of the new technology. The guests include Gerald Brown, a member of the LAB's ethical team, and CNN's legal advisor, Jason Clark.

Henry Townsend, the svelte, silver-haired news anchor with a foxlike face, dresses Clark, a red-haired man wearing round wire-rimmed glasses. Townsend asks Clark if there is anything legally to stop the LAB from pursuing its work. Clark responds, "The current administration hasn't passed any legislation stopping privately funded companies from pursuing therapeutic cloning. However, there is a bill that just passed the House and will be voted on in the Senate. If it becomes law, it will stop all forms of cloning in the United States. This would have serious implications for the LAB."

The camera flashes onto Gerald Brown, the LAB's ethics advisory team spokesperson, signaling that he is about to speak.

Townsend introduces Brown as he adjusts the microphone attached to the lapel of his tweed suit coat. "As a member of the LAB's ethical advisory board, Dr. Brown, how do you view this type of research?"

"This research has enormous life-saving potential. I'd also like to point out the fact that there is sharp distinction in the effort to produce a human baby in reproductive cloning and the research that is known as therapeutic cloning, whose sole purpose is to create stem cells that are identical to a patient's DNA."

"If the goal is to make cloned stem cells, and not to create a cloned human being, can therapeutic cloning be done without pursuing reproductive cloning?" Townsend asks.

"You can help to enforce this, not just by choice, but by creating strict laws that prohibit reproductive cloning."

"Dr. Brown, in the press conference, earlier, we heard Dr. Eastman of the LAB make the announcement that a human blastocyst, or activated egg, has been created. So far there hasn't been enough successful division of this entity to allow for therapeutic medical research. But I'm sure you will agree it's just a matter of time. Aren't there moral and ethical considerations about creating life in this way?" Townsend inquires.

"People whose belief is based on human life beginning at conception may view therapeutic human cloning as ethically wrong or immoral. For them, this type of research might be the equivalent to killing a living child in order to harvest its organs. That's a huge misconception. It's developmentally and scientifically incorrect. Interestingly, many of these same people find it acceptable to conduct research using human stem cells derived from embryos left over from IVF, or in vitro fertilization."

"What's the difference?"

"The stage of development that is needed in order to harvest stem cells for therapeutic medical research is at a cell division much less formed than at the embryonic stage of development. Once an embryo has formed, there is division between the placenta and fetal material and attachment to the womb. At the blastocyst stage we are talking about a ball of cells no bigger than a tiny crumb."

"We know the President supports the use of frozen embryos but doesn't support therapeutic cloning. What's the justification?"

"The justification is that these embryos are going to be destroyed anyway, so at least by using them some good could result in perpetuating human life," Clark replies.

"Even if those who like the President, believe that life begins at conception, isn't it ultimately wrong then to be using discarded frozen embryos to harvest stem cells?"

"It does appear to be an ethical dilemma and counter intuitive if one believes that life begins at conception - then perhaps these frozen embryos should not be used." Clark responds.

"Does the lab support the use of discarded frozen embryos?" Townsend inquires of Brown.

"There are always ethical considerations in scientific research. As a team we have carefully explored all of the ramifications. Currently, our position regarding this is in not using them," Brown explains.

"But not for moral or ethical reasons, correct? You prefer to use therapeutic cloning over frozen, discarded IVF fetuses?" Townsend asks.

"A therapeutic clone is a genetic copy of an individual. Stem cells derived from blastocysts have a much better success rate on many levels not only for finding cures to diseases, but when reintroducing the stem cells into a person's body. They are a perfect match. There is no chance of rejection."

"Dr. Brown, the people doing this research believe that it's both beneficial to prolonging life and that it's not in itself a human life?" Townsend asks.

"They don't believe that entities produced by therapeutic cloning have a moral status—unlike frozen embryos. They believe that the benefit outweighs any moral assignment of this being human life, and that the moral assignment of human life is already being used."

"So in a nutshell, if I understand correctly—and, Dr. Brown, you can correct me if I am wrong—there are those who consider activated eggs as being a human life. But many of these people still support using IVF frozen embryos for stem cell research even though these embryos are a far more developed form of what they would also deem as human life?" Townsend clarifies.

Clark interjects. "If I may jump in here, there seems to be an acceptance to using discarded frozen embryos. It's not illegal to use them, and currently it's not illegal to pursue therapeutic cloning either."

"So, what exactly is the difference between an embryo and an activated egg or blastocyst, and why is it so important to curing disease?" Townsend asks Brown.

"Unlike an embryo, which is a more advanced stage of development than an activated egg, or blastocyst, there is no sperm involved. Therapeutic cloning is a process of growing cells using a patient's own DNA. The DNA is inserted into an unfertilized egg cell to create embryonic stem cells, and these cells hold the promise of repairing the damage of age and disease in humans; so having it as part of the discussion on whether or not its human life is a moot point."

"But the egg used to create a therapeutic clone did come from a person, and the person was created by the egg and sperm uniting at one time in human development. Correct?"

"That's part of the moral debate. So far, as Mr. Clark pointed out, this new type of entity has no legal status or even a moral one. It's not seen as being a human being."

"Interesting. But what if the disease lies in the person's DNA? Would you still want to use someone's DNA to correct an illness?"

"Well, that's where DNA modifications come in."

"Can we do that? Modify someone's DNA?"

"I'm here to discuss the ethics regarding all of this. I can tell you though that there is a company in San Francisco, Cambrian Geonomics that is currently doing this. They are laser printing DNA that removes the error in the code that creates a mutation of Tay Sachs, Parkinson's, and many other types of diseases."

"So why aren't people with genetic abnormalities in their DNA getting this done?" Townsend inquires.

"Because researchers haven't found a good way to get the corrected code safely into a person's body. Soon it will happen, sooner than we think," Brown replies.

"And with it a lot of ethical considerations, I'm certain."

"You know it."

"I'd like to move on to your role as part of a team of ethical advisors for the LAB. To put it bluntly, what is it that you do exactly?" Townsend asks.

"Well, we debate issues like the one you, Mr. Clark, and I are currently discussing. Should a moral status be assigned to activated eggs or blastocysts? I say no. Currently, I and other ethicists on the board have spent the majority of our time creating an ethically responsible egg donor program for this research. We've had many more women than anticipated come forward to participate in this research. Most give the reason for their participation as being a willingness to help friends and family members who might ultimately benefit."

"They didn't just do it for free, though, the women—they were paid thousands of dollars. Correct?" Townsend inquires.

Eastman lets out a low whistle. He turns to Kathryn and says, "I don't like how he's phrasing this. Kathryn nods in agreement. She hopes that Brown will set Townsend straight.

"It takes a significant commitment and involves a certain amount of discomfort to participate in the program. Women who are qualified donors must participate in invasive procedures. They have to inject themselves with medications for days and undergo a procedure in which the eggs are harvested. There is an element of risk involved. Things can go wrong. The women were compensated. All in all, it's a modest reimbursement for their contribution."

Kathryn hoists her beer to the TV screen as she responds, "Well said!" Zorvelli reaches up and taps his beer bottle against Kathryn's, and Anderson follows suit, swinging his beer into the air and waving it in their general direction.

"And compensating them is ethical and legal?" Townsend inquires of Clark.

"Both men and women are compensated for assisting with fertility efforts. Men receive compensation for donated sperm. Women are compensated for being surrogates."

"Dr. Brown, Do you think the LAB published their finding prematurely? I mean, this procedure we're discussing never did produce a blastocyst the size of hundreds of cells needed for therapeutic cloning."

"We could argue that. But look, I don't think so. The LAB's goal was to be as transparent as possible about what they are doing. They have taken the first few and very significant steps in a journey that could help a lot of people. We are continuously doing research to advance medical science on a variety of fronts, but none have been as promising as this. People, who are young and healthy in other ways, are dying every day. Our ability to treat disease often gets obstructed by politics, insurance companies, and drug companies fighting over who owns the right to what drug. Ethically and morally, we should be pursuing the options available to us that have the most potential for saving lives. To stop it doesn't make sense."

"Careful, Gerry," Eastman warns.

"What are you saying about the drug and insurance companies? Do you think there is some conspiracy out there to stop advancement in medical treatments?" Townsend inquires.

Eastman turns to Zorvelli and quietly says, "Gerry's got his balls in a vice now."

"No, no. What I'm saying is that I think there are roadblocks and risks to therapeutic cloning, however if we prohibit therapeutic cloning, we also prevent the development of all these potentially remarkable new cures and therapies. These are the cures that save lives and guarantee a better quality of life."

"Could we agree, Dr. Brown, that there needs to be a line drawn that shouldn't be crossed?" Townsend asks.

"Yes. I would argue that we should draw the line at reproductive cloning. Dr. Eastman and the people at the LAB will not cross this line."

"So what I hear you saying is that you are in support of the LAB's work?"

"Personally, I support it. If medical science can increase people's chances of healthy survival, then this research enhances respect for human life. However, I didn't have an opinion when I was first asked to participate in this. My team and I went into this independently. We were asked by the LAB to debate and arrive at ethical standards for this type of work."

The last scene was of Gerry being thanked for the interview.

"Nice save Gerry. I'm glad I work behind the scenes and I'm not out there on the front lines," Kathryn says with a sigh of relief as Eastman turns off the television.

Dr. Anderson asks, "James, what did you think?"

"I'm hoping that this opens the eyes of members of Congress as to what regenerative medicine is all about."

"Isn't that a bit too much to hope for?" Kathryn cautions.

"Careful Kathryn, your liberalism is showing," Anderson teases.

"I'm a registered independent, a free thinker. I also know the mindset of those who are going to try to stand in our way. There's a huge gap in understanding the difference between fertility cloning and therapeutic cloning."

"Well, let's hope we're much better at getting the information out about the difference between the two than we have been in the past." Eastman states.

"There certainly seems to be a gap in understanding among politicians," Anderson chimes in.

"We all know that this isn't a liberal or conservative fight. In fact, it's one that seems to unabashedly unite people across political party lines, religious affiliations, and humanitarian medical efforts."

"Yeah, and some of them are united against us," Anderson reminds him.

San Francisco, California
Wednesday Afternoon, (three weeks later)

The spacious, red-carpeted room is filled to capacity. Attendance for the United Citizens' Movement Against Human Cloning meeting at the Organic Consumers Association's Conference looked to be picking up since the last one. Tonight's conference began with speaker Lawrence Delano stating, "Human cloning is a crime against human dignity and humanity. It's a step toward the commodification and brutalization of human life. We must not allow ourselves to be pushed any further down this road. If we can't stop human beings from being cloned, try to imagine what we won't be able to stop next."

Delano doesn't mince words as he speaks to the 250 attendees in the banquet room of the Mark Hopkins Hotel. Thunderous applause reverberates throughout the red and gold room and bounce off the crystal chandelier and walls. One of the attendees, a tall man dressed in jeans and work books, gets up and pours himself a drink of purified water. He sips the cool water he holds tightly between his calloused hands as he listens intently as Delano continues. "These scientists have the skills and resources to create human clones. They are operating outside any structures of public or scientific accountability. In a growing number of countries, their efforts to clone human children would be felonies punishable by imprisonment."

The man with the water sets the cup down on the white tablecloth. He's heard enough. He tears his name tag from his brown flannel shirt. Although perhaps never intending it this way, the tag is torn between the first and last names. He gives it to the young girl with the blonde dreads and gray blue eyes framed with too much black mascara. She reads the two pieces JOE SMITH. She smiles up at him and says, "Thank you for attending the conference Joe Smith." He returns her smile and walks out the door. As soon as the door closes his smile is replaced by a scowl.

Smith knows what needs to be done to stop these evildoers, these Satan worshipers. Smith had read about the movement against cloning on the internet. It was a long way to travel but well worth it to among others who feel as he does. Besides, he can write it off his taxes since it was a part of the

Organic Consumers Association, he thinks. He was hoping that the association had a plan for stopping this effort. But after listening to the opening remarks he now knows that there aren't currently any such plans in the works. Conventions and meetings won't stop the effort nor will the Exploratory Initiative that Delano is preaching. No, what is needed is action —swift and final. He'll be the one to get it done. Smith realized a long time ago that if you paid attention in life, you'd notice that there are signs everywhere pointing to the direction you should take. Smith had been seeing the signs for a while now. He's ready to follow them. He knows that he will be the one to stop this abomination while the rest of them are deciding on what actions to take.

Westchester, New York
Monday, October, afternoon (a week later)

"Dr. Eastman, meet Noah," Susan introduces her son.

"Hello there, Noah." Dr. Eastman smiles and nods at the cherubic blond boy sitting on his mother's lap directly across from his big desk in his office at the LAB. Noah smacks a plastic toy truck down on the desk and laughs. Elliot offers Noah a cookie in exchange for his truck. The little boy drops the truck and takes the cookie. "I was able to review Noah's medical records. He's in good health now—correct?"

"Yes, just the usual colds and viruses but no symptoms of ALD," Susan replies with a slight nervous lilt to her voice. She is in awe in the presence of a man who she feels will save her son. She adds, "As you know, the disease may strike at age three or may wait until adolescence or an adult onset. We're hoping the latter."

"It's Susan's and my hope that we will be able to utilize the time we have to discover a course of treatment that will cure Noah."

Eastman sets aside the medical records and looks thoughtfully upon the little family.

"There are drawbacks and concerns. What we're attempting has only been achieved in animals up until now."

"The highest or most evolved animal that this has been performed on, with success for harvesting stem cells has been a monkey, right?" Susan clarifies.

"Yes. Since my initial announcement on therapeutic cloning, we've been able to create a human clone and grow it to the blastocyst stage, much more than the 80 cell division we announced. We've succeeded at 200 cells - a stage at which we now harvest the stem cells. I view this as very encouraging."

"That is hopeful, as you say, but what about gene therapy - the part that follows fter the harvesting of stem cells? Susan asks.

"Are you and Elliot familiar with the process?"

"Elliot and I both know a little."

"How it works is that a normal gene is introduced into the cells of patients who have a defective gene. Once introduced, the normal gene behaves as if there's no defect, and the patients gets better. Although it's a newer technique and a novel one, many scientists are using it to try to find cures for many types of disease. If we do it with your son we would be attempting to find a cure for ALD."

"We believe we don't have anything to lose and everything to gain in trying," Susan states as she reaches over and gently places her hand on her husband's knee.

Eastman is struck and humbled by their plight. He wonders what it might be like to have a child that has been stricken with an incurable illness. He's glad he doesn't really know. The closest he can relate their story to his is in recalling his own mother's death from breast cancer that ultimately led him on the path to his area of expertise. Losing his mom as a child had been painful enough. He couldn't imagine having to face a disease that could take your child's life.

"What you're about to embark on has never been done, at least not to the point at which we can get therapeutic benefits," Eastman advises. He feels a ripple of excitement about the possibility of beginning this journey with the Gaynors, but at the same time wants to honestly prepare them. He believes that Noah and his parents would be a good fit for this part of his work. He also has trepidation. While he wants to advance his work, he feels a responsibility to the parents' emotional states. He doesn't want to fill them with false hope. It's his dream that their hope for this procedure would be realized for their son. However, Eastman knows that the chances of this succeeding, in the time needed to save Noah's life, depends on so many variables that it's truly a journey of faith.

"But it's a start. It's where our best hope lies. We don't have illusions that this will work and that Noah will be spared," Susan replies.

"It's an expensive process. I'm certain you've been informed that there are other treatments that might be of help to Noah in the near future such as cord blood stem cell replacement therapy and bone marrow treatment."

"Elliot and I are aware of all of our options and we plan to pursue any and all possibilities to help our son. The simple truth is that what medicine has to offer Noah right now is a far cry from what he will most likely need."

"Viewing therapeutic cloning as a viable avenue of hope right now is extremely optimistic."

"I agree," Elliot replies. "However, Susan and I have seen this play out with our nephew, Josh, and quite honestly Josh doesn't have much hope left. We don't want the same fate for our son."

"I'm sorry," Eastman replies with genuine empathy conveyed in both his voice and eyes. He pauses and realizes just how much the Gaynors have witnessed the disease first hand with their nephew and are here because they don't have any illusions. They have only hope, faith, and a dream that somehow this might work.

"One other thing I want you to know is that ethical considerations are ones we take seriously here at the LAB. It hasn't been without proper foresight and debate that we've been able to continue our quest in this field. As for problems, they do arise from programming errors in genetic material from a donor cell. When an embryo is created from the union of a sperm and an egg, the embryo receives copies of most genes from both parents. This process is called imprinting. Only one copy of a gene, either the maternal or paternal gene, is turned on. Defects in the genetic imprint of DNA from a single donor cell may lead to some of the developmental abnormalities of cloned embryos. It's not a pure process."

"Is there a way to help prevent this?" Susan asks.

"If we were to use Noah's DNA and if we were able to successfully use the maternal mother's egg, your egg, and that's a lot of ifs, it would significantly increase a successful outcome."

Noah wiggles in Susan's arms. He is clearly tired of sitting in her lap. She places him on the carpeted floor and hands him a cup of goldfish crackers that she had retrieved from the diaper bag. Susan watches Noah and smiles as she notices he seems to enjoy the challenge of picking up the crackers, using his pincer grip, more than he appears to enjoy putting them in his mouth.

"This is akin to taking our best shot in the dark," Elliot says, turning to Susan.

"I agree somewhat with your analogy, Elliot. However, I do believe it's more hopeful than just a shot in the dark for our son."

"Okay, let's start talking possibilities. In order to fully understand what we are attempting to do here I'd like to show you both a film."

"I'm not certain Noah could sit through a film," Susan replies. Eastman nods and asks, "Would you mind if one of our team members takes Noah for a bit?" Susan nods her approval. Eastman presses a buzzer on his desk. A beautiful, tall, svelte redhead wearing a lab coat, black turtleneck, black slacks, and sensible black shoes walks into the room. Susan first notices how her emerald green eyes sparkle against her creamy white skin. A lovely smile spreads across her face as she greets them.

"Hello. I'm Dr. MacMurray, and this must be Noah." Susan thinks that she looks more like a ballet dancer than a physician as she watches Dr. MacMurray gracefully bends to meet Noah. Normally clingy, Noah quickly returns her smile and grabs a handful of her thick, wavy hair giving it a tug and laughs.

"No, Noah," Susan admonishes moving to unclench her playful toddlers hands.

"It's okay," Dr. MacMurray replies standing up. Eastman introduces her. "Mr. and Mrs. Gaynor, Dr. Kathryn MacMurray is our embryologist."

"Please call me Kathryn," she says shaking both of the parent's hands.

"Kathryn, could you please take care of Noah while we watch a film?" Kathryn stretches out a hand to Noah and he walks willingly to her carrying his cup of crackers, much to Susan's surprise.

"Do you like fish, Noah?" she asks scooping the boy up. Noah shows her a goldfish cracker he has in his hand. "Goldfish crackers. I like those too. I have real fish that swim in a tank in my office," she explains as she carries him out the door.

"One other area that we need to address is that the LAB is privately owned and predominately privately funded. You should also be aware of the fact that currently there are no laws prohibiting therapeutic human cloning in New York State and in a few other states, such as California, where you live. We do receive some state funding. However, at any point along the way, the federal government may decide to pull the plug on therapeutic human cloning and make it illegal to pursue it in every state. As you know, the current administration is hostile to this type of research. In all fairness, this has been a bipartisan hostility. Both Republicans and Democrats have spoken out against this type of research. I want you to know up front that there are no guarantees. We have many obstacles to overcome —scientifically, financially, and even politically to advance research and possibly help your son."

"I've heard of cures for other diseases being held up as drug companies fight over the rights to a certain drug, or politics surround the treatment of such diseases as Lyme's, and it's downright frightening," Susan states as she settles comfortably into her chair.

Eastman presses a button on his desk and a large movie screen unfolds behind the Gaynors.

"I'm impressed by the level of technology in your office. Your 'smart room' is outfitted even better than my office," Elliot remarks genuinely meaning it.

"Thank you. Please turn your chairs toward the screen and we will begin the film. his is a video of a cloning procedure recently performed at the LAB," Eastman explains as he presses a button on his computer and the DVD starts playing on the screen.

The Gaynors watch what looks like a round, glowing ball held by a glass pipette. "You're looking at an egg."

"The needle you're watching is extracting the genetic material from the egg. What you're seeing is human material. The therapeutic procedure to create cloned cells for Noah, that we will genetically modify, will be similar to this procedure."

The Gaynors look intently at the screen.

"In this next scene we see a petri dish with a red culture medium. The liquid contains living human skin cells or fibroblast."

"Where did the human skin cells come from?" Elliot asks.

"They came from human donors," Eastman replies and continues, "As the camera zooms in you can see the smaller skin cells that have just finished dividing. They are in a resting phase called G1. They will soon divide again. It's at this stage though that these are used for cloning. Each of the cells contains a nucleus. Within the nucleus are 46 chromosomes. The DNA of each cell holds what I like to refer to as the recipe to create a cloned human embryo. If we clone Noah then we will need to use a three millimeter skin biopsy from a procedure that would be performed by a physician. This is where we'd get Noah's DNA."

Eastman pushes the button again on his desk and off goes the film and on come the lights as the screen retracts back up into the ceiling.

The Gaynors turn around and face Dr. Eastman.

"That part looks easy," Susan remarks.

"It is. The more challenging part is retrieving the eggs."

"Can I donate my eggs?"

"We'd prefer that, Susan. You aren't thirty five yet, and the fact that you are in good health makes it likely that you will be a good candidate."

"What if she can't or decides not to be the egg donor?" Elliot inquires.

"Those of any other young female donor on your side of the family would work well too."

"Why just family? What about other female donors? Aren't there woman who get paid to do this?" Elliot presses.

"We believe that there is no likelihood of an immune rejection response for the patient by taking the mitochondria from the maternal lineage of the patient, because the mitochondria are passed exclusively from the mother to the child. All female relatives with the same maternal lineage possess the same mitochondrial DNA."

"I don't see any problem with me donating eggs."

"I want to caution you, it's not without potential risk to you."

"What kind of risk are we talking for my wife?"

"It's done all the time, right? I mean for infertile couples?" Susan inquires hoping to assuage some of Elliot's concerns and even her own.

"Yes. But there are physical risks that are known as ovarian hyper-stimulation. This can result from the hormone injections you will need to take prior to the egg harvest. There is also a possibility of infection. You may feel bloated and cramping, along with experiencing mood changes and irritability. There are also fluctuations in weight. In extreme circumstances you may experience infertility, and, as with any surgical procedure, there is inherent risk to the patient."

"I don't like the sound of inherent risk," Elliot remarks leaning forward in his seat.

"I'd be carefully monitored, right?"

"Of course. We will go through all of this in detail should you choose to donate your eggs, Susan."

"How much does all of this cost?" Elliot asks.

"It's expensive."

Susan steals a glance at Elliot as he leans back into his chair and she watches him swallow hard. Not only were they talking about turning his son into some kind of science experiment, she thinks, it might bankrupt them too.

Susan quickly calculates their savings. Without knowing exactly what Eastman explains by 'expensive,' she's pretty sure that they might only have enough for one or two attempts.

"The LAB will cover most of the costs, but you need to know that there are no guarantees."

"You mean with the cloning procedure?" Elliot asks.

"I mean with everything. Even when harvesting the eggs—we may get only a few or none at all. We just don't know until we try. In addition, we will need to harvest the eggs out here. That means a fair amount of traveling for Susan."

"Would Dr. MacMurray be the one performing the egg harvesting procedure on me?"

"She most likely will be in attendance, Susan. An OBGYN will retrieve the eggs. After the retrieval, Dr. MacMurray's real work begins," Eastman replies and then asks, "Do you have any more questions?"

"What happens after we have a successful harvest," Susan optimistically inquires.

"We create a clone of Noah, harvest the stem cells and then we proceed to do gene therapy. More specifically, we will take cloned cells in which the ALD mutation has been corrected and create a virus, a way of transmitting that mutation, to shuttle new genes into Noah's body cells."

"How exactly does this work?" Elliot asks.

"The virus infects a cell, carries a therapeutic gene to the nucleus, and inserts it into Noah's DNA at a random location. We will add a functional ALD gene to the cells from his bone marrow. The goal of this is to correct the genetic coding in the cells and destroy ALD."

"I know you haven't done this in humans but gave you had success with this in animals?" Susan asks.

"In all honesty, this type of research is very experimental, and currently we are having difficulty modifying all the cells that need therapy in our animal patients. In addition, there is currently difficulty ensuring reliable long-term expression of the new genes in these animals."

"So it doesn't sound like it's been hugely successful using animals?" Elliot questions.

"Yes and no. We are making progress. And yes, if you agree to the process then Noah will be our first human attempt at gene modification."

Suddenly, it occurs to Susan that they are pioneers in this field, guinea pigs if you will. But this might be the only way to save their son's life, and it scares the shit out of her. It was easy to not think about Noah becoming sick when he was so healthy. When faced with the harsh reality of it all and the fact that the only real therapeutic intervention lay in this new field of medicine, she truly fears that she might not ever see her son grow into a man. She and Elliot very well could lose him before he was even a teen. Intellectually she knows this, but this is perhaps the first time that her heart is breaking because of it. She struggles to cope with her feelings by concentrating on Eastman's words.

"The goal of therapeutic cloning is to provide a pure population of genetically modified cells. Use one modified cell for cloning, and the entire cloned embryo will then carry that modification. So will the embryonic stem cells derived from it and any therapeutic tissues they produce. Alternatively, scientists could do the modification in embryonic stem cells after cloning, and then grow a limitless supply of tissue from one

"I think I understand. You can give Noah the cells that all have the same targeted modification," Elliot states.

"One hundred percent. We consider creating cloned embryos that match patients with a genetic predisposition to disease to be one of the most important therapeutic applications of the technology because it allows diseased tissues of all kinds to be created and studied in the lab."

Susan lays out all of the steps in her mind as if she were looking at a recipe. Noah would be successfully be cloned, the genetic organism would have to continue to divide into a fully formed blastocyst, a*nd* the scientists would have to discover the gene modification that would allow them to attack the ALD disease before it attacked Noah. It sounded like a recipe for success. However, along the way so many things could go wrong, Susan thinks. She looks over at Elliot. Was he seeing the possibilities too?

"And just to reiterate this is purely for therapeutic cloning purposes, not reproductive?" Elliot inquires.

Susan's glad Elliot has asked the question. Even though they had both listened carefully to what Dr. Eastman had explained, they still need reassurances from him that their son wouldn't be used for reproductive cloning purposes.

"Growing an entire human being is currently beyond our abilities and more notably beyond our ethical consideration. The number of cloned cells we'd need to help your son, and to find cures for other diseases, is only the amount that would fit on the head of a pin. This sounds minimal, but in reality we're discussing hundreds. They're also flattened in a Petri dish—thus preventing them from progressing beyond the limited number of cell divisions we require."

"You're talking about a cloned embryo -right?"

"The term embryo or embryonic, Elliot, is a bit misleading. We'll only need to take the embryonic development to a blastocyst stage, or as we also refer to it, an activated egg stage—and then allow it to grow to 100-200 cells."

"The stem cells we derive from Noah's cloned embryos, which will ultimately bear an ALD mutation, will be a significant research tool in helping to cure the disease."

"But ultimately this isn't just about helping to cure our son's disease - you'd be opening the door to find cures for all types of diseases - correct?"

"Precisely, Susan It's our hope that we will be able to cure cancers, diabetes, prevent people from going blind, and also cure many, many life-threatening diseases. If we succeed with Noah, we will have learned how to help millions of other people."

"I think that's truly wonderful," Susan replies.

"You said that the current administration is hostile towards this type of research. I just want to know if it's legal. I mean, would we be participating in anything illegal?" Elliot inquires.

"It's legal. The truth is the House's anti-cloning legislation is designed to make everything we are doing illegal. If the Senate was to pass the bill that recently passed in the House, and we did proceed, we could be prosecuted for therapeutic cloning attempts and you both could be prosecuted for participating in them."

This gives Susan pause.

"We're free to pursue this now. However, this can change. Does this change your minds?"

"No," Susan and Elliot reply almost in unison.

"But what are the chances such a bill would pass in the Senate?" Elliot asks.

"To be honest, I can't give you odds. I can only tell you that as long as we are free to pursue this type of therapy, the LAB's going to pursue it."

"Good. Quite honestly, when Susan proposed all of this to me I didn't see it as an option. It sounded, well, far off into the future type of thinking. After meeting with you, I see the possibilities, and that makes me feel more hopeful," Elliot replies.

"I'm glad. However, do you both want to take some time to talk it over?"

Elliot and Susan look at each other. They both discussed the fact that there aren't very many avenues that hold as much promise available to them in helping their son. They exchange a warm, knowing smile with each other.

"When can we get started?" Susan asks Dr. Eastman.

"I will need to present Noah's case to my colleagues and to the ethics committee. Also, I'll have you go over the medical procedures with Dr. MacMurray, the ones that you and Noah will participate in. I'd like to review all of this in-depth with you tomorrow before you leave."

Westchester, New York
Morning, Next Day

They arrive at Dr. Kathleen Lauderfield's dermatology office at 8:30 a.m. for Noah's procedure. Afterwards, Noah's induced pluripotent stem cells will be frozen until doctors are able to harvest Susan's eggs and attempt the first SCNT process.

Although Susan has reservations about the entire process, she also knows that she will make a pact with the Devil to save her son's life. As she holds Noah on the exam table, she wonders if she hasn't done that very thing. Noah appears to be content sucking on his pacifier and playing with the small plastic fire truck his parents handed to him. He presses the button that makes the alarm sound. Dr. Lauderfield presses firmly, but gently, on Noah's plump pink legs. Noah responds by pulling away and giving her a surprised look.

"Will it hurt?" Susan inquires anxiously.

"He'll feel a pinch and then there will be some pain," Dr. Lauderfield replies and adds, "We need to obtain only a three- millimeter skin sample. It will heal quickly."

Dr. Lauderfield's nurse, wearing a pink scrub top and a big smile, hustles through the exam room door holding a tube of antibiotic ointment and Winnie the Pooh Band-Aids. She's also holding a sippy-cup filled with an orange liquid.

"Nurse Lisa is going to give Noah some Tylenol before the procedure. This way it will start working soon after we finish and help take away some of the distress."

The nurse gives the sippy-cup to Susan and instructs, "Please give this to him now. It will help with the pain and to calm him."

Susan takes Noah's pacifier and truck from him and then gives him the cup. Much to Susan's surprise, Noah tips the cup up to his mouth and willing drinks from it. Then his face scrunches up and he drops the cup.

"I'm sorry," Susan apologizes to Lisa as she hands Noah his pacifier and the truck.

"No worries," Lisa responds as she picks up the cup and sets it down on the counter near the sink.

Dr. Lauderfield moves the instrument tray closer to Noah and Susan.

Elliot stares at the tray and then his face turns white. Susan knows that he rarely accompanies her to the pediatrician for Noah's check-ups, let alone participate in something like this.

"Honey, why don't you wait in the reception area until we're done? I can do this myself," Susan says to Elliot.

"Are you sure?"

"Yes."

Elliot kisses Noah's head and leaves the room. Dr. Lauderfield takes a small instrument from the tray and looking back at her nurse, she shows her the area where the sample will be taken.

"Mrs. Gaynor, please hug Noah face to face with you," Dr. Lauderfield instructs.

Susan takes the fire truck and sets it down next to them. Noah begins to protest as Susan swiftly turns him toward her and hugs him close.

"Like this?"

"Perfect, Mrs. Gaynor," Dr. Lauderfield replies as she pushes up Noah's diaper. "I'm doing it just under the fold of his buttocks so the tiny scar won't be visible,"

Noah lets out a wail. His pacifier falls to the ground. He pushes away from Susan and then melts into her arms as Nurse Lisa dabs the spot with ointment and then applies the Band-Aid.

"All done," Susan soothes as she rocks Noah in her arms and adds, "You were a brave, big boy." Nurse Lisa then surprises Noah with a lollipop; Noah accepts the treat and soon his sobs are sniffles. Balancing Noah in her arms, Susan comes down off the exam table and retrieves the truck and pacifier, placing both in the diaper bag. They follow Dr. Lauderfield out to the waiting area as the nurse tidies the room. Elliot takes Noah from Susan and hoists the now-sticky toddler up into his arms and holds him tight. He kisses his tear-stained cheeks and wipes his nose with a tissue he's holding.

"He should heal quickly, but you can change the Band-Aid as needed," Dr. Lauderfield instructs as she hands the specimen to Susan to take back to The LAB. Elliot glances at it and then looks away. He has no desire to see the sample.

"I'm glad that's over," Susan says to Elliot, who looks as if he couldn't agree more.

"Actually, it's just beginning," Dr. Lauderfield comments with an encouraging smile on her face and adds, "We are all hoping this journey leads to a cure."

Westchester, New York
The Next Day

Leaving Noah with the hotel babysitter is a bit unnerving for Susan. However, the sitter came with excellent references. Dragging a two-year-old around was an exhausting process and both Susan and Elliot know there is no way they can expect Noah to sit through another meeting with Dr. Eastman at the LAB.

The Gaynors have been invited by Dr. Eastman to learn more about the real-life human cloning attempt using donor eggs. This will provide them with an up-close view of the procedure they hope to have with Noah. They are led down a hallway and into the cloning lab's viewing room where they are greeted by Dr. Eastman. Susan is surprised to note that the lab is no bigger than a tiny bedroom. The viewing area where they stand is a bit larger.

"Glad you could get here on time," Eastman greets them.

"Thank you for inviting us," Elliot replies.

"On the other side of the glass window you will see Dr. MacMurray."

Wearing a white lab coat and seated on a stool Dr. MacMurray is looking into a glass dish.

"The dish Dr. MacMurray is scanning holds the ovarian eggs of a female donor," Eastman informs them the Gaynors.

They all watch as Dr. MacMurray hands the dish to her assistant, a young man whose red sneakers add a touch of individuality to the required white coat.

"If you recall the film I showed you, we are performing a similar procedure today. As you can see, the assistant is now placing the donated human eggs into a drop of culture medium at the bottom of a clear plastic dish. He's covering it with a drop of oil to maintain the pH of the culture and to prevent evaporation."

"Interesting," Susan, remarks.

"Take a seat," Eastman offers as he gestures with his hand to the row of chairs arranged in front of a video monitor on the same wall just above the viewing window. The Gaynors sit in unison and watch as Eastman flips on the video monitor.

"We're able to get a better view this way. Looking at the screen you will see a close up of the culture with the eggs in it. You can now see a close up of the culture."

Over the speaker they hear the voice of Dr. MacMurray's assistant, "They look good." "They do Matt," she agrees as she's leaving the lab room.

Susan and Elliot continue to look at the monitor. "Magnified many times over, a human egg is perfectly round and luminous."

"It looks like a harvest moon."

Susan smiles in agreement at Elliot's remark.

"It's the largest cell in the human body," Dr. MacMurray replies entering the room. However, unlike the moon, it's no bigger than a grain of sand."

"You're looking at a close up of one of the eggs we retrieved from a recent donor."

"How many were you able to retrieve?" Elliot inquires.

"We got two viable eggs," Dr. MacMurray replies.

"Only two? Did something go wrong?" Susan asks.

Drying her hands with a paper towel she turns to Susan and replies, "No. On the contrary—two eggs isn't bad. It's not uncommon to get only a couple or even none."

Susan steals a glance at Elliot. Collecting eggs could be a very costly business along with being a risky endeavor.

Tossing the paper towel in the waste receptacle, Dr. MacMurray says, "It's just the way it is. Human eggs are difficult to retrieve, unlike animal eggs, which we seem to be able to retrieve in abundant amounts in only one or two attempts."

"Why's that?" Elliot inquires.

"In human embryology, timing is everything. By the time an egg is collected, it has already started to age. It will lose its viability in the lab within a few hours. The older the egg, the harder it becomes to fuse it with a skin cell and the less likely it is to develop an embryo. We've been trying to get younger eggs, since the cloning procedure can take several hours. We have been timing our retrieval of the eggs closer to the time of the donor's last hormone injection. That's why we need you out here to do this, Susan," Dr. MacMurray explains.

"I see," Susan replies.

"If we go in too soon, the egg may be too immature to be retrieved. It will stay behind in the fluid-filled space in its' ovarian follicle when the surgical team collects the fluid. Today's egg retrieval was something new. We took fluid from more than a dozen follicles. However, we attempted to collect two hours earlier than usual and it didn't work out too well."

Pointing to the monitor with her pocket laser beam, Dr. MacMurray asks, "Do you see the thick capsule surrounding the egg? It's called the *zona pellucida*. It's like a shell for a human egg. This shell, or zona, is flexible and is not attached to the egg itself. Instead, the egg floats freely within it on a thin cushion of fluid."

Elliot and Susan listen intently. Up until Noah's diagnosis Susan hadn't been that interested in science. The doctor's explanation fascinates her. Susan feels as if she is now embarking on a graduate degree in regenerative medicine.

"When we attempt therapeutic cloning, our first step is to remove the egg's chromosomes. We gently anchor the egg with suctioning to a blunt glass tube called a holding pipette. I believe that Dr. Eastman showed you this in the demonstration video you saw using a cow's eggs," Dr. MacMurray explains and nodded in the direction of Dr. Eastman.

Susan and Elliot nod in agreement.

"We then use a micropipette, or needle. The needle is hollow and kind of like a straw. Using vacuum pressure, we can draw things up into our needle straw or spit them back out," Dr. MacMurray continues, "and this is how we remove the egg's chromosomes."

"What happens after the chromosomes are removed?" Elliot asks.

"This is when we will fuse Noah's skin cell with the empty egg, thus creating an embryo of Noah that contains his entire DNA," It's the first step in a long process," Dr. MacMurray explains.

A very long process, Susan thinks.

"As Dr. Eastman explained earlier to you both, we will harvest the stem cells from the clone of Noah and create a genetic modification that will hopefully cure Noah's ALD. We can keep the cloned cells frozen until we are able to discover the correct genetic modification. There is a team of scientists who have already begun work on this process."

"This step in the process seems rather straightforward. I was expecting something much more complicated," Susan remarks.

"Straightforward and complicated, Susan. Finding the right genetic modification may take some time. Creating a cloned cell of Noah is not as easy as it may look," Eastman explains.

"On the day we do the cloning procedure I will be wearing my yellow and blue lucky argyle socks and the locket my aunt gave to me when I was a kid."

"Scientists rely on luck Dr. MacMurray?" Elliot inquires with an arched brow.

"Absolutely. We need to align hard work, opportunity, timing and a healthy dose of luck to achieve success," Dr. MacMurray says with a bright smile.

"What you are doing is so important. I mean, not just for helping Noah, but for all of the millions of people, just like Noah, whose fate is contingent on this research," Dr. Eastman replies.

"Noah's contribution to this research is a contribution to mankind's continued existence," Dr. MacMurray adds.

The doctors' words resonate deeply with Susan, who has begun this quest in order to save Noah's life. Now this quest has taken on epic dimensions according to the doctor. Susan closes her eyes and silently says a prayer asking God to save her son so that he in turn might help others to survive too.

New York City, New York to Oakland, California
Early Wednesday Morning

Aboard Jet Blue red-eye Flight 5327 from JFK to OAK it is pleasantly quiet. Noah, thankfully, is asleep. He sleeps in his car seat, which is securely fastened to the plane seat, flanked by his parents on either side. Bits of cracker crumbs, cookies, and beads of milk that drip steadily from the rubber nipple of a slightly overturned baby bottle cover their seats. Susan leans back against an airplane pillow; she is too exhausted to move and stares at the movie screen that plays on the back of her fellow passenger's chair. She didn't purchase the ear-buds because she'd been certain she had brought some for her iPod. She was wrong. It's okay though because one of her all-time favorite movies is playing. She'd seen Goldie Hawn and Kurt Russell's film *Overboard* so many times she knew it by heart. She actually found herself smiling as Kurt put Goldie, ravaged with poison ivy, into the double bed and Goldie says, "Tell me something about my life. Tell me something that's not horrible," and Kurt proceeds to tell her about the time she became the employee of the month at a local burger joint after saving the life of a kid who had been choking on a French fry. "You were a hero," Russell says to Hawn. Susan thinks about how Noah needs a hero. God knows how much they are hoping that Dr. Eastman and his team at The LAB will fill this role. Susan believes in miracles. If she didn't she couldn't justify putting Noah, Elliot, and herself through this. She'd remain positive and stay focused. To allow her mind to wander to all the ways this great experiment could go horribly wrong is to take away any hope she has at seeing her son grow into the man he has every right to become. For the first time since Noah's diagnosis, Susan feels as if she is shedding the cloak of grief that hangs around her shoulders like a blanket of fog. She feels lighter and happier.

    Elliot accepts another mini bottle of red wine from the flight attendant and quickly downs it, drinking straight from the bottle and not bothering with the cup. Susan isn't keeping count but thinks that he must be up to around three or four bottles now. Susan knows that Elliot isn't particularly fond of wine that opens by unscrewing a cap. They live in wine country and every bottle of wine they drink has a cork. Susan watches him screw the cap back onto the now-empty bottle and wonders how he will get through all of this. She also wonders if their marriage will survive. She has witnessed firsthand what has happened to her sister's marriage while she and her husband are raising a son with a debilitating disease and now watching him fade away. It's one of the worst kinds of hell this life can offer. She turns her attention away from her thoughts and back to the film. Kurt is holding Goldie.

The cabin is dark except for the flicker of individual screens on the backs of semi-reclined cabin chairs and the light strip illuminating the aisle. Elliot and Noah are both now asleep. Susan soon joins them.

Susan dreams that she is in a big room similar to an open warehouse. There are bubbles and blue-tinged lights casting ominous shadows on the cement floor and stone walls. She can hear the "blurp, blurp, blurping" sounds of water bubbling up. A woman in a white coat is taking her through a maze of giant bubbling tubes filled with a blue liquid. Some have shapes inside she can't quite make out. She has a sense of both excitement and trepidation. She can hear the soft whir of machines in the room. They sound as if they keep the liquid in the tubes moving. The room is sterile and slightly cold. She follows the woman deeper into the bubble tube maze.

"Where are we going?" she asks her.

"To see your son," she replies.

Susan can't figure out what her son is doing in a bubble maze. But somehow it makes sense. She knows that she's taking her to see Noah. The woman stops at the end of a long row of bubble tubes. She stands aside and gestures with an open arm to a very large cylindrical glass container that stretches from the floor to the ceiling. Susan stares as she tries to make out what is inside. All of a sudden she can see it. It's kind of like looking at the picture of the sonogram they had done when she was pregnant. It's the shape of a fetus. But it isn't really a fetus. It's fleshy and curls up into a position that looks like a giant question mark. It's floating in liquid and reminiscent of an effervescent jellyfish in the large cylinder. The cylinder is filled with bluish water that appears to glow. Taking a closer look, Susan realizes that it's more developed than a fetus. It's actually the body of a small boy with blond hair who has Noah's features.

"What the hell?" Susan exclaims and jumps back as she watches the bubbles blow upwards from the boy's mouth through his pale lips.

"We grew him big," the woman in the white coat remarks.

"Grew who big?"

She looks at her in perplexity and says, "Why Noah, of course," adding, "It's better this way to harvest the parts."

Susan screams.

Elliot startles awake, hearing Susan crying out and notices her squirming in her chair. She is still asleep and appears to be having a bad dream. Elliot gently shakes her awake. "Susan, it's all right."

"What?" Susan asks blinking her eyes and pulling herself upright trying to place her surroundings.

"You just had a bad dream," Elliot replies soothingly.

Susan looks around and remembers that she's on a plane.

"I need to get off the plane," she says with a panicked edge to her voice. Her palms are sweaty and her heart is beating rapidly. She takes a deep breath in through her nose and slowly lets it out through her mouth. *This doesn't happen to me. This happens to Elliot,* Susan thinks. Elliot soothingly says, "We're almost home. Look out the window; you can see the lights below."

The pilot's voice is authoritative and cheerful. Resounding through the speakers, she informs the cabin, "We are beginning our descent into Oakland. We will be touching down in twenty minutes. The weather is a clear fifty-two degrees. Flight attendants, please prepare passengers for landing."

The cabin lights come on as the head flight attendant walks the aisle, giving the passengers directives for putting up tray tables and storing loose items. She watches as the passengers adjust their seats to their upright positions. The passenger directly behind Noah's seat accidently kicks it and Noah lets out a frustrated cry. "It's okay, Noah," Susan says and then realizes that it's the pressure in the cabin affecting his ears. Noah pulls on them and thrashes his head about and then reaches out his arms toward Elliot.

"Up, me up! Uppy!" Noah cries.

"No, little buddy. You have to stay put until landing," Elliot firmly tells his son.

Noah's crying hits a fevered pitch and Susan can feel the cold stares from the passengers around them bore into her. Susan's frustrated and angry. *It isn't Noah's fault. He's most likely in a lot of discomfort.* She looks to Elliot to help her. He looks as if he's had enough too.

"Elliot, do something," Susan snaps.

"What do you want me to do? I can't pick him up!"

Susan reaches into the diaper bag and retrieves Noah's pacifier. "Try to get him to suck on this so his ears pop," she instructs.

Noah slaps the pacifier away, from Susan's hand. It lands on Elliot's lap. Elliot picks it up and pops it into his own mouth and begins sucking. He looks so funny that Susan starts to laugh. Noah looks at Susan laughing and stops crying. He looks over to his daddy. Noah pulls the pacifier from Elliot's mouth. "Mine!" Noah commands and places it firmly into his own mouth. Soon a look of surprise comes over Noah's face, and Susan realizes that Noah ears have thankfully popped. The pressure is relieved in more ways than one.

Despite the lighthearted moment, Susan still feels caught in that fog of unreality between sleep and wakefulness. Her mind races with so many concerns, she can't seem to land on just one. Susan gathers Noah's toys, juice bottle, and snacks and places them into the diaper bag.

As the wheels hit the runway with a thud, Elliot lets out a sigh of relief.

Susan joins him. She is glad to be home but wonders if her nightmare is a harbinger of the beginning of worse things to come for their little family.

Westchester, New York
Saturday

The boy on the bike darts out in front of Eastman's car. Eastman swerves to the side and skids to a stop. The street is slick with a fresh dusting of new snow. The boy keeps riding down the middle of the street. After his heartbeat slows to a normal pace, Eastman continues down the residential road at a snail's pace. The boy is to the left of his vehicle, not making much distance on this slick road, and still in the middle of the street. What is he thinking? Eastman notices the grimace on the boy's face. He appears pissed off that Eastman almost clipped him. Incredible! Eastman speculates that the boy is no more than twelve years old. His bike is too small for him and his pants are too large. The crotch is down around his knees, the same knees that ride high above the steering wheel with every pump of the pedal. The kid acts as if he owns the street.

"Arrogant little brat," Eastman mutters under his breath.

Almost immediately, he reminds himself that it's probably the kid's neighborhood and he has a right to ride in it freely. He also notices the kid isn't wearing a helmet, just a navy blue cap that stretches tight over his ears.

Eastman recalls never wearing a helmet when he was this kid's age either. *We weren't educated about safety back then.*

This child apparently isn't either, or maybe he is and he didn't give a shit. Eastman wonders if the kid's parents did. He thought back to a letter he had received from the parent of a child with a spinal code injury. The parent was inquiring about the advancement of stem cell research for these patients. His child had been hit by a car and became a paraplegic as a result. Well, a helmet wouldn't have prevented that type of injury, but riding in the bike lane might. Eastman entertains the thought of saying something to the kid, but lets it go when he realizes he's late in picking up Kathryn. He's also lost. "Where in the hell is Picane Place? I see Picane Court and Picane Circle, but no Picane Place!" He says out loud to himself.

Pulling up alongside the boy on the bike, Eastman rolls down his window. "Hey kid, do you know where Picane Place is?"

"Two streets and take a right."

"Thanks," Eastman says and then impulsively asks the kid, "Where's your helmet?" The kid flips him the bird. Eastman chuckles and shakes his head.

Eastman pulls up to Kathryn's house to find that she's right on time. She looks cold as she stands on the sidewalk hugging her- self. He feels bad that he's late. Always punctual—that was his Kathryn. *His Kathryn.* Now why did he think that? He leans over and opens the door for her. "Hey, I'm sorry. I got lost."

"Oh my gosh. I thought I was going to freeze," Kathryn replies as she slips onto the leather passenger seat. Eastman can't help but notice how beautiful she is. He's awestruck. But it's the little imperfections in her features, her ever so slightly off-center nose that keeps Eastman from stumbling over his words. He watches as she gives a quick shake of her head, shaking her auburn curls loose over the shoulders of her wool coat as she clicks her seatbelt locked. Conscious of Eastman's attention, Kathryn flashes him a quick smile as he punches it into first and pulls away from the curb. If he hurries they will be in time to do a little "meet and greet" before dinner. God, how he hated fundraisers, but they're vital to the survival of the LAB. Currently he's taking just enough money to live on. This didn't leave anything for fun but most of his "fun"—if you could call it that—is in attending fundraisers these days. Usually they were held in posh hotels scattered throughout the country or in someone's grand mansion of a home. Tonight's soirée was at the home of a Westchester judge, Jonas Abrams.

Eastman looks over at Kathryn and smiles. The color of her dress matches her emerald green eyes. He couldn't afford to pay her much these days and wondered how she managed to look so damn gorgeous for these events.

"Hey, thanks for agreeing to be my date tonight," Eastman says.

"Date, lab assistant, embryologist, whatever it takes to keep things going," she replies easily.

Eastman considers that keeping things "going" would be easy if he weren't attracted to her. He didn't need or want the complications that a relationship would bring especially with a colleague. Keeping this in mind he refocuses his attention on the road.

Santa Rosa, California
Saturday Afternoon

Susan chases Noah around the yard on a mild winter afternoon. Susan zips up his lightweight jacket. She's concerned about the shorts he insisted on wearing in this chilly weather. It's a California thing; her friends from the Midwest often called this manner of winter dress. Northern California could be very cold at night, but most of the time the winter days were of moderate temperatures. Noah giggles as he falls into the tire swing that hangs on a sturdy oak tree branch near his plastic turtle sandbox. All too soon the laughter turns to tears and Susan cradles him in her arms.

"Owie hurts," Noah says as he touches the Band-Aid that covers the scrape on his knee he got the day before.

His shorts ride up to his buttocks and Susan sees the tiny round scar from the tissue puncture. Her heart skips a beat thinking back to that day in Dr.

Lauerfield's office. *It's only the beginning*, Susan recalls her saying. Susan kisses her fingers and touches them to Noah's owie. "All better?" She asks. Noah flings his arms around her. She hugs her little boy back with all of her might. Her heart hitches a bit. *Normalcy has flown out the window*, Susan thinks as she recalls the procedure. Sometimes, like now, she just wants to have a few moments of no realization, to be a mother playing with her healthy two-year-old in their backyard. But she knows that those days are gone forever. Keeping things "normal" for Noah will be a challenge.

"You hungry baby?"

"Cookies."

"Maybe just one and after lunch," Susan answers scooping him up in her arms and carrying him into the house.

Westchester, New York
Saturday Night

The reporter from *Parade Magazine* introduces herself to Dr. Eastman as he places his hand on the expansive curved iron railing mounted on the wooden staircase that leads to the restroom upstairs in Judge Jonas Abrams' home. The one off the foyer seemed to be forever filled with women. After his third attempt for a place in the line, one of the guests waiting in line suggested that Eastman find a restroom someplace else. Looking for a place to set his second glass of champagne, a bubbly brunette with a mane of untamed, curly brown hair haloing her heart-shaped face approached him.

"May I hold that for you Dr. Eastman?"

"Sure, thanks. Do I know you?"

"Abby Snapple," she replies and extended her hand to take Eastman's glass.

"Like in Snapple teas?" Abby wants to roll her eyes but refrains. If she had a dollar for every time she'd been asked this question, she would be wealthy as an heir to the Snapple fortune. She gives an easy laugh and replies, "No. I'm not that fortunate to be in the family of a multimillion dollar company. I'm a journalist. Actually, Dr. Eastman, I'm interested in the work and research you do."

"At the moment I'm researching an available restroom. If you can wait a few minutes I'd be happy to speak to you when I get back."

Just then Kathryn approaches the pair with a small plate of curious edibles. The curious thing is that although Kathryn's plate looks as if it held four mini-works of art, none of them looks appetizing.

"In the meantime, let me introduce you to the LAB's embryologist and my right-hand person, Dr. Kathryn MacMurray. Kathryn, this is Abby Snapple, journalist for?"

"*Parade Magazine.*"

Kathryn extends a manicured hand, her delicate wrist adorned with a silver bracelet.

"Dr. MacMurray can answer your questions until I return," Eastman says and mounts the stairs, taking note of the enormous crystal chandelier that hangs next to the staircase. The light reflecting through the crystals makes unusual patterns on the wall. They look like images he'd seen on slides under the microscope. As he searches the doors in the hall for one that might be the entrance to the restroom, he wonders if he's destined to relate most observances back to his work. *I need a vacation,* he thinks. Bermuda was close—just a quick plane trip away—and he'd never been there. Maybe Kathryn would like to come too? *She deserves to get away as much as I do.* He opens the third door on his right and discovers a bathroom so big he can fit his entire living room in it. It's the kind of bathroom that makes him uncomfortable. The guest towels were too nice to use and the toilet too nice to take a piss in. Oh how he hates these meet-and-greet, kiss-ass, events. He longs for a night in front of the TV with a six-pack of Corona and a deep-dish pizza. *I wonder if Kathryn likes to watch sports?* Funny, they never talked about it at the LAB. The truth was they seldom talk about anything outside of their work. *Is this intentional? Stop thinking about Kathryn!* Eastman scolds himself. *Maybe I just need to get laid.* Once finished, Eastman looks around as he rinses his hands under the gold faucet. The entire bathroom is done in a Safari motif. Each guest towel has the image of a zebra, and the wallpaper is black with gold foil lions randomly embossed near green bushes. *It's hideous.* Maybe black and gold speckled bathrooms are the new thing for rich socialites who have nothing else to do with their lives but decorate, throw parties, and support their spouse's causes.

What a waste of money, he thinks as he aces the shot of a wadded up paper guest towel into the black and gold receptacle. If he could use the money they sank into this house, it would go a long way to help people who are counting on a miracle of science for themselves or for a loved one.

Santa Rosa, California
Same Night

Susan looks past Kim, through the French doors, and out onto the patio of Kim's backyard. She watches as Jake and Elliot swig IPAs by the barbecue and grill the burgers. It almost looks like a summer barbecue except its winter and the guys are wearing jackets. She looks up to the leaf bare Maple trees that line the back of her sister's yard. She notices crows the size of small black cats scattered among the branches. How she loathes crows. The sounds they make remind her of every scary movie she's seen. Just this thought sends a shiver down her spine. She notices that Jake has made a fire in the outdoor fireplace where her niece, Cameron, sits toasting marshmallows. A seemingly normal Saturday routine, yet as she turns away from the French doors she sees that inside the house Josh's appearance is a startling reminder of how un-normal things have become.

"Why do I have to stay here? I promised Sarah I would come to her party," she pleads with her mother.

"Because we're having a *family* dinner."

"Some family, Mom!"

"Grace!"

"All I want to do is go out with my friends. I'm sick of having to do everything you want. I want to do what I want for once." Grace storms out of the room.

Kim appears to be upset by Grace's behavior. Susan wonders if fourteen years from now she'll be having a similar exchange with a sixteen-year-old Noah. Just as quickly she realizes, *I should be so lucky*. Does anyone ever think about having a terminally ill child when they fall in love with the idea of having kids? She fights back tears as she glances over at Josh who's asleep in his wheelchair. Susan wonders which child Noah will become—a healthy kid with a rebellious attitude or one who won't live to see his tenth birthday? They don't have a choice, though. They will all have to deal with what has been handed to them. *What if I lose Noah? Stop this, gf!* Susan silently scolds. *You need to stop thinking negative thoughts.* Susan didn't know when she had begun giving herself silent pep talks and even more curiously when she had begun referring to herself as "gf." The acronym was easiest enough to understand—"gf" was for girlfriend. Somewhere along the line, Susan realizes, she has become her own best friend. Maybe it was when Elliot had stopped filling that role. Susan was feeling anger and resentment towards him more and more these days. She feels as if he has the luxury of checking in or out. Noah's care has fallen squarely on her shoulders ever since he was born. Now that they were dealing with their son's terminal diagnosis, Elliot often avoids having to make decisions and attend physician visits. He often uses the same excuse of being too busy with work.

Susan is shaken out of her deep thoughts when she hears Kim say, "I don't like to give in to her when she's acting like this. I do think she needs a break, though, and I understand why she wants to go."

"Tell her to go, really, it's no big deal, she should have some fun."

"Yeah, let's wait and see if she apologizes for making a scene and then I can tell her," Kim says and then adds, I know she's a great kid. Her behavior is just reflective of all of the stress we are living with here. I feel like it's the progression towards the end, like I'm on some weird walking escalator that keeps moving us forward toward more pain and sorrow. It's the long goodbye and I'm powerless to stop it from happening."

Possibly sensing Kim's sadness, Noah toddles over to her and gives her his stuffed bunny. She takes it and thanks him. Then she tickles him with the furry, well-loved toy. Noah giggles and squirms. Kim laughs along with Noah. The laughter feels good to Susan too, and in this moment there is lightness in the air, she thinks as she looks through the French doors out onto the patio where the guys are grilling.

"How are you holding up, man?" Jake inquires of Elliot as they grill up the rest of the burgers.

"We're going to start Noah on Lorenzo's oil soon."

"That's good. I wish we'd known in time to try that with Josh. Noah's still asymptomatic, right?"

"Yeah." The question makes Elliot feel uncomfortable. "This is one of the few times we've talked about Noah in a conversation that places Noah in the same boat as Josh. It's something I never imagined. Maybe I've been denying the possibility. You know, I've always had empathy for you when we discussed Josh, but now that we're discussing Noah too, I almost can't talk about it."

Silence floats in the air between them like the smoke rising up from the grill.

"Having a sick kid is kicking our butts," Jake blurts out and adds, "Susan probably told you about the next round—the bone marrow treatment. We got the test results back and learned that Grace is a good match for donating, which is good news. I don't know how in the hell we're going to pay for it. I've taken a second mortgage out on the house already—insurance only covers so much and Josh's been sick for so long. We are maxed out," Jake says and adds, "I know what I'm about to say next will sound cold and even selfish, but I don't want to do the bone marrow treatment."

Elliot carefully considers Jake's words. "Do you need a loan?

In all honesty, given Noah's recent diagnosis I'm not sure I should offer, but I want you to know that we will help you guys with whatever you need."

"We don't have any more money to pay for any of this. The best we can hope for is that we will be allowed to pay for it over time, or we will have to consider bankruptcy. But no, I don't want a loan. What Kim is failing to realize is that more than money, this is about quality of life. Josh's quality of life—of course—and Kim's, Grace's, Cameron's, hell, even mine," Jake says and continues, "Josh has been through enough. The odds of him surviving the transplant and it working are not good. He's getting weaker and will have to go through ten days of chemotherapy before having the bone marrow stem cell transplant procedure."

Elliot empathetically nods. "Shit, man, it all just sucks."

"Josh's time here with us is brief. I want to spend what time we have left together not making him into any more of a God damn fucking science experiment!"

Elliot places a comforting and sturdy hand on Jake's shoulder. Jake gives an acknowledging hit to Elliot's other arm and says, "I'm glad you guys came tonight. I finally feel like someone else on this planet understands what we're going through."

"Hey Elliot, those look almost crispy on this side—shouldn't we flip em?"

"Do the honors Jake. Have you talked to Kim about foregoing the bone marrow treatment?"

Jake's face cringes at the thought as he flips the well-done meat over to its pink, fleshy side.

"Shit, I can't even go there with her. She'd be so pissed if I even brought it up." He adds with even more pain in his voice, "She can't let go. She won't let herself really believe that Josh is going to die. She's focused on giving him every possible chance there is. You know, she's right in a way too. I can't take away any chance for him to have a longer life. I'm not God, and so I go along for the ride. I gave up control over things like finances, a happy marriage, and my own quality of life long ago. He's our son."

"What does Josh want?"

Elliot watches as Jake holds the spatula above the burgers and then looks at him as if he'd never considered the idea. It was an important question. It was Josh's life. Not Jake's, not Kim's. It was Josh's—Elliot thinks. "He's still a little boy and one whose disease has taken away most of his cognitive abilities. A little boy who can't choose, but if I had to guess, Josh would want to be with us—without the pain. I don't want him to suffer. If I could trade places with Josh, I'd do so in a heartbeat. He's imprisoned in a sightless, soundless world without the ability to control even his bowels," Jake says and turns his back to Elliot trying desperately to control the sobs that roll out of him in waves of emotion. Elliot places a hand on Jake's back once more and squeezes his shoulder a couple of times. Elliot stands there with him until Jake composes himself. Jake turns around and upon seeing the overcooked, charred burgers on the grill says, "Shit. I can't do anything right."

Westchester, New York
Later Saturday Night

Dr. Eastman returns to the ballroom to find Kathryn still chatting with the journalist. He notes Kathryn's brilliant smile as she chats with ease, a champagne flute hardly sipped in one hand and a small silver bag in the other. The plate of edibles had been discarded. Her back is turned toward him. The silk dress drapes effortlessly around her curves. He notices her delicate white neck adorned with a silver chain. He follows the curve down the small of her back to her perfectly shaped buttocks where his gaze lands.

"Like the view?" Jon Mallored's deep voice jolts Eastman from his forbidden thoughts and back to reality. "Hey, Jon," Eastman acknowledges extending his hand.

"I thought she was a colleague. Your assistant, I presume?"

"Dr. MacMurray?" Eastman asks self-consciously.

"Must be distracting to have *her* around the LAB."

"Dr. MacMurray is our embryologist. How are things at Merck?" Eastman inquires switching topics.

"Apparently not as interesting as they are at the LAB," Jon says with a nod in Kathryn's direction.

"Interesting yes, but not in the way you're referring to them."

"Are you working on something, other than the lovely embryologist?"

"Let it go, Jon, you are way off here. And yes, if you have a pulse you already know that I'm working on something."

"Anything I can assist you with?"

"Since you work for such a wealthy SOB, I'd be foolish not to mention that I am working on funding for therapeutic cloning."

"Me likes. So how can Merck help?" Jon asks as he grabs a glass of champagne off the tray of tall flutes a waiter is carrying. The waiter offers Eastman one too.

"No, thank you," Eastman says to the waiter and then to Jon, "Anyway, not sure there's much in it for Merck."

"You never know. Disease and cures are definitely our business, and what a business it is."

"You ever get tired of working for a corporation that screws people Jon?"

Feigning shock and then hurt, Jon places his hand to his heart and replies, "We help people."

"Yeah, but wouldn't you rather help them without reaming them in the ass too?"

"Now what fun would that be?"

"If that's your idea of fun."

"What the hell is bugging you tonight? Sounds like you've got something up your butt, James."

"I'm just frustrated."

"I can see that," Jon says, nodding in Dr. MacMurray's direction.

"Give it a rest Jon. I'm sorry if I offend you. It's not you."

"Is this where I say, 'It's not you, it's me?' Lighten up, you're gonna kill this over-the-top fab party with lots of hot and rich chicks to be had," Jon warns and adds, "That gorgeous brunette by the fireplace is looking lonesome. I'll see you around."

Eastman cruises over to the sofa to rescue Kathryn from the *Parade* journalist. He places a hand lightly on her shoulder and asks, "You ready to go?"

Kathryn smiles and replies, "Sure."

Abby looks to Eastman and inquires, "Aren't you staying for dinner?"

"No. I've got an early morning."

"I really wanted to talk to you too."

"Come by my office this Wednesday at noon, and we'll finish the interview. No photographers; just come yourself." He hands her his card, shakes her hand, and turns to escort Kathryn to the car.

The drive home is long and wordless. Eastman is exhausted and by the looks of it, Kathryn is too. She's sound asleep. Her shallow breathing is the only thing breaking the silence inside the dark car. Eastman wonders if he has succeeded in boring her to death. He realizes he's working her and the rest of the team members too hard. Everyone who works at the LAB seems to have a passionate calling for the work and maybe this is what kept them from complaining or burning out. His thoughts fall back to his own drive—the memory of his mom. He swallows a lump in his throat as he recalls her bright, encouraging spirit, all extinguished through breast cancer. It's an insidious disease that had robbed him of precious time with her. He was very young at the time of her death. However, he recalls the feeling of helplessness, anger, and frustration he and his father experienced in the process of losing her. His work was a way to honor her. If he's being honest with himself, it's also a way to protect him. He can turn all of the feelings he had with the loss of his mom and turn it into something meaningful—he'd find the cure for breast cancer and in the process so many other diseases too.

Kathryn stirs in her seat. He finds himself longing to touch her. It'd been a long time since he last felt any kind of romantic longing. Until now.

Eastman pulls up to the front of Kathryn's craftsman cottage. *A renters dream*, he thinks. There's a beautiful stone path leading to the steps of the porch and a heavy wooden door, all beautifully maintained. These were some of the things he hadn't noticed when he first came and was in a rush to get to the fundraiser.

Eastman gently wakes Kathryn by placing his hand on her arm. Her eyes open and to her horror, she notices she's drooling. She takes a tissue from her purse and dabs at the corner of her mouth while Eastman gets out of the car.

He opens her door and extends his hand for her to take. As she steps out onto the sidewalk she steadies herself on her four-inch heels.

"Thank you. Sorry for nodding off like that. I make great company, don't I?"

"My pleasure," Eastman replies as he walks her up the stone path.

"Really, James, it's not necessary. I can find it from here."

"No problem. I just want to make certain you get inside safely."

"Um, okay, that's nice of you."

Thank you for coming with me tonight, Kathryn."

Kathryn retrieves her key from her purse. "Good night. I'll see you tomorrow," she says as she unlocks her front door.

"Right. I'll see you bright and early," Eastman replies.

Kathryn turns toward him and Eastman stares at her.

What am I waiting for? But he knows—*A kiss.*

Kathryn moves inside, smiles, and closes the door. Eastman hurries down the path somewhat sheepishly. He climbs back into his car feeling lonelier than he can recall. He realizes, *Something has to change.*

Santa Rosa, California
Saturday Night

Susan watches as the white foamy blob she spits into the stainless steel sink is pushed down the drain by the rush of the running faucet water. She rinses her toothbrush and taps it twice against the basin, hoping to dry it, then plops it into an *I Love Lucy* toothbrush holder. The fluffy white towel feels soft as it brushes past her plump pink lips and soaks up any missed wetness. A tear escapes her eye. She's scared to her toes. If things were normal, she realizes, she'd be thrilled to be pregnant. In her heart she's ready for another baby. However, being pregnant means that she can't participate as an egg donor. Helping the child she already has is her prime concern and responsibility. Also, she's sure she and Elliot should never have another biological child because it too could be afflicted with ALD. She attempts to snap herself out of this anxiety provoking train of thought.

Come on Susan, you're assuming you're pregnant. You haven't even taken a test yet! You just missed your period. It's probably due to stress…You should tell Elliot.

She looks into the mirror and mentally rehearses her words—the ones she will say to Elliot, and then terror rushes from her beating heart to the tips of her pink painted toenails.

Santa Rosa, California
Sunday Morning

"I'm late," Susan says with her back to Elliot as she spreads butter over wheat toast at the kitchen counter.

"For what?"

"My period," Susan says a little sheepishly and slowly turns toward Elliot.

"Have you seen my keys?" Elliot asks and takes a bite of the Cheerios Noah offers him from the tray of his high chair.

"Mmmm," Elliot says to Noah, who smiles and puts a spoonful into his own mouth.

"Why? Where are you going?" Her words come out harsher than she intends.

"To the office, I've got a lot of paperwork I need to get a jump on for this week," Elliot explains as he spies his keys next to the coffeemaker on the counter.

Susan gives him a quizzical look. "Aren't you going to say anything?"

Elliot stops short of giving her a peck on the cheek and replies, "It's probably just stress. You'll get it soon. Let's talk later." He grabs his keys and waves to Noah as he hurries out the door.

Susan watches as Noah flips Cheerios, with the teaspoon he awkwardly holds in his hands, all over the kitchen as he does his best to maneuver his spoon. Thankfully, a few pieces land in his mouth. *It must be really tough struggling to use a spoon.* She couldn't remember not knowing how to walk or talk or feed herself—yet she had to learn these things. Watching Noah achieving each of these milestones gives her tremendous respect for all that's involved in mastering these tasks—ones that make him independent and able to care for himself one day. Tears swell in her eyes as Susan remembers watching her nephew master the use of silverware and then lose his ability to feed himself within a mere six years. *Everything he has learned he's losing.*

"Please don't let this happen to Noah," Susan whispers.

Butlerville, Indiana
Sunday Evening

Gwen is holding a pen to the journal she keeps. She's shared all of her thoughts about how her quilting circle is creating a lovely, warm quilt they hope to raffle off at the church to benefit Hope House, a place for elderly Butlerville residents. Gwen pushes aside the dirty coffee cups and pie plates at the kitchen table, clearing a place to set the journal and patiently waiting for Joe. "Some nights, Joe, getting you to share is like extracting teeth."

Joe sits across from her and pulls at the skin on his neck in thoughtful contemplation and says, "I thank the Lord for my good health, a good soybean crop this year, the farm, and for you." Gwen beams at Joe's last thought. Silently, Joe adds another blessing he feels Gwen wouldn't understand. *Neither Dr. Eastman nor anyone else has actually cloned a full human being.* He adds the word *yet* to his silent thanks because he knows Eastman is getting close. Too close. He's going to be stopped. Smith knows this for certain. He feels it in his bones. There's one other final blessing he doesn't share that he's particularly grateful for—*God is talking to him again.* When out in the barn this morning, God told Joe that he has a plan for him. Joe's excited about this plan and doesn't want to fail. He tries hard to mask his excitement as Gwen quickly writes everything Joe has just shared with her in the journal and asks, "Have you shared everything you'd like to, Joe? I feel as if you're holding back." Holding back is an understatement, Joe thinks. He's almost giddy with joy knowing that he's the chosen one.

New York City, New York
December

It had been a blessing when Susan finally got her period a few weeks earlier. If she hadn't she would not be able to donate her eggs to help Noah. Susan isn't sure whether it was the egg harvesting or the five-plus-hours commute to do the procedure that is wearing on her. The holidays are taxing her too. It's the first year Noah's been able to really participate in them. It was so much easier when he was a baby. She and Elliot had taken Noah trick or treating. She dressed him as a lion. People come from all over Santa Rosa to trick or treat on their street. McDonald Avenue is known for doing Halloween decorating up big. Every homeowner must participate. This year she and Elliot were required to make their house one of the Wizard of Oz themed venues. Somehow they managed the expectation. Thankfully, Thanksgiving was celebrated with her sister and her family. Now Christmas was upon them. So far she and Elliot hadn't gotten a tree, and she hadn't done any shopping. She hopes that Elliot will get the tree while she's away. Maybe a tabletop one that Noah can't easily reach and one that won't cost very much, Susan reminds herself to tell Elliot. Jetting off to New York again to donate eggs for a second time was placing a crimp in their budget. Christmas would be a modest this year. It was also one that would be bittersweet.

Looking out of her hotel window, Susan recalls her plane trip from the previous day. On board the airliner, Susan had faithfully thrown herself into the first twenty pages of a new thriller. However, her grief over what would soon be the complete loss of Josh proved to be a worthy opponent in terms of competing for her attention. She had given up reading and closed the book. Her mind had drifted back to her sister's family. Her heart is heavy. Caring for her sister during this time has been emotionally exhausting. She had supported her in the best way she knew how— spending hours listening, sharing tears, reframing the events, going back over decisions that had been made, acknowledging and validating the bottomless depth of pain. They all were grieving Josh before he actually dies as he's now in a vegetative state. Susan also knows that this might someday be her own experience. Josh's demise was expected given the fact that they had run out of options for treatment. His disease had advanced quickly, and they weren't even able to try the bone marrow treatment. Susan is eternally grateful that she still has the opportunity to try to save Noah.

Susan and Elliot decided he should stay at home with Noah and Susan should make the trip alone. Besides, the trip was on their dime, and they needed to keep expenses down. Elliot also needed a break from Susan. They both knew this without ever speaking the words. The hormones she'd taken prior to the procedure was making her moods swing from one end of the spectrum to the other. It, of course, upset Elliot when she snapped or burst into tears for no apparent reason. Pregnancy had been a bit like this for her. She wonders how Elliot had survived nine months of it.

The third-story Upper West Side hotel room window looked out onto the lawn of the Museum of Natural History. Although she had spent the morning in her warm room, it appears to her to be very cold outside. Passerby's are bundled up with hats, scarves, and gloves. She sees a couple sharing a drink from the Starbucks around the corner. The steam from the cup floats up around their faces. There isn't a flake of snow on the ground though. Susan is disappointed, as she's been looking forward to seeing the snow at Christmastime. It's something she didn't get to experience often living in California. Her thoughts shift to the procedure she is about to endure. It isn't just the discomfort of the procedure, although Susan thinks the word "discomfort" should be replaced with pain.

Susan recalls an intimate conversation she had had with a friend who is a breast cancer survivor. Susan had witnessed her friend's chemotherapy treatments and the surgery and then reconstruction of her breasts. Susan remembers the nausea, the fatigue, the violation of her friend's body all in a heroic effort to save her life. She confided in her friend that she'd feared that she wouldn't have the courage to go through such a process. Her friend had told Susan that she was doing what she had to do for the sake of her children. Susan embraces this thought. Will she continue to be able to find the strength and courage to do what she needs to do to save Noah's life? Yes. She wasn't comparing her experience to that of a breast cancer survivor. However, she and her friend share a bond of empathy that requires finding the courage and strength to persevere in the face of daunting obstacles, setbacks and a goal of a longer, good quality life. Susan squares her shoulders and decides that after the procedure she will reward herself with a tour of the museum.

She had always wanted to go to the Natural History Museum in New York. She'd taken Noah to the one in San Francisco. Noah had seemed enthralled. There's a poisonous frog exhibit here at the one in New York. Now, this might be fun. She can tell Noah about it and maybe find a book to bring home and to read to him about the frogs. Susan realizes just how much she's missing her son. Every day with him has become precious. She allows the thought to slip in, and in turn, it makes her wonder how she will ever survive missing her son all the days of her life if it comes to this. She knows she is strong, but is she strong enough to live without Noah? She thinks not. Unlike Susan, Kim must survive for Cameron and Grace. Susan knows that Kim will fight to survive the ultimate loss of Josh for both of her daughters' sakes. Susan believes that she'll need this kind of anchor to tether her to the Earth. She feels hurt and angry that not only is she facing her son's illness and possible demise, but now she and Elliot most likely won't ever be able to have another biological child. They wouldn't risk it. A boy would have a significant chance of acquiring the disease and girl could be a carrier. ALD is robbing them all of so much.

Susan looks out the window and sees a black sedan parked at the curb in front of the hotel. She wonders if it's the one the LAB is sending for her. If it is, it's right on-time. In a flash she grabs her purse, coat, and room key and exits the hotel. When she approaches the car, the driver acknowledges that he's there for her and holds the door open as she climbs into the backseat. She's both excited and nervous to be on her way to the OB-GYN's office for the egg harvesting procedure. She prays for a good, viable harvest.

Westchester, New York
December, Same Day

As promised during their last interview, Dr. Eastman gives Abby Snapple a tour of the LAB. It just happens to be on the day they are first attempting to create a clone of Noah. Eastman hopes that the journalist will fully understand the urgency of what they're attempting to achieve. Abby brushes back the curly tangle of thick, brown hair that falls loosely onto the shoulders of her pink blouse tucked neatly into her jeans. She carries with her a small yellow legal pad and a pen that she seems to click every couple of minutes. *A nervous habit?* Eastman wonders. He tries his best to block out the distraction of the clicking sound as he explains the purpose of the LAB's work. "I'm looking for one of the greatest gifts that can be offered to mankind," Eastman explains. "I want to give families who are living with life-threatening diseases both hope and a cure. I believe that many cures can be found in this type of research." He walks over to a container and motions for the reporter to follow. "Over here is the area where we keep the child's skin cells that will be used for the cloning," he says. "He's the little boy I told you about when we last spoke, who has ALD."

Abby jots more notes as she follows Eastman around the LAB. Eastman notes that the atmosphere in the LAB is tense. People seem uncharacteristically quiet for such a facility and very focused on the tasks at hand. He's glad that Abby is respectful and avoids interrupting anyone's work.

"The child's mom is having her eggs harvested today and they will be used in the cloning attempt. We're waiting on word as to how many eggs were retrieved," Eastman informs Abby.

Abby looks at her notes and then says, "So let me get this right. Ultimately you are using the child's skin cell and the maternal mother's egg to create a cloned embryo. If all goes well then you will extract, the now five day embryo's stem cells and grow them here at the LAB. After that you will create a sort of cellular therapy - a perfect genetic match for the child - putting these cells back into the child to cure his disease?"

Before Eastman can reply his attention is abruptly refocused onto Kathryn who is fast approaching the two.

"Excuse me," Kathryn says to Abby as she takes Eastman by the arm to speak with him in private.

"No problem. I'll just review my notes."

Eastman and Kathryn move over to a corner of the room near the door she had just come through.

"James, I just got off the phone with the OB-GYN. Dr. Ball says they were only able to retrieve two viable eggs from Susan."

"The results are disappointing, but not unexpected."

"James. The eggs are on their way and should be here soon."

"Have everyone ready to begin the procedure right away. I want to make the attempt as soon as we know the eggs are viable."

Zorvelli sees Snapple standing alone looking down at her note pad. He walks over to her and says, "Excuse Ms. Snapple. I'm Dr. Paul Zorvelli the LAB geneticist. I'll be happy to answer any questions you may have."

"Nice to meet you, Dr. Zorvelli. I do have a question. Can you define morula stage for me? I sort of remember this from the conference but I'm not fully clear on the concept."

Snapple flips to a clean page on her note pad and positions her pen.

"Ah, yes, the *morula* is Latin for *mulberry* because it ends up looking like one," Zorvelli says with a bit of flare.

"That sounds like the simple answer. How about a more detailed one if you don't mine."

"A morula is an embryo at an early stage of development. It consists of cells called blastomeres in a solid ball contained within the zona pecullucida. The morula is produced by embryonic cleavage, the rapid division of the zygote. Once the zygote has divided into 32 cells, it no longer looks like the berry. Within a few days after fertilization, cells on the outer part of the morula become bound tightly together with the formation of desmosomes and gap junctions, becoming nearly indistinguishable. This process is known as compaction. How am I doing so far?"

"Great, Dr. Zorvelli. Please continue."

"The cells of the morula then secrete a viscous liquid causing a central cavity to be formed, forming a hollow ball of cells known as the blastocyst. The blastocyst's outer cells will become the first embryonic epithelium. Some cells, however, will remain trapped in the interior and will become the inner cell mass, or ICM. These are what we refer to as pluripotent. The ICM will ultimately form the "embryo proper," while the trophectoderm will form the placenta and other extra-embryonic tissues."

"I'm sorry, but do you mind giving me a quick definition of the trophectoderm?"

"Trophoblasts are cells forming the outer layer of a blastocyst. They provide nutrients to the embryo and develop into a significant part of the placenta. They are formed during the first stage of pregnancy and are the first cells to differentiate from the fertilized egg. This layer of trophoblasts is also collectively referred to as 'the trophoblast' or, after gastrulation, the trophectoderm."

"Your hand okay?" Zorvelli asks Snapple whose shaking her hand so hard that it appears to be suffering from writer's cramp.

"It's a lot to write down."

"I'm happy to be speaking with a reporter who has the ability to understand and put this all together. That's truly important when working with journalists. Publishing information that's incorrect or misunderstood can go against our efforts to proceed."

"Thank you. It's important for me to get it right too. Please continue."

"The trophoblast later forms the placenta. Another thing you should know is that the trophoblast surrounds the inner cell mass and a fluid-filled blastocyst cavity known as the blastocoele or the blastocystic cavity. The human blastocyst comprises seventy to one hundred cells." Zorvelli pauses and asks, "You got all of this?"

"I'm keeping up. Please go on," Snapple says and adds, "I'm using my own creative shorthand and I'm taping it as back up, she taps her pocket where the recorder has been running."

"Is taping it okay with you?"

"Sure, sure. Now where was I? Oh, the blastocyst formation begins at day five after fertilization in humans, when the blastocoele opens up in the morula, a process known as hatching."

"In order to clone you don't need to go beyond the blastocyst stage, is that correct?"

"Yes. For therapeutic cloning, which is what we are doing, that's true."

"Would that be considered the beginning of human life, Dr. Zorvelli?"

"The real question is—does a blastocyst meet the criteria of a human being?"

"Does it?"

"The best way to answer, I believe, is to discuss the core criteria that comprise a human being and use this understanding to discuss the point."

"Explain, please."

"Okay. Let's consider some of the things that would comprise parts of a human being, but not be considered human beings themselves."

Snapple nods, encouraging Dr. Zorvelli to continue.

"An example would be a biopsy. Unless your argument is that the tissue removed during a biopsy is a human being, your criteria for what makes up a human being would be considered vague. I personally think the idea of a biopsy being considered a human being is ridiculous, and I think that's a sentiment that is universally shared."

"But this isn't tissue from a biopsy."

"No, it's not. To me, it's less than the tissue removed during a typical biopsy. It's enough cloned cells to fit on the head of a pin, and those cells are then pressed flat into a petri dish so there is no further development. That's all we need to harvest cloned stem cells for therapeutic purposes."

"Interesting," Snapple says and nods to Eastman, who is rejoining them.

"Hi James, I was just explaining the development of a human embryo to Ms. Snapple."

"Please continue. We have time. And that's if Abby is still interested?" Eastman smiles wryly knowing how Zorvelli was considered a bit of a loveable wind bag around the LAB.

"Oh I am, please go on, Dr. Zorvelli."

"Before it's even a week into development the human embryo, or blastocyst as we prefer to refer to it, is round and has a fluid filled inner core. We call this the inner cell mass. The outside of it will eventually, if allowed, develop into the placenta."

"So the inner part is what ultimately develops into a human fetus?"

"Yes, that's correct. Eventually all of this material will become more than two hundred types of cells in a human body,"

"And this is where you can get human embryonic stems cells-the kind you need to form tissues and cells in the body,"

"Yes. With the right coaxing, they can develop into new tissues and neurons," Eastman says excitedly.

"That's pretty mind blowing," Abby remarks.

"It is," Zorvelli agrees.

"When does embryological development cross the line from therapeutic cloning to reproductive cloning? Is there an exact stopping point?"

"That's a great question. We have very specific thoughts on this. I'll let Dr. Eastman explain the LAB's view," Zorvelli replies turning towards Eastman.

"In the first two weeks of development, an embryo can still divide and become identical twins. Also, these two embryos can fuse into one and eventually become one person. However, it isn't until the primitive streak formation that an individual person is mapped out. At this point, there isn't a brain, any sensation, or memory. I would characterize it as having the potential to become an individualized human when it evolves to the primitive streak formation. I wouldn't touch it at this point."

"So this is where therapeutic cloning leaves off and reproductive cloning begins. There seems to be a lot of misunderstanding about this. There are members of congress who want to make it illegal," Snapple offers.

"Even the National Institute of Health, agrees with what I just explained to you. If the president and members of Congress fully understood this they would support therapeutic human cloning. It would be much like the way Great Britain views this type of pioneering research. Somehow we have to be better at educating people about what we are doing," Eastman replies.

Their conversation is interrupted by Snapple's cell phone vibrating. She looks at the caller ID and says, "Excuse me," as she answers the phone. "Yes?" Eastman stands close by, not sure if he should wait or excuse himself. "I just sent the story on stem cell therapy in time for tonight's deadline. I want to let you know, though, that I've been invited by Eastman to stay for the therapeutic human cloning procedure."

Eastman can't help but overhear Snapple's conversation. He figures she's talking to her editor.

Dr. Anderson's voice comes over the loud speaker, "James, we're about to start the procedure.

"I've gotta go," Snapple says into her cell phone and presses the end call button.

A lab assistant enters the room and whispers something into Eastman's ear. "That's not the news I was hoping for," Eastman replies and his face reflects the disappointment in his voice.

"What's going on?" Zorvelli asks Eastman.

"Only one of the eggs is viable."

"Shit. So this is our only shot?"

"Unfortunately."

Abby walks over and joins Zorvelli and Eastman.

"Dr. Alan Anderson will be assisting Dr. MacMurray with this attempt. The two have worked together on numerous attempts using bovine material and were successful in the first human clone," Eastman informs Snapple.

The room is small and is filled with the LAB members in the gallery who aren't directly involved in this attempt.

Eastman motions to the monitor overhead, which displays an up-close view of the procedure.

"Dr. Anderson is adding the little boy's, Noah's, skin cells to the droplet of medium that contains the egg Dr. MacMurray has just readied for the procedure. The skin cells are impossible to see as they are a hundredth the size of the egg," Eastman explains.

"What is Dr. MacMurray doing with the needle?" Snapple inquires.

"She's drawing a cell up into and then releasing it through an opening drilled in the egg's zona. What she's hoping to do is place it snuggly between the egg and the zona," Eastman explains punctuating each important word with each step he sees Kathryn take.

"The DNA of his mother's egg has been removed already -right?"

"Yes. We are hoping to fuse Noah's DNA with mother's egg," Zorvelli replies.

"You say the little boy's name is Noah? May I use it in my article?"

"Let me ask the parents. I don't think it's a problem if you don't use the last name - which you don't even know - right?"

"No. I have no idea who the parents are," Snapple replies.

Over the loud speaker the gallery can hear Dr. Anderson say to Dr. MacMurray, "Keep nudging the zona with the needle."

"I'm trying but it's not working. The egg isn't making contact with the skin cell."

"How about trying from another angle?" Anderson suggests.

Moving from another direction, Kathryn says, "Yeah, okay the cells are touching now."

"It's your lucky locket," Alan offers.

Eastman notices that the room is dead quiet. *It's more like a morgue than a lab*, he thinks.

"What happens next?" Snapple whispers.

"They're going to try to get the cells to fuse using electricity," Zorvelli replies in a normal tone of voice.

"Too little current and the cells won't fuse, too much and the egg fries. If they succeed the genes that make the skin cell a skin cell will be deactivated or muted, and other cells will enter the gene to initiate early embryonic development," Eastman explains and adds, "If all goes well the nucleus of the reconstructed egg will enlarge dramatically by tomorrow."

"This is exciting!"

"It is. However, it doesn't always work on the first attempt," Eastman says.

"Didn't it take over 200 attempts to clone that first sheep?"

"It did."

"So, two eggs aren't great odds for getting it right?"

"This is our only shot today. Sadly I was informed by this turn of events just prior to the start of the procedure."

When they look back at through the window and then up at the monitor screen they see a microscope platform.

"You're looking at a fusion chamber. You see that round shallow dish with the two wires on the bottom?" Zorvelli asks Snapple.

"I do."

"That's it. Dr. MacMurray is placing the egg between these wires."

Dr. MacMurray peers at it through the microscope. She looks up and says, "It looks good. The egg is round. There is a uniform cytoplasm and a perfect space between the zona and the egg."

Dr. MacMurray looks back under the microscope and prods at the egg.

"What she's doing now is difficult to see. She's using a glass rod with a rounded tip to position the egg between the electrodes in the dish. She's going to try to ensure that the current goes directly through the cells pushing toward each other getting them to fuse."

"I'm going to turn the current on now," MacMurray says to Anderson and it's carried over the loud speaker.

"Too much current and the egg will cook," Zorvelli tells Snapple.

They watch as Dr. MacMurray flips a switch and begins pulsating electricity through the cells.

"If all goes well we will have a clone," Eastman states in a hopeful tone.

"The cell is running away from the egg!" Kathryn exclaims in surprise.

"That's not supposed to happen!" Anderson exclaims.

Dr. MacMurray moves so Dr. Anderson can look through the microscope.

"It looks like the zona's disappeared."

"That just can't be," MacMurray replies.

Anderson moves over and MacMurrays takes the dish. She places something into it.

"What's she doing?" Snapple inquires tentatively.

"She placed dye into the dish. She's checking it with the UV light now. Without a zona there will be nothing to hold the cell to the egg."

Dr. MacMurray looks up from the microscope and dejectedly states, "We didn't get fusion."

Fuck! Eastman shouts inside his head. He's painfully aware that everyone is staring at him expectantly. After briefly meeting Kathryn's eyes through the glass, he turns to his staff and Snapple. "We will try again."

Santa Rosa, California
January

Elliot wraps his arms around his wife as she folds the warm towels straight from the dryer and kisses her neck.

"That tickles!" Susan replies with a giggle.

"Hey, you feel like you've put on some weight."

"Is that your way of being romantic? Cuz it's not going to get you anything but a frown," she says turning to face him.

"No, I meant it's a good thing. I was concerned. You had lost quite a bit recently."

"Well, I guess feeling good makes you want to eat."

"You know I think things are better too. It feels; well, more normal - like how it used to be."

Susan kisses Elliot's lips and turns back around to focus on her folding.

"I don't want to get my hopes up but the Lorenzo's Oil seems to be doing its job," she replies as she places the folded plum colored towel into the basket sitting on the floor.

"We're participating in what amounts to be the great experiment," Elliot reminds and adds, "We're part of a team that's continually learning from our failures which will move us forward to ultimate success."

"Wonderful analogy, honey, which reminds me, it's time for Noah's oil."

"I'll feed it to him," Elliot offers as Susan hoists the basket of folded towels from the laundry room floor to her hip.

"It's a deal."

As they leave the laundry room and enter the kitchen Susan remarks, "You know I've been thinking about the last time I donated my eggs. I hope that I'll be able to provide Dr. Eastman with a lot more this next time."

"I think the less you worry about it you might just find that when the time comes you are able to."

Susan knew that what Elliot was really saying is that he's enjoying the break from the manic franticness they've experienced ever since Noah was diagnosed with ALD. Although the thoughts and fears of what might come were only a breath away - Susan's determined to give her family what it needs - a break.

She watches as Elliot takes the vanilla ice-cream from the freezer and sets it on the counter next to Lorenzo's Oil.

"I hope you have better luck than me feeding him the stuff, you know some days it's a real battle," she remarks as she places a few folded dish towels into one of the kitchen drawers.

"I have the magic ingredient," Elliot replies with a smile as he grabs a bottle of confetti colored sprinkles from the counter.

"Noah loves sprinkles on his ice-cream. I'm going to let him sprinkle them this time."

"He'll like that and with all of that sugar it might just mask the bitter taste of it.. You just may be a genius!" Susan says with a smile and turns to leave the room to put away the bath towels.

The phone rings and Elliot answers it.

"Gaynor's residence."

Susan pauses halfway between the kitchen and the living room to see if it's for her.

"That's good news. I'll look for the email with all of the info. Thank you so much," Elliot says as he hangs up the phone.

"What's good news?" Susan inquires as Elliot approaches her.

"Noah's been accepted into the U.S. Lorenzo's oil clinical trials!" He exclaims as he lifts her off of her feet laundry basket and all.

"When?" Susan asks as he sets her back down.

"They are sending us an email. It'll have all of the info."

"What a birthday gift! I can't believe I'm saying this. I always thought we'd get Noah a tricycle for his third birthday," Susan realizes she is rushing her words together.

"We can do that, too." Elliot says still grinning from ear to ear.

Just as quickly Susan's thoughts turn dark and she thinks to herself, *Well maybe not a tricycle. I mean we still have to watch for the fact that the oils may cause thrombocytopenia, a lowering of platelet count. He won't want to ride his trike if he's fatigued, or his nose and gum bleeds, or he experiences bruising of the skin. All of the possible symptoms the doctor warned them about.*

"Susan. Are you okay?"

Not wanting to spoil the moment or jinx it either Susan brightly replies, "How could I not be with such wonderful news."

Westchester, New York

Dr. Eastman leans back in his black vinyl desk chair. He takes a sip of what he jokingly calls a "dirty latte," a latte with one pump of chocolate syrup. Kathryn calls it "mocha light." He tries to calm the beginnings of a headache centered in the middle of his forehead with the heel of his left hand. He's hoping that the caffeine will stop the throbbing. It's been a long day and he doesn't plan on going home anytime soon.

Dr. Anderson sticks his head in the door. "You don't look so hot."

"I'm okay. Just tired. What's up?"

"Dynamic Innovation, you know, the lab in Texas, just reported that they succeeded in cloning a cat."

"Good for them," Eastman replies flatly and drank some more of his dirty latte. "Where did you hear this?"

"I talked to Dr. Eric Groeber at DI about ten minutes ago. He says he wants to break the news to us before it goes public."

"Which will be when?"

"In about twenty minutes when the journal *Science* hits the stands."

"Nice of Eric to give us a heads up," Eastman says. Finishing the last few drops of coffee, he places the cup on his desk and then stretches both arms over his head.

"Yeah, I thought it was something you'd wanna know," Anderson replies.

Standing up, he walks around his desk and over to Anderson. He extends his hand to Anderson to shake while replying, "Congratulations, Alan. You laid the groundwork for their successful attempt."

Anderson shakes Eastman's hand. "Thank you."

"Did he go into specifics?"

"Not much, some. We discussed the number of attempts, a little bit about what worked and didn't work."

"Let me know if you learn anything more," Eastman says.

"I will."

"Do we know whose cat it was?"

"Yeah, some wealthy oil tycoon whose cat died. He's going to put up all of the money."

"Do they look the same?"

"Nope, this one's a different color."

"I hope he's okay with that."

"I'm sure Eric braced him for the possibility."

"Cloning cats is many, many steps away from cloning dogs or humans," Eastman reminds him.

Eastman considers the news to be a reality punch to the gut. The honeymoon of the twenty-five-cell division was definitely over. It's time to step up their game big time. Eastman says goodnight to Anderson and walks into the laboratory. He discovers Kathryn sitting on a stool at a computer terminal. "Kathryn, I'm surprised, it must be almost ten." Kathryn spins around on her stool and smiles.

"I was just reading something you might find interesting. It's a report on the trend in pet guardians to clone their pets. One man's given millions to the Texas lab in the hope of cloning his dog."

"Interesting about the dog. The place where Alan used to work successfully cloned a cat," Eastman says as he sits down on the stool next to her.

"Things are changing exponentially in the field of science. I wonder if people really understand it," Kathryn says.

"It's a lot for the average person to wrap their brain around."

"Cats and dogs are one thing. I quite honestly don't think that people really care about whether or not they're cloned. There do appear to be very divisive concerns over cloning humans and what defines a human being, for that matter," Kathryn remarks.

"Nothing new about that debate," Eastman agrees.

"There's that bill that's been proposed in the Mississippi state legislature. The media's discussing how it may affect abortion rights, but they haven't even mentioned how it might impede our work if this thing passes."

"I doubt it will pass. But you're right. Just the fact that there's discussion and proposed legislation stating that an egg and sperm uniting is the equivalent of a human being is kind of crazy."

"Kind of crazy? It's downright certifiable!" Kathryn says jumping up out of her seat and placing her hands on her hips. She notes Eastman's look of surprise at her passionate response.

"I can see I just struck a nerve with you."

"I'm really fired over this. I mean, I would actually go to the mat to protect a woman's right to choose. And can you imagine if this thing does pass? What's that going to do? You'd have all sorts of people arrested for murder, not just physicians who perform abortions and women who want them, but what about women who are accused of somehow inducing a miscarriage by something they did or didn't do, not on purpose, but inadvertently during their pregnancies? This is scary!"

Eastman looks at Kathryn with a mixture of respect and curiosity.

"Don't you feel the same way?" she asks, sliding her hands into her lab coat pockets.

"Yes and no," Eastman replies as he places a steady hand on her right shoulder. "You know my background, I mean, much of it." Kathryn looks at him skeptically, but nods for him to continue. Eastman removes his hand. "Well, this may be something that surprises you. I used to be one of *those* people who protested at abortion clinics."

Kathryn doesn't hide her surprise and says, "You were? I mean I know where you stand on the beginning of life, but I just never imagined that your views were so different from mine. I didn't think you were pro-life."

"I wouldn't be doing what I'm doing if I wasn't pro-life. Neither would you."

Kathryn pulls her hands out of her pocket and sits back down feeling thoroughly confused. "Now wait a minute. You can't tell me what I do and don't support. I am pro-choice. I believe in a woman's right to choose."

"And I respect that."

Kathryn is beside herself. "You just said *I* am pro-life, James!"

Eastman takes Kathryn's hand in an effort to calm her. "I want to help extend life, not impede its progress or destroy it. This is where we have common ground. We both believe in creating life and helping to extend it. Where we may differ is our belief on when life begins though."

Taking back her hand she replies, "Well, I can attest to the fact that it doesn't start with the sperm and the egg. I mean, that's just the beginning of the *possibility* of a human being. It's a start."

"I agree."

"Well if you agree, then what is the difference in our views?" Kathryn asks, cocking her head to one side.

"I don't think that human life begins until after the placenta and what will become the fetus separate. Until then, it's a ball of cells. Once the two separate, that's when I believe human life begins."

"Yes, yes, the primitive streak formation when the placenta and fetus separate. That's as far as we need to go to get viable cells for human cloning. We all agree on that at the LAB. I agree with that. But, I also believe that a woman should be able to *choose* if she wants to carry a pregnancy to term or not."

Eastman is momentarily lost in Kathryn's beautiful green eyes backlit with the fiery passion for what she believes. He reminds himself to focus on their discussion and to answer her carefully. This is a discussion he hasn't had with any of the colleagues who work for him. He also doesn't want it to result in damage to his and Kathryn's friendship.

"Look, I don't have all of the answers. I just know that my passion and mission is to support life, to help cure disease and extend lives. I may not share your exact views, but I believe in what we do."

"Do you think I'm impassioned because of some personal experience?"

"Aren't we all? A large part of my motivation to succeed comes from my own personal experiences," Eastman states.

"Oh?" Kathryn inquires tilting her head to the right.

"It was in watching my mom suffer,"

Eastman watches as Kathryn's demeanor changes from one of challenging him to full empathy. "She died from breast cancer when I was fifteen. I desperately wanted to help her. I was angry at the doctors, at God; hell, I was angry with *her* for dying. I felt helpless as I witnessed my father's pain and my mother's death," Eastman says and pauses as the images from so long ago dance through his head. He remembers coming home from school and finding his mom in the bathroom pulling out handfuls of her gorgeous chestnut-colored hair. Her hazel tear filled eyes illuminated as she looked into the mirror and saw her son watching her. A smile parted her lips as she shook the hair from her fingers into the sink. "I think it's time for a wig, don't you, James?" she asked him through her tears. The thought passes and he says quietly, almost inaudibly, to Kathryn. "There was nothing I could do for her." Eastman's own eyes fill with tears as he recalls his mother's dignity and bravery during the last months of her life and his helplessness in having to watch her die. Moved by his words and the visible emotion rippling through Eastman's body, Kathryn reaches up and gently wipes away a tear that spills from the corner of his left eye.

"I'm sorry," Kathryn says. The air between them stills, and all that can be heard was the constant low hum of the computers. Quietly, as to not intrude upon the intimacy of what just passed between them she says, "My story isn't personal. It's just how I've always felt. It's what I believe. I worked in a clinic when I was doing my rotations in medical school. What further cemented my belief was seeing twelve-year-old girls pregnant. I also spoke with rape victims who were pregnant by their rapists. There are things in life that no girl or woman should have to psychologically put herself through."

"I do understand and respect your views, Kathryn."

"Do you?"

"Of course."

Kathryn relaxes a bit more and replies, "As an embryologist, I helped to make many dreams come true for all sorts of people who years ago wouldn't have been given the opportunity to raise a child from birth to adulthood. I helped same-sex couples, infertile couples, people who really, really wanted to be parents. I enjoyed it. I took great pride in what I was doing. Their fetuses were precious to me. But I also saw the other side. I also witnessed a darker side, one in which women had abused alcohol and drugs. They were damaging their fetuses in utero. Their addictions were more important than the fetuses they were carrying. I also saw what damaging effects poor nutrition and no prenatal care had on fetal development. In a nation where food is abundant, it's heartbreaking to witness the consequences of hunger," Kathryn offers.

"I can only imagine what that must've been like."

"In my work I also helped determine which fetuses had Down's syndrome and Edward's disease. The women carrying these fetuses desperately wanted to have a baby. However, some didn't want their children to be born with a lifetime of complications. They also didn't want the stress and strain that having such a child would place on them and their relationships. Most marriages that involve raising a special-needs child fail."

Nodding, Eastman acknowledges what Kathryn has just shared. "I've never been in your position or the position of a person having to make such a heart wrenching decision. I very much believe that all life is precious. In the cases you speak of, and in other cases, I ask myself how much pain a life should endure."

"And how much pain is that James?"

"This isn't something I have an answer for. I believe it's up to God."

"When I hear people say, 'it's up to God,' I can't help but think this is a cop out. It's up to the person having to face this. People need support and they need to know that they have a choice."

Eastman thinks carefully about Kathryn's words. He realizes that while they both viewed things differently their constructs about life shares many common areas. He feels as if in many ways he understands the human condition and strives for the best human potential science and medicine can offer. What he chooses not to say to Kathryn is that that he wonders if some of the woman weren't cold hearted in their unwillingness to give birth to and raise a child with physical and genetic abnormalities. He had known several families who had children with Down's Syndrome, Russell Silver Syndrome, and other disabilities, who loved their children and couldn't imagine life without them.

"Did the women whom you provided with information about their pregnancies always terminate, or did some choose to carry to term and raise their children?"

"The women grieved their losses when they were told of the abnormalities. Some chose to carry to term. Others, I believe, suffered greatly when choosing to abort. There isn't much sympathy or even empathy for women who make the difficult choice to terminate a pregnancy when the fetus has abnormalities. Many who did make the choice to terminate the pregnancy simply stated to friends and family that they had suffered a pregnancy loss rather than go into the details of their choices and have to contend with the opinions of those who had disapproved. These weren't people who wanted a perfect child. They were people who wanted a child that had a fighting chance in this world. Many consider children with Down's Syndrome to be just different looking and slow. However, they don't understand the host of physical problems that accompany such a child and the procedures a child like this must endure. I'm not saying I always fully agreed with their choices. It wasn't my job to counsel them on what to do. As you know, my job was to study and then later to assist in the creation of a healthy embryo. I don't really care about 'when life begins.' I just wanted to assist in creating a life that is wanted and cared for," Kathryn explains placing her hands on her knees.

"Thinking about the beginning of life and our genetic lineage is one of the most profound things we can wrap our brains around. It makes me think of Jack Reimer's . . ."

"*Jewish Insights on Death and Mourning*?" Kathryn interrupts.

"I haven't met very many people who are knowledgeable about this book. I'm impressed. It made a lot of sense to me at a time when I was searching for answers about human existence. There's a quote I embraced and memorized from the book."

Kathryn gives an encouraging nod, and Eastman recites a passage he has memorized: "I am what I am because of the first amoeba that developed into a more complex form, impelled by the divine imperative to grow. As I think of the long line stretching far into the past, I also cast my glance forward. The line into the future is just as unbroken. It moves through me into generations yet unborn. And as I think of this, I am comforted. I am a point in that line, and the course of existence travels through me. I have inherited from all the past and I will bequeath to all the future. In the movement of that line lays the secret of immortality, and I am a part of it.'"

"We even carry within us atoms from stars before the Earth began," Kathryn says thoughtfully. "He's talking about a kind of immortality. And doesn't having children afford a person a certain kind of immortality?"

"It does."

"Have you ever thought about having a kid?"

Eastman looks at her intently, but before he answers, Kathryn blushes awkwardly and says, "Maybe that's too personal a question."

"I have," Eastman replies. "But my work has been my child, or my immortality, if you will. It's been my life. I live for my work. I haven't made room for more."

Kathryn looks into his eyes. "I understand."

Eastman knows in his soul that she is one of the few people who truly did understand. Despite all of the compelling reasons in his head not to do so, Eastman gently wraps his arms around Kathryn and strokes her cheek with the back of his hand. To Eastman's delight, Kathryn relaxes into his warm embrace. They eagerly find each other's lips and softly kiss. Kathryn sighs.

"I know," he murmurs against the pale flesh of her neck as he drinks in the fresh scent of her hair. This moment has been too long in coming, Eastman's heart rejoices but his head wonders if this might ultimately hurt their working relationship.

Westchester, New York
Next Morning

The world of cloning is set on fire with the latest achievement. Anderson approaches Eastman in his office at the LAB with more breaking news. He looks at his iPhone as he reads aloud from an article. "SEOUL, South Korea. A South Korean team led by disgraced stem cell scientist Hwang Woo-suk is claiming to have cloned coyotes for the first time. The Sooam Biotech Research Foundation says Monday that eight coyotes were born in June as part of its efforts to clone various species of animals in cooperation with South Korea's Gyeonggi Province."

"The province says it'll raise the coyotes but will later donate them to zoos at home and abroad," Anderson paraphrases.

"Remember when Hwang scandalized the international scientific community in 2000 when his breakthrough human cloning research involving embryonic stem cells was found to have been faked?" Anderson asks but means it more as a statement of fact.

"Has the coyote clone been confirmed?"

"Not yet."

Eastman takes a bite of his spinach croissant and speaks around the pastry in his mouth, "If it's true, then good for him."

Anderson shrugs. "Well, coyotes are a ways off from humans."

"Yeah, but we've got to keep the wolves or the coyotes at bay."

"Good one James; that's real funny—not!" Anderson states and more solemnly asks, "What wolves are you currently trying to keep at bay?"

"You know - the usual suspects. Creditors, political zealots who don't approve our work here," Eastman replies with a sigh.

"Do you ever feel like jumping ship?"

Eastman looks at Anderson thoughtfully. "You got something you want to tell me?"

"No, not me. So far, I'm good. I just mean, well, I'm sure you've been approached. Any scientist worth his weight has been, at one time or another."

"Don't even go there."

"I didn't mean to poke a stick in a sore spot. It's just that Hwang doesn't have to fight. He gets to focus on his work. No bullshit fundraisers, meetings with the press to swing popular support. The advancement of science and medicine are too often pawns in a political arena, not to mention financial shortfalls in this country. It makes it difficult."

"The grass is always greener. But we both know that's not the whole truth," Eastman says with a sigh and adds, "I am getting sick of all of the crap we are currently encountering. The anxiety of waiting to hear what stance the current administration is going to take is busting my balls."

Anderson interrupts, "Do you think they'd actually pull the plug?"

"You know, that's always a risk, but this isn't the first time I've actually had a butt load of anxiety over it. I was born in this country; I love what we've built here.

I won't abandon my work, though, if it comes down to it. It's my mission. I'm not willing to abort." Eastman stands and gathers his laptop and notepad from his desk.

"Where are you going?"

"To the conference room. Aren't you coming too?"

"It's already ten?" Anderson asks as the two head out the door and down the hall.

"Time flies and I'll be damned if we hear that the South Koreans beat us to therapeutically cloning the first human no matter how much damn support they get," Eastman replies.

"We're up against it on all sides," Anderson acknowledges.

Eastman remarks, with a hint of mounting frustration, as they enter the conference room, "Let's see if we can figure out how to knock down some of these brick walls. I promised a little boy's parents I'd do everything I possibly could to save him."

Butlerville, Indiana

"You fucking bitch!" Joe shouts at his wife of twenty-five years. Gwen sits perfectly still at the old wooden table that was handed down to her by her grandmother. Her right index finger traces a deep scratch in the oak wood made long ago by some other member of her family—perhaps even before she was born. Now in her early forties, she distracts herself from Joe's tirade by thinking about the countless meals at this table as Joe paces the floor like a caged animal. Gwen controls her fear by silently reciting, "God Grant me the serenity to accept the things I cannot change, the courage to change the things I can, and the wisdom to know the difference."

Gwen knows all too well that this is one of the things she cannot change. She has no doubt that God can, though. It will pass. It always passes. Gwen thinks back to the time it first began. Joe returned home from the military a few years after they were married. She didn't know what it was called but later learned it's called post-traumatic stress disorder (PTSD). However, the definition for PTSD didn't explain all of Joe's peculiarities. His mental illness appeared to Gwen to be getting progressively worse especially over the last couple of years.

It was almost as if Joe failed to recognize her at times. He saw her as someone bad, perhaps even evil, Gwen thought and then suppresses a shudder. Although Gwen doesn't dare utter a sound, Joe seems to be hearing her say things. How could that be? He's answering her as if she's talking to him.

"So that's all you have to say for yourself? Is it! Well to hell with you!" Joe shouts.

Gwen wonders what's wrong with her husband. She and Joe didn't have a particularly affectionate relationship. He kept to himself a lot. It's just his way. They had always gotten along except for what she refers to as "Joe's flare ups." Sometimes Joe would insist that he heard things such as scratches under the house that Gwen never heard. Gwen believed Joe. He was very emphatic about what he says he heard and saw. She didn't want to distress him by admitting to him that she didn't share his reality. Last summer he seemed to be the most insistent about a creature under the house; she had one of the farmhands check under it for a critter that may have been trapped there, but he reported finding nothing. That same summer, on a particularly warm night, they were lying in their bed and just about to fall asleep when Joe said that there were people talking and laughing outside. He and Gwen went to see who was there, but once again there was no one. Now this. Joe had taken to swearing at her. It was humiliating. Even worse, she had begun to fear Joe.

Joe slams his hand down hard onto the table right in front of where Gwen sits. Startled and frightened she jumps up.

"Get out of my fucking house before I kill you!" Joe rages as his eyes bore into the depths of her soul. Gwen sees pure evil in the man she once admired, trusted, and loved. She believes Joe when he says he will kill her. *Remain calm*, she silently tells herself as her body shakes. Slowly she walks toward the stairs. *I'll pack a bag and drive the truck to my sister's house in Speedway*, she says to herself as she takes the first tentative step up the wood staircase that leads to their bedroom. Suddenly, Gwen feels herself being pulled backwards by her hair. "Stop it Joe," she cries as her hands fly up to her hair. But Joe yanks her harder by her hair and she hits the ground hard. "Joe, no!" Gwen screams seeing his fist comping down her face. As the first blow slams into her nose, she hears the crunching sound her nose makes as it breaks and she tries to recoil. Her tongue finds something floating in her mouth. *My tooth*. Feeling the empty place where it once was attached. She notes the coppery taste of blood as she chokes on it and spits out the tooth. *Joe's going to kill me.* She feels another blow landing just below her chin. Searing pain roars throughout her body and then blessedly nothing.

Westchester, New York
Same Day, January

Eastman, along with the core staff at the LAB celebrate the news he's just heard on CNN. The anti-cloning bill failed to pass the Senate. Perhaps their little celebration is premature, Eastman considers; they are still waiting to hear the President address therapeutic cloning, but he hopes the Senate's actions foreshadow support for their work. There was another bill introduced in the House that Eastman and his team were hoping would die too. He pops open a bottle of Korbel Brut sparkling wine, a favorite. "That's one small step for man, one giant leap for mankind," Eastman says quoting Neil Armstrong, as he raises his plastic cup up high. The team moves into a circle and touch their plastic cups together in a toast before taking a sip. "Therapeutic human cloning research lives to see another day," Zorvelli says with a bit of a chuckle.

"I'll drink to that!"

"You'll drink to anything, Alan," Kathryn remarks in jest and everyone laughs at the truth of her statement.

"Especially if it involves beer - preferably pale ale," Alan clarifies.

Butlerville, Indiana
Two Days Later, January

Joe had discovered Gwen at the bottom of the stairs with dried blood smeared across her face. Her nose was almost flattened to one side and her mouth didn't close or align correctly. She looked to Smith like a broken doll. She was badly bruised. He considered that she may have taken a tumble down the stairs. But a tumble down the stairs wouldn't have accounted for all of the injuries, especially the ones to her face. Sitting in his truck in the hospital parking lot, he replays all the events leading up to this moment. He had rushed Gwen to the hospital soon after he discovered her. The extent of her injuries, according to the attending physician, amounted to a broken nose, broken jaw, broken teeth, concussion, and various bruises. With her mouth wired shut, Gwen had to write down what had happened. She wrote one version she gave to the doctor. She wrote another for Joe. The note to the doctor stated that she had slipped and fallen down the stairs in the middle of the night. When the doctor took it and read it he just shook his head and left the room.

Gwen handed Joe the second note she had written. This one meant for his eyes only. He had read it at her bedside earlier that morning. It was painful for him to read as Gwen had detailed the events of the prior evening. It was apparent to Joe that because she didn't provide this information to the doctor she wanted to protect him. She stated, in the note he read that she believed God would help him. She wanted him to pray. Gwen said she was praying for him. She also told him to talk to the psychiatrist she had insisted that he see when he first started hearing the voices that no one else heard. She wrote that if he promised to get help, she would not press charges against him and possibly even return home. Joe couldn't believe that Gwen wasn't coming home. It was almost too much to bear. He promised Gwen that he would see the psychiatrist. He didn't quite believe that he actually did this to her. He truly had no memory of it at all. If it was true, and he had no reason not to believe Gwen, his behavior must've been a fluke. Maybe it was some rage he felt from Eastman's evil doings that came out on Gwen. He thought that if it's possible that God is using him for good, maybe he was temporarily possessed by something evil. How he wished he could tell all of this to Gwen. He knew that she'd believe he was hearing God's voice because she believed too. But he also knew that she wouldn't understand the things that God had wanted him to do. For Gwen, God was gentle and compassionate. Well wouldn't she like to know that he had a wrath that squarely placed Joe on a path of destruction - the destruction of the clone and the scientist who created it?

Gwen had once told him that she believed he was suffering from schizophrenia and post- traumatic stress disorder. She had read all about it on WebMD. That's when she made him see the psychiatrist. Gwen refused to believe that he was special, and this bothered him more than anything else. Joe knew he had no intention of seeking medical help this time. He didn't mind the psychiatrist but when God calls you though you listened. What he needed was a spiritual cleansing. God would see that that was done. Soon, very soon, Gwen would see him in the powerful light that surrounds him like a shining cape. Once God's work was done, she'd finally understand him and revere him. Joe wishes he could tell Gwen about the first time God had spoken directly to him. He somehow knows that she would only relate it the delusions the psychiatrist said he had.

Recalling the first time, Joe fills with a sense of awe. His feelings of anger and shame dissipate with the memory. He was in the barn feeding the horse when God spoke to him. The sun was beaming through the cracks in the boards in the barn's ceiling high above him. It was almost mystical the way the rays of light illuminated the inside of the barn. Joe felt as if he were lit up like a heavenly angel. Then he had heard God's voice. He dropped to his knees on the dirty, hay-strewn floor and bowed his head. God told him that he was to get his gun and to meet up with Dr. James Eastman. He was to "put the fear of God into him." Joe had acknowledged God's will and then just as God stopped speaking, the beam of heavenly sunlight was blocked by clouds and the barn was cast into a dark gray haze.

Taking one last glance up at Gwen's third floor room Joe starts his trucks engine and thinks, *I'm going to miss you Gwen. One day you'll understand and you'll come back to me. Now I'll go home and wait for God to tell me when to leave for New York.*

Santa Rosa, California
Same Day, January

Susan sits at her kitchen table and hears the drumming sound of the rain pelting against the kitchen window as she absently swishes her teabag in her cup of hot water. The chamomile scent fills her nostrils as she thinks back to all that has happened over the past few months. The holiday happenings were usually a happy distraction, but this year there was too much pain. Pain etched in the faces of her sister, brother-in-law, and their girls. Her own pain and the pain she sees reflected in Elliot's eyes when she looks too closely makes her want to push it all away. Still, she allows the events to unfold in her mind.

Susan used to think that there was nothing worse one could experience than the death of your child. She was wrong. Watching your child suffering—dying a slow and torturous death, robbing him of dignity and joy burned one's soul. As far as she was concerned there was nothing worse.

The family stood by helplessly as Josh became blind and deaf and lost all control of bodily functions. Susan watched as Kim held her son and rocked him like the baby he'd been several years earlier. Susan recalled Kim telling her how much she wanted Josh to feel her presence and her love— it was if she were pouring all that was good, all that unconditional love she had inside of her into Josh—maybe to save him—maybe to take with him. Jake responded the opposite of Kim. He seemed to distance himself from his son in the final days of his life. He confided in Susan that he viewed Josh as already gone. He believed with all of his heart that his son's spirit no longer resided in his broken body and that he had been grieving the loss all along. He tried to focus on and comfort Grace and Cameron. Josh died just before his eighth birthday.

Susan recalls that it was now almost a week ago that they had all come together to lay Josh to rest, although in some ways it felt like it was yesterday. The funeral was somber and so very sad. She thinks back to the overcast foggy morning. Their entire family and close friends remembered and mourned Josh at his burial in a cemetery not too far from their home. Elliot placed a DVD player at the gravesite and played the song Kim had requested, "Everything I Own," by Bread. It was all Susan could do not to fall into a puddle of tears when it played. She had held Noah tightly and while praying for her nephew's soul, she also prayed that Noah would be spared. A spray of white baby roses and blue carnations draped the coffin. The night before, after the viewing, Josh's sisters, Cameron and Grace, had filled Josh's forever resting bed, as Grace had lovingly referred to it, with all of Josh's favorite things. There was a book titled *I'll Love You Forever* that Susan had given to

Kim at her baby shower; his stuffed dog, Rufus; Matchbox cars; Sour Patch Kids candy; and Legos. They took markers and colored his white casket with everything they could recall that Josh had enjoyed in his life and personal messages of love.

Susan remembered Kim sharing with her that she had decided on a burial site instead of the cremation that Jake had wanted, because she said it was important that she be able to have a place to go and sit and talk to Joshua. She talked to Susan about how Elizabeth Edwards (whose son Wade had died as a teen) had sat by his grave and read the entire recommended school reading list of books to him. Kim says she envisioned carrying out a similar act of love with Josh. Susan thought it allowed her sister some kind of connection, perhaps a reason to just sit with her son's body as it decomposed into the earth.

"Children shouldn't die before their parents do. It's unnatural and wrong," she remarks out loud, but there's no one to hear her. A boom of thunder jolts her fully upright and she wipes away the tears streaming down her cheeks with a crumpled dish towel piled on the table next to her tea cup.

Washington, D.C.
February

In the House of Representatives chamber of the United States Capitol, the stage is set with an unlikely cast for one of the biggest human cloning debates that has ever been held. Never would Eastman and his associates at the LAB (and throughout the world, for that matter) have imagined that Greenpeace, the Sierra Club, the Catholic Church, Christian Conservatives, and other groups form an alliance against therapeutic cloning. On the opposite side, in support of the practice, are both Republican conservatives and Democratic liberals. The entire issue has become a political hot button, and it seems that everyone has a dog in the race. It's an issue where people have come together despite all sorts of opposing lines drawn in the sand to unite for a cause. Interestingly, those who united in their opposition to this debate and those who were for it might not have agreed on anything else but this one issue.

President Kenny Longran's approval rating is at an all-time low. Many are anxious to hear how he will straddle the issues of regenerative medicine and therapeutic cloning, as his constituency is split down the middle. There is a parsing of the issue. The American people wonder if Longran will support research on existing embryos and stem cell lines. They also wonder if he will support new stem cell cultures. Will he choose to stop all forms of stem cell research? Also interesting to his political constituency is the fact that the President is hoping for a second term and some of his wealthiest supporters consider stem cell research on existing embryos to be the moral equivalent of grave robbing.

Recently, congressional members Kathleen Sullivan (D.LA) and Senator Rick Morales (R. KS,) had introduced another bill called the Respect Human Life. If it passes it will outlaw all types of cloning and any therapies that could be developed from therapeutic cloning. This is all despite efforts by moderate Republicans and many Democrats to allow therapeutic cloning and stem cell research, using cloned embryos. It is an all-or-nothing bill in which there would be no hope for any type of therapeutic cloning research.

Westchester, New York
February

On the evening of the President's State of the Union address, Eastman and the staff gather in front of the TV and watch as the President prepares to speak. This is an important day for Eastman and his associates, since the President will address the issue of human cloning. Given his voting record as Governor and his stated position on stem cell research, everyone in the LAB is fearful that the President will set the wheels in motion to stop therapeutic cloning research by helping to guide the legislature.

Senator Quinton Matthews (R., Utah) is a right-to-life supporter who has joined forces with two of the nation's most liberal Democrats, and unlikely trio, to sponsor legislation that will sanction the cloning of embryos for research purposes. However, the sanction will be limited. The new legislation will outlaw placing a cloned embryo into a human or artificial womb. The research will have to be approved by a professional peer review board before being undertaken. This is the bill that Eastman and his colleagues hope will pass. However, Senator Matthews has been vilified in the media and by many of his past supporters. Unfortunately, he is viewed as supporting what the President has referred to as "embryo farms." This couldn't be farther from the truth.

The Senate is evenly divided between the two competing bills. One bill supports therapeutic cloning the other one would outlaw it. Each bill has approximately forty supporters. There is eager anticipation experienced by all involved waiting to see how this turns out.

Santa Rosa, California

The Gaynors and their extended family are gathered together in their living room to watch the presidential address. Susan sits next to Kim on the sofa. She feels the anxiety and trepidation radiating from her sister as they await the President's address.

"Can they do it, Elliot? "Can they ban cloning?" Kim asks.

"They can, but it's a process. They'll have to enact a ban into a law. Thankfully the wheels of Congress move very slowly."

"They may pull federal funds, but places like the LAB may continue to be privately funded," Susan informs.

"What if they succeed in outlawing it?" Kim asks.

"Not unlike state marijuana laws," Elliot remarks.

"Unless the feds come into the states and shut it down," Susan replies.

"Could that happen with therapeutic cloning?" Jake inquires and takes a seat next to his wife on the sofa.

"Yes. But we are getting ahead of ourselves here," Elliot says standing in front of the TV.

"I hope this doesn't go against our efforts. I mean, why do medicine and medical technology have to be linked to politics?" Kim asks.

"I know that our fight isn't the only one that's hindered because of politics, religion, and money. Look at the whole Lyme's Disease mess," Jake states.

"People still don't get the kind of medical care they need who have Lyme's," Kim agrees.

"There are so many people who have a dog in this race. Also people who have Parkinson's disease, diabetes, heart disease, cystic fibrosis, and multiple sclerosis, everyone afflicted could potentially benefit from therapeutic cloning." Susan says.

"Let's hope they make their voices heard," Kim state.

Elliot turns up the volume on the TV just as the President comes on to address the nation.

Westchester, New York
The LAB

Eastman grabs a slice of pizza, his own creation: ranch dressing, feta cheese, pineapple, and artichokes. He tucks a can of Coke and a napkin under his arm and takes a seat next to Kathryn. His knee accidentally brushes up against hers, and he feels a flush of excitement and just as quietly hides the emotion to honor the unspoken agreement between the two of them to remain professional at all times in front of their colleagues. Anderson adjusts the volume on the TV using the controller, taking the open seat on the other side of Kathryn just as CNN announces that the President is about to speak.

"Here we go, folks," Eastman says with nervous laughter as the room quiets.

Eastman watches as President Longran, who is seated behind his desk in the Oval office, looks up into the cameras. "Good evening," Longran smiles as he begins reading the teleprompter.

"We gather together, in this room and across our great nation, to address the state of our union. The majority of us, especially in this Congress, in my Cabinet, are looking toward the decisive days that lie ahead. One of the most compelling issues we face is that of eradicating disease. We'll work together to help those whose lives are threatened by disease. We will work side by side to obtain prosperity for all Americans. A significant component to this is education. Our ability to compete and remain leaders in this world rests upon the education of our future generations."

"I hope this isn't long. I just want him to get to the part on human cloning," Anderson remarks around a mouthful of pepperoni pizza.

"We have successfully worked together to be the change that we have wanted to see in the world. We have achieved many amazing things in which we can all be proud. We have helped millions of Americans by cutting taxes. This has helped to rebuild our economy. We have grown the economy by providing jobs for all Americans who want to work. When citizens' work they have money to spend and this along with tax cuts helps to ensure a healthy and prosperous nation."

"Hooray for tax cuts," Zorvelli tips a slice of veggie pizza on a paper plate to the television screen.

"Put a lid on it, Zorvelli," Anderson instructs.

"You against tax cuts, Alan?" Zorvelli says and took a bite of pizza. To everyone's surprise he begins to choke.

All eyes turn to see if Zorvelli is all right. His face turns red, then purple. Upon seeing the change in color, Kathryn, Eastman, and Anderson jump up in unison and rush over to him. Eastman mentally rehearses the steps of the Heimlich maneuver and is ready to perform if necessary. Anderson stands in front of Zorvelli just in time for Zorvelli to cough up a blob of cheese mixed with dough and sauce that lands on the top of Anderson's shoe. Anderson looks down at the mess on his shoe. "Crap!" he says with disdain. Tears spring from Zorvelli's eyes and he bursts into laughter. Anderson grabs the napkin from Zorvelli's lap and wipes up the mess. "I'm glad you're okay and that you think this is funny," Anderson says as he crumples the napkin-filled mess and tosses it into the garbage.

"Yeah, yeah. Thanks," Zorvelli replies as Eastman and Kathryn return to their seats, turning their attention back to the President.

"We will continue to work toward offering affordable healthcare to all American citizens. Our healthcare system is revered throughout the world and is a model of excellence in which we can be proud. Without healthcare insurance many Americans rely on emergency room care for minor ailments such as a cold. This drains the systems and leaves too many Americans out in the cold. We can do better."

Eastman leans forward in his seat and anticipates more discussion on healthcare. He listens intently for the mention of stem cell research and regenerative medicine.

"To a large degree we didn't have this problem in veterinary medicine," Anderson remarks to Kathryn.

"Why's that?"

"It's affordable. My patients received the same high quality healthcare and sometimes even better than human healthcare at a fraction of the cost. People can afford veterinary medical care. Human medical care should take a page from our book."

Eastman shoots Anderson a look imploring him to be quiet in case they were getting close to hearing the fate of their business.

"We must put the physicians, nurses, healthcare workers, and patients in charge of a system that is inclusive of all citizens. We must begin with our seniors and reforming Medicare. We want our citizens to receive the same good quality health coverage and care that members of Congress receive and to have access to innovative technological medical advances and new medications."

"What about regenerative medicine then? Surely this is the newest, if not most important, advancement in healthcare options?" Eastman questions.

"Frivolous lawsuits have held our American doctors hostage in fear of being sued. The costs of healthcare have risen because of excessive litigation. Liability reform must be passed by Congress. Tonight, I am announcing a six-hundred-million-dollar program to help Americans addicted to both prescription and illegal drugs so they can receive treatment. In helping parents who are addicted, we will be helping their children to have safer, happier, and healthier lives. Coming to the aide of children, who are some of the most vulnerable of our citizens, speaks to our values and morals, and supports our image as one of a welcoming society. When I speak of the most vulnerable I am including the unborn. I ask you to protect fetuses and infants by ending the practice of partial birth abortion."

Kathryn leans into Eastman and whispers, "He makes it sound like it's an everyday practice when in fact partial birth abortion is extremely rare."

Eastman feels the warmth of Kathryn's breath on his ear and smells her fresh scent. It reminds him of a summer day and makes him long to hold her.

"And because no human life should be started or ended as the object of an experiment, I ask you to set a high standard for humanity, and pass a law against all human cloning. The Respect Human Life legislation is a bill I support and I urge congress to hurry and pass it so I can sign it into law. No human life should be terminated or begun as a scientific experiment. For this reason I implore every one of you to embrace humanity by passing a law against all types of human cloning."

"Shit," Eastman remarks under his breath.

"Does this mean they're going to try and outlaw the use of leftover, frozen, IVF embryos?" Kathryn asks.

"More importantly, are they going to try and shut us down?" Anderson asks the question that is on everyone's mind.

"The President says *all* human cloning. He doesn't draw a distinction between therapeutic and reproductive," Zorvelli replies.

"They're going to try, aren't they?" Kathryn asks Eastman.

"I believe so," Eastman somberly replies.

A low rumble reverberates throughout the room as side conversations start among the team as the President continues with his address.

"Nearly thirty million men, women, and children on the continent of Africa have been diagnosed with the AIDS virus. Three million of these people are children. In many African countries one-third of the adults carry the infection. Sadly, only fifty thousand are receiving the medicine they need to survive—the rest are being turned away. No person, in this day of miraculous medicine, should be told to go home and die."

"No, no one should be told to go home and die, and we are trying our best to change that," Eastman echoes with an edge of anger to his voice.

"Medications such as anti-retroviral drugs can extend the lives of people with the HIV virus for up to twelve years or more. We have an opportunity through the drug companies to help these people, and we have a moral obligation to do so. We will continue to fight HIV/AIDS in other countries as well as our own. I propose the Emergency Relief Plan for those suffering from AIDS. This plan will help to prevent millions of new HIV infections and provide humane care for those suffering from the disease," the President continues.

"Yeah, and the work *we* do can find a cure for AIDS and HIV, not just slap a Band-Aid on it," Anderson says evenly.

Kathryn turns to Eastman and says, "Jesus, there's no vaccine against Ebola. Remember the few times we had an outbreak in this country and were just barely able to contain it? That was years ago. The virus has gone airborne, at least with primates in the Texas lab, while our efforts to find an effective treatment for it, let alone a vaccine against it, have had little traction."

"All of this discussion about the advancement of medicine and no support for the research we do—the research that can actually lead to cures?" Eastman remarks.

Eastman notices that most of the people in the room are now involved in side conversations and no longer watching the rest of the President's address, since the question they were most interested in had been answered.

"What about support for AIDS?" Zorvelli asks and adds, "Remember when that was a taboo topic for the President and Congress? We were all waiting for politics and prejudice to be placed aside in order to help people. Now our President proudly announces that we are going to help people who are HIV positive and prevent its spread. How times have changed."

Kathryn, picking up on the thread of Zorvelli's comment, thoughtfully replies, "We have to do the same thing with therapeutic cloning. We have to make it popular, respected, and something that helps the world."

"Yes. It's all of those things, but people don't know it yet. They have doubts, just like they did about AIDs research and helping HIV-positive people," Eastman replies.

Eastman knows it's time to talk about what this might mean to the LAB and their jobs. He stands up and turns off the television using the controller. He looks to his colleagues and the rest of the LAB's employees. Clearing his throat he says, "Could I have your attention please? I know this is depressing news. In many ways it's expected, though. We had a feeling where the administration stands with our work. There's still much ignorance about what we do, the potential to extend life that our work holds. But it's not a death sentence for us."

Zorvelli, who is usually calm and prone to choosing his words carefully, is openly angry.

"The hell it isn't! I'm sorry for being so riled up, but I see this administration as equating the work we do with abortion. They are *not* synonymous. We try to prolong life, not end it."

"Exactly, and everyone here agrees with you," Eastman replies.

"Maybe it's time we give a little push back. I mean, the press can be a powerful ally," Anderson offered.

"There are millions of people out there with diseases or with loved ones who have diseases that our work could ultimately benefit. We need to get that message out," Kathryn says.

"There are members of Congress who can relate to therapeutic cloning as a potential cure for disease for themselves and their loved ones too," Anderson reminds everyone.

"It's time to hire a PR firm," Zorvelli says.

"Too bad we can't hire a lobbyist too. Politicians tend to swing their support where the money is," Kathryn muses.

"It's interesting how the President doesn't distinguish between therapeutic cloning and reproductive cloning. He lumps the two together, giving the impression that all cloning leads to experimentation on fetuses," Anderson says.

"We all know there's a huge educational gap and misconceptions that we need to overcome," Eastman says.

Despite his encouraging tone, it's apparent that the team is downcast and deeply concerned by the looks on their faces and by their body language. Eastman can't recall the last time he'd seen so many arms crossed on chests and jaws firmly set in anger.

"Look, it's not over 'til it's over. The President doesn't condone this type of research, but he doesn't currently have the full ability to stop it either. Passing a law to ban cloning could be a ways down the road. If the current bill out there were to pass both the House and Senate, there would most likely be appeals to the U.S. Supreme Court by the states, like ours, that currently support therapeutic cloning. I also heard from a friend of mine on the hill that the Senate, thankfully, doesn't have enough votes currently in favor of passing the Weldon bill either. As for now, the LAB is free to move forward with our work. Is everyone on board?" Eastman asks.

A rumble of approval rolls throughout the room with some people saying "yes," others applauding or nodding yes.

Zorvelli stands up waving around a magazine in his right hand and raises his voice above the murmurs. "While Washington is dicking around with basically what amounts to a lack of federal support for our work, the rest of the world moves forward."

"What are you holding?" Anderson asks.

"The most recent copy of *Nature*. We're basically sitting with our dicks in our hands, waiting to hear our fate, while Japan supports its scientists through a major achievement. They've grown a human liver," Zorvelli remarks.

The gallery is now with Zorvelli. Heads were nodding in agreement.

"Hold on, let's not jump ship. To be clear, they've induced stem cells to create a human organ that doesn't quite work," Eastman remarks.

"Yeah, well, in your playbook, that's close enough to the truth, isn't it?" Zorvelli retorts.

Eastman arches a brow at Zorvelli's dig regarding what most of the LAB considered a premature announcement.

"You had the LAB go on record stating that we cloned the first human. I think we jumped the gun, and now we may be facing a shit-storm of backlash because of it," Zorvelli coldly replies.

Eastman can't believe what he's hearing. Zorvelli's blaming him in front of everyone for the President's stance? What the hell? He sits back down in his chair feeling inwardly distressed.

"We all agreed to announce it. Our country should be supporting our work and other scientists like us, like the work being done at Boston Children's Hospital, as much as Japan and Korea and other countries are supporting scientists like Takanori Takebe. We just moved the discussion forward," Anderson came to Eastman's defense.

"Move it forward? Forced the issue is more like it. I mean, why the hell couldn't we just have said somatic cell nuclear transfer, or SCNT? You know the word *cloning*, even with *therapeutic* in front of it, upsets the top brass," Zorvelli counters.

"Wouldn't they have known that the two are the same?" Kathryn inquires.

"Highly unlikely," Anderson says and adds, "except maybe the more learned among them. People just don't follow things that closely."

"They don't understand it."

"Then we need to educate them," Kathryn offers, looking at Eastman who feels angry and a bit betrayed in front of their colleagues by Zorvelli's remarks. He wants and needs Zorvelli squarely in his corner encouraging the team towards success—not making them wonder whether or not they should even be on the team.

Cambridge, Massachusetts
February

A dispirited Eastman travels to Harvard to meet with his old professor and mentor, Dr. William Barrett. Eastman isn't certain why he is making this visit. He feels he needs something that only this man can give to him, but he doesn't know what it is. Eastman realizes it's been many years since he and the professor have spoken. He's both excited and a bit nervous at seeing him. A visit to a man he admires and respects is long overdue.

Eastman recalls Professor Barrett's research that helped to develop the micro cytotoxicity test in the 1960s. All heart, kidney, liver, lung, and bone marrow donors and recipients have been typed using this test. He's a man who dedicated his life to research and then went on to not only teach, but to encourage others in their own work.

Sitting in Barrett's office, Eastman feels small in front of the mahogany panels, the floor-to-ceiling windows framed by wine-colored velvet drapes. He admires the opulence of the sparkling Steuben glasses sitting next to the Waterford crystal brandy decanter on the sideboard. The aroma of pipe tobacco, worn leather, and brandy combine into one powerful scent that brings back many memories. *It's amazing how a scent can transport you back in time*, Eastman thinks. Suddenly Eastman feels every bit the student he had been and none of the accomplished, confident scientist he's become.

It used to unnerve Eastman to come in here. He'd never been comfortable sitting in such grandeur. Yet Barrett had a way of making you feel welcome when he wanted to, and fortunately for Eastman this is one of those times.

Professor Barrett enters his office. Eastman rises from his chair and greets the man who is now in his late seventies and still sporting a thick head of gray hair but carrying twenty pounds more than he should.

"Professor, thank you for seeing me," Eastman says extending his right hand.

Barrett takes Eastman's hand and instead of shaking it, he pulls him in close for a hug.

"Wonderful to see you," Professor Barrett replies slapping Eastman on the back.

Eastman takes his seat as Barrett walks around his desk and lowers himself into a chair that after years of wear engulfs the man like a hug. Eastman is glad to see that the two still share a genuine fondness for each other.

"It's been a long time, Professor."

"Well, it's nice of you to visit an old man," Barrett wryly replies with a bit of twinkle in his eyes.

Eastman enjoys the small talk they banter around for a few minutes. After catching up with each other, Eastman plunges into the immediate. "As you are aware, I've had some success with what I've achieved. But it's not enough."

Barrett leans forward in his chair and makes direct eye contact with Eastman through dirty wired-rimmed glasses.

"A bit of humility now I detect?" The professor says and chuckles. "I remember you always were a bit of a cocky student." Leaning back he adds, "You could afford the attitude. You have talent. Under this bravado was a deep insecurity at the time. However, despite your being your own worst enemy, you are someone who possesses perseverance and determination. This combination trumps talent any day. But to possess all three is remarkable. I've been watching, waiting for remarkable. Remarkable takes guts, though. It takes risk."

Barrett's comment wasn't lost on Eastman.

"Surely you know I take risks?"

"You've taken quite a big risk announcing a successful human clone. Do you think your risk paid off?" Barrett asks.

"I think so. My father always told me that if I was going to take a risk to make it a big one. I also remember you telling me that Salk said risks were worth taking because they *always* pay off. Maybe not in the way you want them to, but at the very least in learning what to do and what not to do."

"And what was Salk working on when he died?" Barrett asks.

Of course, Eastman knows the answer and says, "A vaccine for AIDS."

"I do believe he would've eventually gotten there, just as he did with the polio vaccine, had he not been at the end of his life."

Eastman decides he has had enough of the around-the-barn sort of discussion Barrett is known to engage in, and cuts to the chase. "What's your point?"

"My point? You've learned from some of the best and brightest scientists in the world. You come here appearing the lost student. You aren't lost. You just need to trust."

"Trust who?"

"Isn't it obvious? Yourself," Barrett answers.

Eastman allows the comment to sink in. Was he here because he feels he may have lost trust in some close team members such as Zorvelli? Does he doubt himself?

"It's hard to trust when you aren't one hundred percent sure," Eastman replies.

"Do you think it was easy for Salk? No. His vaccine wasn't perfect. It helped so many, but at first it actually caused polio in some. It had to be worked out. But if he didn't take the risk we may never have benefited from the preventative cure. What a different world we'd live in without Salk's polio vaccine, Edleman's discoveries on the structure of antibodies, and Skinner's contribution to understanding human behavior. They all took risks. This reminds me of Bob Edwards, a colleague of mine, who you'll recall created the first test-tube baby."

"Yes. A true genius."

"He got Louise Brown with only one embryo. He got one embryo that day. He went ahead and made the attempt and succeeded."

"I understand what you're saying. After taking such a significant risk I feel like a man without a compass. I'm feeling my way through the thick woods, and there are many fallen trees blocking my path," Eastman replies.

"Yes, you've stepped up to a daunting task," Barrett acknowledges.

Eastman nods his head in agreement.

"Reminds me of one of Robert Frost's poems, "The Road Not Taken. Barrett remarks and gestures to the framed poster recanting the poem directly on the wall behind him.

"Yes, I remember this. You've had this hanging in the same place from when I was your student," Eastman says.

"Well, read it," Barrett commands.

Eastman pulls his cheaters from his pocket and leans forward for a better look and then recites;

Two roads diverged in a yellow wood,
And sorry I could not travel both
And be one traveler, long I stood
And looked down one as far as I could
To where it bent in the undergrowth;

Then took the other, as just as fair,
And having perhaps the better claim,
Because it was grassy and wanted wear;
Though as for that the passing there
Had worn them really about the same,

And both that morning equally lay
In leaves no step had trodden black.
Oh, I kept the first for another day!
Yet knowing how way leads on to way
I doubted if I should ever come back.

I shall be telling this with a sigh
Somewhere ages and ages hence:
Two roads diverged in a wood, and I—
I took the one less traveled by,
And that has made all the difference.

"Being older," Barrett says.

And wiser, Eastman thinks as it truly related to his present situation.

"Affords me a perspective I didn't have when I was younger and heavily engaged in my own work."

Eastman raises his eyebrows in a gesture of encouragement for Barrett to offer his insight.

"At the time, I was often too narrowly focused on my work and, at times, missed the obvious. If you recall when you were a student I referred to it as the 'laser beam blindness,' the inability to take a step back and to look at the whole picture. Sometimes we need to step back. I assume that's why you are here?" Barrett inquires.

Eastman thinks about this for a moment. A smile slowly parts his lips. He stands up and reaches across the desk and shakes the professor's hand. "Thank you, Professor Barrett."

"I don't have to wish you luck. You have what you need to accomplish your goals. I'm glad that I got a visit out of it too," Barrett says.

"Thank you for allowing this visit. It's helped me to take a step back and to see the bigger picture."

Leaving the professor's office, Eastman realizes his work boils down to saving one little boy. *To hell with the rest of the side shows*. His focus will solely be on saving Noah, and if he succeeds, then he will have unlocked the door for saving millions of others. *I'm on the road less traveled and sometimes it's lonely at that*.

Westchester, New York
Westchester Outpatient Clinic

"Susan, open your eyes. Susan, can you hear me?" She hears a man's voice in the recesses of her mind.

"She's slow to come around. I'll keep talking to her and see if I can get her to wake up," Susan hears the voice say. "Susan, it's all over. You did great. Open your eyes." Susan opens her eyes and sees a dark-haired man in scrubs standing over her. "You're awake! Good. How do you feel?" Susan notices his laminated badge hanging around his neck. It reads Jonas Applebaum, RN, Westchester Outpatient Surgery Center. "How many eggs?"

"Doctor Daniels is coming in, and I'll let him tell you all about it."

Susan's heart sinks as she fears the doctor will have to be the one to break the bad news. The nurse sees her expression of dread. "I'm not supposed to say anything but I want you to know it's' all good," he says with a smile.

"Really?" Susan asks in a raspy voice.

"Can I get you anything?"

"Some ginger ale would be nice. I'm so thirsty."

"You've got it," Applebaum replies and turns to leave just as Dr. Daniels enters and greets Susan. "Hello to our star patient." Susan brightens at the compliment, hoping its good news. Daniels is a handsome middle-aged man with chiseled features and short-cropped blond hair. He came highly recommended and had agreed to be Susan's OBGYN in New York and perform the surgery that Dr. MacMurray was present for. In fact, Dr. Daniels performed most of the egg harvesting surgical procedures on donors volunteering for the LAB.

"I'm happy to report that we harvested ten eggs this time. I also expect you to recover nicely."

"Ten? Is that enough? I mean, I know two was barely enough."

"Well, if you don't believe me you can ask Dr. MacMurray."

On cue, she walks into the room. Dressed in her green surgical scrubs and wearing a rainbow-colored cap, Dr. MacMurray acknowledges Daniels as he steps back from Susan's hospital bed. "Susan, I'm sure Dr. Daniel's told you the wonderful news. How are you feeling?"

"It's ten, ten eggs, right? Are they all viable to work with?"

"We will know soon enough. Ten is excellent! We consider that very good with humans."

"Humans? Well then I wish I were a cow," Susan says sarcastically.

Dr. MacMurray replies with a laugh. "You rest and listen to the nurses. They'll take good care of you."

"Thank you," Susan replies and inquires, "Dr. MacMurray, you will let me know right away how many are viable, right?"

"I promise."

As the two doctors leave the room, Susan begins thinking about all of the possibilities. Her thoughts race to the day when they will be able to offer a cure for Noah. With this thought she feels a longing in her heart. She misses her beautiful ball of energy—Noah.

Santa Rosa, California

"Yeah, I think we have some here somewhere," Elliot says to Noah's pediatrician over the kitchen phone as he searches the cabinets for Pedialyte.

"Daddy!" Noah cries out, standing in the middle of the kitchen floor, and then vomits all over his pajamas.

Elliot ends the conversation with the doctor and hurries over to his son. "Hey little buddy, it's okay. Daddy's going to clean you up and help you to feel better," he says as he wipes his son's mouth with a dishtowel from the counter and begins stripping Noah of his clothing.

"No big deal," Elliot says as he tosses the pajamas into a pile on the floor along with the dirty dishtowel. Elliot feels that Noah's skin feels hot. "Wow, you've got a fever too.

"I want Mommy!" Noah sobs. "I want her too," Elliot replies, feeling as if he might start crying also. "The doctor said to give you some special stuff to drink. I think we have it somewhere in the pantry. Let's look," Elliot says taking Noah's hand and leading him into the pantry. Elliot scans the shelves and sees a bottle of the stuff. Reaching for it he says, "You'll drink this and feel better."

"No!" Noah says. Elliot takes the bottle and Noah follows him into the kitchen. "How about if I put it into one of your bottles for you? I think we still have one of those around here," he says as he searches the cupboard where they keep the cups. "Bingo!" Elliot exclaims as he finds a blue plastic bottle with a nipple attached. "Gimme!" Noah says reaching up for the bottle.

"First I have to pour this special drink into it and then you can have it," Elliot explains as he goes about the task of preparing Noah's bottle. He hands him the bottle and remembers that he should give him some liquid Tylenol for the fever. Noah sits on the floor sucking the bottle as Elliot prepares a dropper full of the thick orange liquid. "Here you go," Elliot says as he approaches Noah with the dropper. Noah turns his head and swats at the dropper sending the gooey orange liquid all over Elliot. "Crap!" Elliot exclaims and Noah starts crying again. Elliot sets the Tylenol down on the counter. He scoops up his son and the baby bottle filled with Pedialyte. "I'm putting you back in bed," Elliot tells Noah. On the way he opens the fridge and retrieves a beer. Noah stops crying and reaches for the beer. "No, little guy, this is daddy's bottle."

Elliot kisses the top of Noah's head and heads to the nursery. "As soon as we both calm down I need to give you your medicine. You want to be feeling good when Mommy comes home? Right Noah?" Noah sucks on his bottle and nods his head. "I can't wait for your mommy to get home either," Elliot says placing Noah in his crib. Elliot takes a seat in the rocking chair next to his son's bed, twists off the beer cap and swigs down the cool amber liquid. The truth was he couldn't stand to see his son sick. It made him feel helpless. He wonders how he will be able to endure it if Noah does succumb to ALD? *I don't think I could be that brave.*

Westchester, New York

The eggs were now safely inside an incubator plugged into the cigarette lighter of the car and resting on the car's passenger seat.

"The drive isn't a long one from the clinic to the LAB—less than 30 minutes. So we should get there pretty quick," Zorvelli says from the driver's seat.

"Good," Steve Landers, the middle aged guard sitting in the car's backseat replies.

"Carrying thousands of dollars of precious cargo always makes me a bit nervous. I take turns doing these egg runs with Dr. Anderson. Have you gone on a run with him before?" Zorvelli asks.

"No. This is my first run with the LAB," Landers says as he runs a meaty hand through is graying hair. "As a retired cop working security now, I've protected jewels and sizable amounts of cash, but this is the first time I've sat with precious cargo being human eggs."

"Hey, maybe we should get one of those Baby on Board signs to hang in the window—but instead of it saying *baby* we can get one that says Eggs on Board," Zorvelli says and then chuckles at his own joke.

In an attempt to humor Zorvelli's lame joke, Landers replies, "That's a good one, but I don't think we want to call attention to what we're carrying. How many do you have in there?"

"About ten. We're hoping they're all viable but we won't know for certain until we get back to the LAB."

"If they're viable?"

"They're worth a bundle."

"How's the gas?"

"Full tank."

"Just curious? Ever run into a problem on one of these egg runs?"

"Not that I'm aware. I know there have been car-jacking's but no eggs or organs involved."

"Well, when you're transporting big ticket items it's always good to have some protection in case of the unexpected. Besides, you don't want these to get into the wrong hands."

"Damn straight," Zorvelli agrees, turning onto the final, long, road that leads to the LAB.

"The scariest part, or should I say, the most anxiety-producing parts are the pickup and drop off. Anything could happen when the eggs in the incubator are exposed."

"Kind of like the Brinks guys picking up and dropping off the money."

"Yeah, like that. Hey, maybe we should have an armored car. I'll talk to Eastman about that," Zorvelli says with a laugh.

"What the hell?" the guard says, looking out of the back window.

"What's wrong?" Zorvelli asks quickly glancing up into the rear view mirror.

"This truck has been following us since we left the clinic. It's still following us after you turned off the freeway and onto this road."

"They're going in our direction all right. I want to know why," the guard says as he turns around and to monitor the situation.

The truck pulls right up behind their car and then passes them.

Landers puts a hand on his gun ready to take action if necessary.

The truck cuts in front of Zorvelli, and he hits the brakes nearly missing the truck.

Fuck!" Zorvelli says as the incubator lurches forward in the seat.

"Asshole!" Zorvelli angrily states flipping the truck driver the bird.

Zorvelli brings the car to a stop on the side of the road. The incubator is wedged between the dash and the seat.

"Thank God it didn't hit the floor," Zorvelli says with relief flooding out of his voice.

"Get back onto the road," Landers instructs holding his cocked gun in both hands.

"I will, I just need a minute."

"Now!" Landers dictates seeing the truck driver pull a U-turn and head back towards them.

Zorvelli pulls back out onto the road and proceeds cautiously.

"Goddamn shit head!" Zorvelli fumes.

Just then the truck swerves toward them.

He's going to hit us head on! Zorvelli thinks, as there is no time to speak.

Landers leans out the back window and takes aim.

Seeing the gun, the truck driver veers off to the right at the last second before he would have plowed into them. Zorvelli jerks the steering wheel hard toward the gravel shoulder. They go into a slide and Landers misses shooting the truck. They smack hard against the shoulder's guardrail. The incubator tips to the right and then to the left on the seat, only to be fully upright by the time they stop. Seeing that the incubator is safe, Zorvelli says, "What the fuck?"

Landers looks over to see the truck back on the road and speeding away.

"You did great," Landers remarks.

"What the hell was all that about?" Zorvelli inquires, his own voice sounding distant to him, overpowered by his heart beating like a drum in his chest.

"That's what I'd like to know."

Washington, D.C.
March

Senator Brice (D., CA) was quick witted and stylish. Her chief of staff Amy was not. The humor challenged 33 year old was relatively calm, mostly dull and a talented researcher - all qualities that Brice needed to keep her focused and to keep her on track with her work. The Senator had canceled her first morning meeting in order to meet with Amy. Amy, who was dressed in a sensible brown suit and low heels, and is sitting in an overstuffed chair doodling on a yellow legal pad while waiting for the Senator to finish her mocha.

Brice, sitting on the sofa, directly across from Amy, looks fashionable and svelte in her blue blazer and matching pencil skirt. Unlike the majority of Washington DC female fifty somethings, Brice's best years weren't behind her - she played tennis and had a figure and legs that showed it. Leaning forward Brice sets her empty Starbucks cup down on the glass coffee table between them.

"Amy, have you been following the human cloning debate?"

"You mean here in Washington?"

"Well, of course, Amy. I didn't mean in Boston."

"Yes, ma'am, I am well aware of the pending legislation. As you know, a proposed bill, the President Longran is urging support of is the Respect Human Life bill."

"Catchy name and a bit misleading," Brice replies.

"The panel the president had appointed to look into the moral, and ethical implications of human cloning are heavily stacked with "experts" who don't support this type of research."

"Yes. I know that. What I want is a complete understanding of therapeutic cloning. .Do you have one?" Brice inquires.

"You mean the kind that could ultimately eradicate disease in humans and animals?"

"Yes, I'm currently leaning toward supporting the bill Senator Matthews is sponsoring. This legislation that will sanction the cloning of embryos for research purposes However, I don't like that the research will have to be approved by a professional peer review board before being undertaken - I mean that can be a slippery slope depending who is on the board."

"I agree," Amy replies.

"What I want from you is for you to put together a sort of crash course in the concepts for me. I want to fully grasp what it is we are debating here. I'm not interested in anything about reproductive cloning. I'm opposed to that completely. But I do need to come to an educated decision about Matthew's bill. Can you do that, Amy?"

"Of course. How soon do you want it?"

"Yesterday."

"I understand, ma'am."

"Oh, and Amy, can you run through what you do know with me now?"

"Yes. Do you want me to draw you diagrams?" She asks officiously.

"I'm not a fucking moron. I just want you to explain what you know in layman's terms."

Amy flinches ever so slightly at the Senator's abrasive comment. "Yes, ma'am. Would it be okay if I *did* include diagrams and drawings in the briefing I'm putting together from the research I've done? It helped me to gain a better picture in my mind of what is all involved."

"That would be fine. Now start by telling me everything you know."

Westchester, New York
March, Same Day

Zorvelli, carrying the incubator in his hands as if it were a newborn king, walks with Landers close by his side. They enter the LAB through the front door. Zorvelli notifies the guard at the security desk that they're taking the eggs to the room where they will be processed.

"I'm going to hang out in the reception area for a bit just in case there's any more trouble," Landers informs Zorvelli.

"Good idea. Could you also call the police and make a report?" Zorvelli inquires just as he sees Eastman and Anderson walking quickly towards them down the hall.

"Yeah, I was going to," Landers informs as he turns towards the reception area.

"Great timing. Everything go okay?" Eastman inquires.

"We had a little incident with some asshole truck driver. The incubator got shaken around a bit," Zorvelli replies.

"Are you okay? Shit, I hope the eggs are okay," Anderson states.

"Thanks for placing your concern about my welfare before the eggs," Zorvelli sarcastically replies and not waiting for a response from Anderson adds, "I'm okay. My shoulder is a little sore. What isn't okay is my car."

"What's wrong with your car?" Eastman inquires.

"Lets' just say it's a little worse for the wear," Zorvelli informs as the three head on down the hall toward the room where they'll deliver the incubator.

Westchester, New York
Two Hours Later

Eastman was overjoyed with his good fortune. There are several viable eggs to work with. The procedure to insert Noah's DNA into one of the eggs in which the DNA will have been removed can be attempted more than once, if needed. Eastman watches the big screen hanging on the wall in the sterilized room in which Dr. MacMurray prepares for the procedure. The television monitor provides an up-close view that can't easily been seen through the glass.

The team inside the gallery watches Dr. MacMurray and hears her announce through the loudspeaker, "I'm about to start the procedure." She takes a deep breath, lets it out slowly, shakes out her gloved hands, and then carefully proceeds. Her focus is laser-beam intense. Eastman and the rest of the team turn their attention back to the big screen as Dr. MacMurray carefully uses suction to draw the egg into the needle; the egg elongates. Dr. MacMurray holds her breath, fearing that it might burst. However, something occurs that hadn't happened last time. Instead of the ball of cells "running away from the suction," fusion ensues and the cells are extracted.

Eastman and the others watch this on the television monitor. However, Eastman waits for the final confirmation from her.

After what seems like an eternity, Dr. MacMurray looks up at Eastman, pulls off her face mask, and gives him a huge smile.

"Success!" Eastman joyfully exclaims as Dr. MacMurray gives him the thumbs-up sign through the glass window. "Now we must wait and see what happens to the reconstructed egg in the morning," Eastman remarks to the staff in the gallery, "We will hope that it grows very big by tomorrow."

There are handshakes and back slapping all the way around. "Way to go, Dr. MacMurray!" the crowd cheers through the glass window. Dr. MacMurray smiles and clasps her hands in a victory sign above her head.

Kathryn fucking did it! Eastman happily thinks and then excuses himself to make an important call to Susan. He can hardly wait to share the good news.

New York City, New York
Same Evening

Susan is trying not to let her emotions ride too high as she packs to catch her long flight home. Still, she can't help but smile when she considers the news. They're on their way to really being able to help Noah. She thinks about the growing ball of cells that is the first significant beginning in a long but promising road to finding a cure. *It's a hopeful start*, she thinks and reminds herself that anything can go wrong. She can't wait to share the news with Elliot. She hopes she'll have time to do that before she boards the plane. Right now she's running late. As she looks inside the closet for any clothes she might've missed, she's jarred from her thoughts by a loud knock on the door of her hotel room.

"Who is it?" She inquires before opening the door.

No reply.

"Who's there?" she repeats a bit louder this time when she notices an envelope being slipped under the door. Bending to reach for it, she thinks it might be the bill but then wonders why they'd bring the bill when she called the front desk earlier and told them she'd stop by on her way out. *Maybe it's a mistake*; she considers as she picks up the envelope and tosses it into her purse. She'll open it at the front desk. She glances at the clock on the nightstand. *Oh no, I've gotta go!* She realizes she should've checked out fifteen minutes ago if she wants to make the flight. Grabbing her purse and her suitcase she rushes out of the room and toward the elevator. She notices the doors on the elevator are closing when she shouts, "Wait!" A tall, weathered looking man wearing jeans, a John Deer cap, and work boots holds the elevator for her. "Thank you," Susan exclaims breathlessly. The man who appears to be dressed more for work on a farm than a hotel in New York City nods. "Main floor please," Susan tells the man as he presses the button for the doors to close. Susan gives an uncomfortable smile as the man is silent and looks straight ahead. Just as they reach the main floor the man glances at her open purse. "You might want to open that envelope before you leave," he tells her as the elevator doors open.

But before she can reply he's gone, lost in the crowd of people in the lobby. *Why would he say that?* Susan wonders as she heads toward the front desk. Retrieving the envelope to see if they already charged it to her credit card, Susan stops dead in her tracks. Her heart races and her knees buckle. She reaches for the marble pillar to her right. Inside the envelope is a flier with her son's picture; above his head is the boldly typed word, "STOP," and below Noah's chin, it reads, "NOW!"

Westchester, New York
Later the Same Evening

Eastman and Kathryn stay in the LAB until well past midnight. "Go home," he urges Kathryn.

"Oh no, I'm too excited to sleep."

"There's nothing more to do. You can't sit here waiting for cells to divide."

"Is that your way of saying a watched pot never boils?" Kathryn says smartly, wrinkling her nose. Despite her fatigue she feels a current of excitement racing through her veins in anticipation of what might happen with the blastocyst. There's something else going on too. Kathryn doesn't want to leave Eastman. She found a kindred soul in him. They have shared their passion about their work almost to the exclusion of everything else around them. There is something extremely desirable, perhaps even sexy, about this for Kathryn. She feels herself drawn to him over and over again in so many ways.

"Seriously Kathryn, you should go home and at least rest before tomorrow."

"Are you going home?"

"In a while."

"Well, then, I'm staying too. Besides there is something we both can do. Something I've been doing all day."

"What's that?"

"We can both pray."

"Pray?" Eastman says raising his thick, dark eyebrows.

"Yes, pray. It was kind of mandatory at parochial school."

"I see. So you're a Catholic girl?"

"Irish Catholic," Kathryn says mockingly in an Irish accent.

Eastman thinks back to a song he knows, and a smile pulls at the corners of his mouth and crinkles the corners of his eyes.

"What?" Kathryn curiously inquires cocking her head to one side.

"That Billy Joel song popped into my head." Eastman proceeds to sings the verse, "Come out Virginia, don't hesitate, Catholic girls start much too late."

Kathryn lightly punches him in the arm. "If I had a dollar for every time I've heard that, I wouldn't have to work here."

"Have to work here? I thought this is your calling - your passion."

Kathryn arches a brow. "Okay, you got me there."

"I feel as if we are on the verge of turning the page and entering into a whole new phase of medicine. If we can help Noah, we open the door to helping millions of people," Eastman states with a hint of excitement rolling through his voice.

"Not unlike the biblical Noah, who was told by God to preserve all the animals," Kathryn offers.

Eastman ponders this and then says, "Well, what do you know? We do have our own modern-day Noah helping us to preserve the human race."

Westchester, New York
Next Day

Eastman startles awake by the sound of his neighbor's leaf blower. The guy often used it to clean out the dirt in his garage. *Why the hell can't he use a broom?* Eastman thinks. He sits up in bed and sees that it's light outside. It's too light. Damn! The clock on his nightstand reads 9:15 a.m. *I need to get back to the LAB. How had I slept so long?* He thinks and then smiles at his next thought. *There's just something about being with Kathryn that relaxes me. I haven't slept this good in a long time."*

Time was something he was painfully aware of this morning. Eastman grabs his cell off the nightstand and punches in Kathryn's number. She answers on the third ring. "Are you at the LAB?"

"Hey, I was just about to call you. Yeah, I've been here all night. If you're coming back in now, I'm starving. Will you pick me up an onion bagel with cream cheese and lox? Oh, and don't forget the capers. I like lots of them. I love capers. They remind me of little balls of cells sitting on the head of a pin. Have you ever thought of capers sitting on cream cheese like that?"

Eastman pulls the phone away from his ear and looks at it and thinks. *Kathryn sounds positively loopy—lack of sleep does it every time.*

"Yeah, I'll get you the bagel, but what's going on with our blastocyst?"

"I was just about to check it again."

"Okay, call me after you check it?"

"You'll be here soon. I'll tell you when you get here."

Eastman hangs up and grabs his jeans off of the back of the chair next to the bedroom door, regretting his promise to get the bagel. He feels an urgent need to get back to the LAB.

Westchester, New York
Morning

"Well?" Eastman blurts as he sidles up to Kathryn, who is sitting on a stool looking through a microscope in the LAB.

"Did you get my bagel?" Kathryn inquires looking up.

Eastman hands her the bag. Kathryn takes it from him and opens it. "Did you get cream cheese?"

"See for yourself."

"What about capers? Did you get a hundred capers?"

"I don't know if there are a hundred, but there are lots. Now what's going on?"

"We have a cell division to one hundred!" Kathryn exclaims with a bright smile spread across her face.

"Holy shit! Are you certain?" Eastman let out a long whistle through his teeth.

"Yes, I've checked several times and it's continuing to divide."

"We have a blastocyst?" he inquires, cautiously.

"It looks that way. But just in case, I've got everything crossed including my toes."

Kathryn stands up and faces Eastman. She tilts her head in a quizzical fashion. "I thought you'd be over the moon with this news."

Eastman steels a glance around the LAB. He notices that they are alone in the room. Impulsively he gives Kathryn a big bear-hug and lifts her feet off of the ground.

Kathryn tosses her head back and laughs. Eastman sets her back down and she adjusts her lab coat.

"Was that the reaction you were looking for?" Eastman happily inquires.

Santa Rosa, California
One Week Later, Sunday Afternoon

While Susan changes Noah's diaper on his changing table, positioned just under the nursery window that looks out onto their backyard, she looks down at her son who is playing with a small, blue ball he holds high above his head. She can feel the warmth of the sun coming through the nursery window kissing her face. "Do you want to play outside, Noah?"

"Ow thide!" Noah parrots.

Susan smiles at her son and allows her thoughts to dance through her mind. Things were going well. Noah had started preschool at the College Oak Montessori School, not too far from their home, despite Susan's concerns about having him out of their sight. Elliot insisted that they lead their lives as normally as possible despite the frightening flier Susan received in New York. She had reported the flier to the police and to Dr. Eastman everything she could recall about the man in the elevator. The truth was there had been nothing remarkable about him. When she mentioned that he looked like a farmer the two officers had exchanged glances. Well, how many farmers might be deranged stalkers? Chances of finding the man weren't great. Susan fears that he will show up again, and this scares her to her toes.

Susan is jolted out of her thoughts by Noah dropping the ball on the changing table.

"Uh oh."

Susan picks up the ball and hands it to him. She pulls up his little jeans over his big diaper.

Noah squeezes the ball again with both hands.

"Wow buddy, you're strong," Susan tells him.

"Song," Noah tries to repeat the word but comes out lacking the str sound.

Her mind wanders to the article about cloning Noah that ran in *Parade Magazine* last Sunday. Susan prays that Noah's identity would remain a secret. After all there was really nothing that would signal that it was their son. Still, she had an uneasy feeling in having done the interview. *Too late now,* she thinks. *It's been a week and nothing. So it's probably fine.*

"Ow thide, Mommy," Noah reminds.

"Almost ready Noah," Susan replies. As she tosses the soiled diaper and dirty wipes into the garbage something catches her eye through the window. "What the hell is that?" Susan asks out-loud. She sees a camera lens peering over the top of the fence in the backyard. Squinting she takes a closer look. To her horror—a man's head pops up with a camera.

"Oh my god!" she exclaims as she quickly scoops up Noah and carries him out to the living room where Elliot's asleep on the sofa. "Elliot, get up!" Susan shouts. Startled, Elliot jumps up off the sofa and stumbles into the coffee table, smacking his shin. "Shit! What's going on?" he asks as he rubs his sore leg.

"Someone's outside taking pictures of us!" Susan exclaims.

"Not there, out back. He was over the fence in the Wilkerson's' yard!" she tells him.

"Are you sure? Why would someone be taking pictures of us?"

"I have no idea. You need to go over there and find out what's going on," Susan says urgently hugging Noah close to her.

"Okay, let me get my shoes."

Susan follows him to the kitchen door where his sneakers sit next to the back door.

"The Wilkerson's aren't home. They're in Hawaii," Susan reminds Elliot and adds, "Maybe you shouldn't go. Maybe we should call the police."

"I'm sure it's nothing. I'm going to check it out. You stay here," Elliot says firmly as he hurries out the door. Susan watches Elliot making his way across the yard from the kitchen window. Susan sees Elliot approach the fence and then go around the other side into the Wilkerson's backyard. It seems like an eternity before she finally sees Elliot approaching the door. She rushes over to the door, still holding Noah who clearly wants down as he wriggles in his mother's arms. "Did you see anyone?" Susan asks Elliot.

"Yeah, some guy with a camera getting into a car. He took off before I could approach him. I'm calling the police."

Later That Morning

Elliot was livid. He put in a call to Eastman after calling the police and soon after the phone call the Gaynors and Eastman are Skyping.

Susan and Elliot position the laptop on the coffee table in the living room. The two sit on the sofa as Noah played near them on the floor. They watched as the image of Eastman's face came into view.

"Susan and Elliot let me first say how very sorry I am that this is happening."

"Yeah, it kind of sucks big time," Elliot agrees.

"Why would a photographer be taking a photo of our son if they didn't find out somehow that he was the boy in the Parade article?" Susan asks Eastman.

"That's a good question. We could assume that he found out. I'll contact the reporter and see if there was a leak," Eastman offers.

"What should we do?" Elliot inquires of Eastman.

"For everyone's safety I think we just want it to go away. For now we do nothing." Eastman replies.

"Safety? Do you think Noah's at risk of being harmed?" The fear and concern in Susan's voice was apparent to all.

"Quite honestly, I don't know. There was the threatening note you received in the hotel, and there have been a few questionable things that have happened here which deeply concern me."

"Whoa, back up. I'm still worried about the note—but nothing has happened since then to us. I didn't know about anything on your end, though." Elliot says, a bit shaken.

"No direct threats. There was an incident with a member of the team transporting the eggs, but we weren't certain it was someone who knew what he was carrying or someone who was expressing road rage. I probably shouldn't have even mentioned it. The point is I think it's best if we just let this story die down and go away. It's better to keep things quiet."

Turning to Susan, Elliot asks, "Okay with you?"

"I'm not sure, what else we can do for now."

"You did contact the police about the photographer, correct?" Eastman asks.

"Yes. They're coming to our house to take a full report," Elliot replies.

"Keep me posted about how things progress," Eastman says and after saying goodbye they all sign off Skype. Susan is scared for her son, for her family, for the people who are helping her to save her son's life. She can feel it in her bones that this isn't just going to go away. This is the beginning of bad things to come.

Susan has just put Noah down for a late morning nap when detectives Zachary Hannis and Molly Malone arrive. The two detectives stomp the wetness from their boots at the door as Elliot invites them to have a seat in their living room and Susan offers coffee. Detective Malone's unruly red hair was protruding from beneath her police hat. Susan notices that she has warm, gray eyes that show her sensitivity. In that instant she takes a liking to the detective.

Elliot produces both the *Parade Magazine* article and the *World News* rag for the detectives as the downpour outside pellets the living room windows and casts dark shadows across the room. Not wanting to confirm or deny the truth, Elliot chose a middle ground. "Our son is named Noah. His cousin and our nephew, Josh, died from ALD. I think someone took a leap of faith and tied the two together and now assume the story in *Parade* is about our son."

"Mr. and Mrs. Gaynor, I understand that you want to protect your son. I also understand your concerns about being stalked. However, in cases like these, the level of intrusiveness often increases if there is any truth to the story," Detective Hannis explains as he removes his police hat and sets it in his lap. His thin, blond hair was plastered against the sides of his head.

So much for being diplomatic, Susan thinks.

"Our first concern is for the safety of you and your son. Any information you can provide us will assist us in doing our jobs," Detective Malone says.

"What if this story is true? What if it is about our son?" Susan asks.

"It's best to trust us and to tell us the truth. What you say to us will be kept confidential from the media," Detective Malone assures them. "However, we need to know exactly what we are dealing with here."

Elliot and Susan exchange a concerned glance. Susan nods to Elliot, giving permission to tell the whole truth. They both realize that they have no choice but to explain the situation.

"Our son was diagnosed with ALD. Our nephew, as I says, recently died from the disease. We are pursuing all medical avenues available to us, not only in caring for him but in the hopes of saving his life."

"Just so I'm clear, you are cloning your son?" Detective Hannis inquires as he strokes the day-old growth on his chin.

"We are attempting to, yes," Susan replies. Looking at both of the detectives' puzzled faces, she quickly adds, "Look, it's hard to explain. It's not some voodoo type of medical experiment. We're not hoping to create a whole new person. It has to do with stem cell therapy and regenerative medicine. You've heard of that, correct?"

"Of course. Look, Mr. and Mrs. Gaynor, We aren't here to judge you. We're here to protect you. What I do know about human cloning from recent news is that there are some people who are vehemently opposed to it. We've unfortunately seen this with some anti-abortion groups."

Malone adds, "We'll keep a close eye on your home. You both need to keep a close eye on your son and on each other."

Hannis stands and Malone follows his lead. He hands Elliott their cards. Elliot accepts them as he walks the two to the front door.

"Call us anytime if you have more problems or questions. Hopefully, this thing won't evolve beyond the 'just curious' stage," Malone says.

You and me both, Susan thinks.

A cold shiver crawls up Susan's spine as Elliot closes the door behind the detectives. Suddenly she wants to check the window in Noah's nursery to make certain it's locked. *Make that every window and every door in the entire house.*

Westchester, New York

After the story broke in *Parade*, the LAB, too, is flooded with phone calls, letters, emails, and faxes. It's too much for the team to keep up with. Yet Eastman is feeling more confident than he had in a long time. They have almost enough cell divisions to clone Noah. They choose to keep this information close to the vest, difficult as it is for Eastman to sit on it. He wants to publish his work. He is afraid, though - afraid for the Gaynors. The story in *Parade* had caused some anxiety, curiosity, hate mail, and angry phone calls. He hasn't planned on their identity being exposed. This concerns him greatly. He is also concerned about what the current administration would do if they knew that he and the LAB had progressed this far. His pledge not to concern himself with such issues was now eroding. He has grave concerns, and they are about the safety of his colleagues and staff. He hires extra security for the LAB. The upshot of all this publicity, though, is that they receive more private funding.

The silver lining in the black cloud.

Butlerville, Indiana
One Week Later

Joe places the lock box on his bed and opens it. He pulls out the semi-automatic Glock pistol and carefully loads cartridges into the sleek 15-round clip. It feels heavier in his hand than when he had been practicing with it on the farm just last week. It felt powerful. *This might get the good doctor's attention. Good doctor,* Joe smirks at his play on words. *Evil doctor is more the truth.*

Joe tucks the gun into his jeans and puts on his hunting jacket. He has a couple of days' drive ahead of him and a lot of time to think and to plan for his meeting with Dr. Eastman. He feels a sense of purpose, something he hasn't felt for some time. He smiles a knowing smile as he tosses his duffle bag of clothes and the paper bag of sandwiches he has made on the front seat of his blue Ford pickup. No one knows where he's going. He did tell the farmhand he placed in charge of the farm that he was going to a growers' meeting in Chicago and would be home in a few days. Joe climbs into the driver's side and puts the key in the ignition. He closes the door and turns the key. Putting the truck into drive and stepping on the gas, he sees a cloud of dust kicking up behind his truck in the rear view mirror as he rolls down the long, dirt road that will take him from the farm to the interstate. It was the first step in a long journey.

Eastman needed to realize that there are consequences for going against God's will. Joe's excitement grows as he presses the gas pedal down on the road and makes up a song. *Put that pedal to the metal all the way to New York. Put the lime in the coconut and drink it all up. Put the petal to the metal and blow it all up.*

Santa Rosa, California

Elliot breezes in through the front door as he arrives home from work. Immediately he's taken aback by what he sees all over the floor.

"What's all this?" Elliot asks as he sets down his briefcase next to the ottoman and sheds his coat on a living room chair. Susan is sitting among a massive pile of letters strewn about on the large Persian rug. Noah's tossing a few of the envelopes in the air. "Listen to this, honey," Susan says and reads the letter she's holding in her hand: "Dear Mr. and Mrs. Gaynor, I'm writing to tell you how much I appreciate your efforts and your willingness to pursue therapeutic cloning. I am the mother of a son who was recently diagnosed with ALD. I am a devout Christian and pray every day for a miracle. I think what you are doing is very brave and selfless. I, too, want a chance for my son. I know that while people fear cloning might result in the creation of a baby, I believe that therapeutic cloning is the answer to my prayers. I just wanted to thank you and let you know that my family and I are praying for your family. God Bless, Megan Bylund."

Elliot is surprised. Most of their experiences so far had been negative. He is touched that someone would take the time to write something so supportive.

"They can't all be like this, can they?" Elliot asks as he walks over to Susan and sits down on the floor next to her.

"I haven't opened them all, but many are. Some are mean and hateful, but so far people from all around the world have sent letters of support discussing their own health struggles with family members and friends. They are hoping for cures for so many diseases." Susan's tears in her eyes spill down her cheeks as she leans into Elliot for support. Noah hands Elliot an opened letter. "Thanks, buddy."

"Some have put cash and checks into the envelopes. Others have put pictures of their loved ones. Some have written about family members they've lost.

It's overwhelming—the amount of support we are receiving," Susan gushes. Susan is overcome with emotion. For one of the first times since they started this journey, she feels as if she's wrapped in a blanket of support with expressions of kindness and generosities covering her. Although she has her sister and other family members who are kind and caring, Susan realizes that she, Elliot, and Noah are all connected by a bond of empathy to so many people they never knew existed until now. It is overwhelming and empowering. She knows she's not alone—there are so many others who share their journey.

Elliot hoists Noah into his lap and kisses him. He sits him back down on the floor next to Susan and asks, "And what about the not-so-nice letters?"

"When I read the first line and it's negative or hateful, I toss it," she replies, nodding to a wastebasket filled to the brim in the living room. "These letters, the opened ones we are sitting in, are all letters of support."

"Well then, I think we should use them to paper the den," Elliot replies and winks at Susan. She smiles back at his joke.

"We'll give the money to Dr. Eastman."

"How much is there?"

"I haven't added it all up, but it's significant. Some people sent a dollar, and some sent checks in the amount of a thousand dollars. They are made out to us. Can we sign them over to the LAB?"

"There's a way to do it. I'll ask our accountant, Ernie, at the office tomorrow. He'll know how it's done." He looks more closely at the letter Noah had handed him. It looks as if it had been addressed by a child using a crayon. He opens it and white powder puffs up into his face.

"Holy shit!" he exclaims, and reads what is written: "Consider yourself warned. The words appear to be cut from magazines and pasted onto the paper.

Elliot quietly and firmly says, "Susan, pick up Noah and move out of this room now! And call the police. I think we may have been exposed to a toxic substance!"

Susan looks at Elliot and sees the powder sprinkled on his shirt and tie. "Elliot, what is that powder all over your shirt?" Susan questions with alarm.

"Move. Now." Elliot's voice booms authoritatively.

Susan hurriedly picks up Noah and sprints out of the room.

Her hands are shaking as she fumbles to hold onto Noah and grab her cell from the kitchen counter. She punches 911 and listens.

"Nine-one-one. What's your emergency?"

Westchester, New York

Eastman stretches out on the orange sofa inside his office. It's late at night and very few people are at the LAB. He likes this time. It's peaceful and he can think a thought without being interrupted. However, the thoughts he's ruminating about tonight seem to bring more anxiety then resolutions. He was worried - worried about the LAB's budget. It was tight and it showed. Personally, he was taking just enough of a paycheck to pay his bills. Despite the recent infusion of private funds the LAB they were barely making payroll and paying the bills. The scientists who worked there all recently took a ten percent pay cut and some research had to be put on hold. The human cloning experiment was top priority. He could feel in his core that they were on the verge of a real breakthrough and this excited him. He'd continue to solicit funds from private investors by speaking to privately owned corporations and by talking to reporters and trying to educate people about the LAB's work. Actor and stem cell advocate Michael J. Fox had lent his celebrity to the cause by shedding light on it. Stem cell research could very well lead to a cure for Parkinson's disease, the disease Fox had. Eastman hopes that this will result in the LAB receiving more private funding.

He sits up and rubs the temples on the side of his head. He's got the beginning of a headache. *Time to go home and get some sleep. Stop worrying. It doesn't do any good. Remember your mantra, "Cure the disease and the money will follow."* Eastman, says to himself. *It isn't rocket science. Just standard knowledge.*

There were so many other 'what ifs,' Eastman thinks as he pops the top from the bottle of Advil and tosses three tablets into his mouth. He washes it down with a lukewarm cup of tea sitting on the table next to him. He shudders at the bitter taste realizing he had left the tea bag in the cup. What is that his mom always told him? "Count your blessings, James." One blessing was that the team at the LAB wasn't in it for just a paycheck. They were doing research in order to cure diseases. This was the core of their philosophy and the heart of their work. They had all watched people they loved become sick and die. They were a unique team; they all worked well together and felt immense respect and loyalty toward each other.

As soon as one blessing was counted another worry popped up. Eastman thought about the next one as he bent down and reached for his shoes.

To date, the federal Food and Drug Administration has claimed authority over regulating human cloning. However, Congress has not passed legislation confirming the FDA's authority. Eastman believes that this won't happen as long as the bill banning all types of cloning isn't passed. It is another reason to light a fire moving the conversation forward. Letting things sit is not only threatening research, it is stalling progress. He made a mental note to contact his friends in DC and see if he could help swing the vote in favor of the bill supporting therapeutic cloning.

The thought of another blessing followed. For now, cloning can be pursued in some states, but not all. New York, where the LAB was located, and California, where the Gaynors live, both encouraged embryonic stem cell research. No federal law currently exists that will ban human cloning. However, the vast majority of researchers, Eastman and his colleagues included, support only therapeutic cloning; they do not support cloning for infertility purposes. Defining personhood was still an argument for public debate. It needed to be decided if blastocysts, embryos, or fetuses are to be considered human beings and afforded all of the rights and protections of a human being.

What scared the shit out of him was those "personhood amendments," popping up in a couple of states. Fortunately it had been voted down in the state of Missouri. However, if it had passed, the laws would change. In cases of abortion, or even with the use of the "morning-after pill," women who take action to stop an embryo from developing into an unwanted pregnancy ultimately might be tried for murder. It is a slippery legal slope that many of those who do not support the personhood amendment want to avoid. Eastman had taken a stance against abortion long ago. However, in his mind there were some exceptions. Women who conceived through rape or incest, or need to abort to save their own lives, should be able to make this choice. However, women would be prevented from doing so if such an amendment passes. One senator went as far as stating that in the case of a "legitimate rape," the female body had a way of preventing a pregnancy. If a woman found herself pregnant after rape, then it wasn't a legitimate rape. This sent women's rights advocates crying foul and they went after elected officials who espoused this belief. This thinking was just crazy to Eastman.

Santa Rosa, California
Same Evening

Police in hazmat suits with take-charge attitudes invade the Gaynors' home. Susan is doing her best to control her emotions. Doing something normal, such as feeding Noah in the kitchen, helps to keep her grounded. Noah's too distracted by the hazmat team to eat much. Susan watches his head turn in all different directions as he tracks the team combing through their house. Susan places cheese slices and crackers, Noah's favorite foods, on his high chair tray while she and Elliot flank him on either side.

Detective Hannis sits across from Susan at the table. He looks like he's dressed for a mission to Mars rather than an interview with a distraught family. Hannis has just finished informing the Gaynors that they are going to the hospital for observation. Hannis' voice is muffled by the visor covering his face. Thankfully, Noah thinks this is funny and he let out a giggle. Susan's glad to hear Noah giggle. She doesn't want him traumatized by the event.

"Alright, let me gather some things together. Would it be okay if I went upstairs?" Susan asks as relief washes over Susan as she learns that they will be leaving for the hospital soon. She wants reassurance that her family isn't exposed to a harmful toxin. *Please God let it be some horrible prank*.

"That's fine. I'll escort you," Hannis replies.

As she takes a damp wash cloth and wipes Noah's hands and face she thinks about how just before this scare unfolded she was feeling optimistic. The letters and notes of support, along with the money, made her feel as if people were cheering her little family on. Unfortunately, it was all interrupted by this stupid stunt. Well, she hoped it was a stunt and nothing more. She wouldn't allow herself to even entertain the idea that her family was attacked on purpose. The thought makes her hyperventilate out of fear. It also angers her. How dare someone attack an innocent child in all of this!

Elliot lifts Noah out of his highchair and follows Susan and Detective Hannis over to the stair case that leads from the kitchen up to the bedrooms. Just before they take their first step a tall, cordial man wearing a white hazmat suit, enters the kitchen, his brown eyes look soulfully at them through his visor, and introduces himself to the Gaynors. "I'm Agent Cory Matthews. I'll escort you to the hospital. We have an ambulance waiting." To Susan he appears to be kind.

"I'll help the Gaynors to gather a few things upstairs to bring to the hospital. Wait down here. We will be right back," Hannis instructs Matthews.

Noah reaches out to FBI Agent Matthews' visor with his little hand. "Spaceman!" Noah says with delight.

Susan and Matthews smile at Noah's pronouncement. She recalls that the last time she had heard the name Cory Matthews was when it was the lead character's name on the popular 1990's television show *Boy Meets World*. *How sweet if life was as simple as one of these sitcoms*, Susan muses as they all, but Matthews, walk up the staircase.

"I'll grab Noah's diaper bag and a blanket from our room. Elliot can you pack our toothbrushes and grab my purse?" Susan asks her husband.

"What do you need your toothbrush for?"

"I just want to be able to freshen up if we're at the hospital for a while," Susan says shooting her husband a 'don't ask anything more' look as all four of them climb the back stairs.

"Mr. Gaynor, I need to ask you a question," Hannis states as they reach the upstairs hallway.

"Shoot," Elliot replies.

"Were you the only one to touch the envelope and the letter?"

Elliot touches Susan's arm and she stops walking toward their bedroom. Elliot turns back toward the detective to address him, "I think Susan, Noah, and I all touched the envelope—and of course the mailman—but I was the only one to touch the letter."

Susan nods in acknowledgment.

"We'll need all of your fingerprints," Hannis informs the Gaynors.

"Now?" asks Elliot.

"No, at the station. Soon after the hospital releases you."

"If it's tonight, can we do it in the morning. We are all exhausted," Elliot inquires of Hannis.

"That'll be fine."

"How soon will we know if we've been exposed to something dangerous?" Susan asks, hugging Noah close to her.

"If you were exposed, you can expect to see symptoms within the next three hours," Matthews says.

"What are the symptoms?" Susan asks.

"Well, if it's ricin, which is popular now and fairly easy to obtain . . ."

"Ricin!" Elliot blurts.

"Or Anthrax. However, that's much harder to obtain."

Susan looks at Noah and is glad he was too young to understand what was being said. She is certain he's feeling the anxiety though. She shoots Elliot an imploring glance to tone it down for the sake of their son.

As they enter the master bedroom, Hannis says, "Inhaled ricin usually involves flu-like symptoms, cough, fever, stomach pains, dehydration, vomiting, and low blood pressure."

"Can it be treated?" Susan asks.

"Ricin can be fatal," Hannis flatly remarks.

"If you're trying to scare the crap out of us you're doing a good job!" Elliot replies.

"How long before we know." Susan squeaks out as her throat began to tighten.

"I'm not trying to scare you, just give you the facts. As far as lab results on the powder, we should be able to turn those around within the next 24 hours."

"We could be dead by then!" Elliot states the obvious. "I've got court in the morning," he says almost absently.

Susan is alarmed to see Elliot sway back and forth on his feet. She grabs his arm to steady him.

"God, help us," Elliot says as Susan helps him to the edge of the bed.

Westchester, New York

It is technically now spring throughout much of the country but still very cold on the East Coast. The frigid night cuts straight through Eastman. He marvels at the snow coming down and how it creates a gorgeous white blanket that covers the dirty Westchester sidewalks and streets. Eastman thinks it looks rather magical. It's a night in which one might expect the unexpected. A miracle, perhaps? Did he actually believe in miracles? Maybe. There were events that were elusive to being explained by science. However, his own personal experience with miracles seemed to evade him. Where was the miracle his mom needed when she died from cancer? Eastman tucks his hands deeper into the pockets of his long wool coat in an attempt to keep them warm. Instinctively he hunches his shoulders up under his ears and shudders as he feels the first biting sting of cold. He curses himself for not bringing a hat and hurries to the car. He's tired after meeting earlier in the day with possible donors in New Jersey. On his way home he had stopped off at the LAB to retrieve some papers that are now tucked inside the breast pocket of his coat. The sidewalk is slippery and twice his right foot slid out from underneath him. The metal keys in his hand are cold to the touch despite the warmth of his pocket. *Why hadn't I had the foresight to wear gloves and a hat?*

He presses the clicker on his keychain and watches as the lights on his car blink on at the same time the doors unlock. Soon he's inside and starts the engine. *It can't get warm fast enough!* Eastman turns the heat on full blast. For a moment only cold air streams out, making him shiver and take notice of the steamy exhale of his breath. *Cold as a witch's tit!* He presses the button for his seat warmer. He switches on the radio and jazz music fills the vehicle. Leaning back, placing his head on the headrest he waits for his heater to catch up with his seat warmer. His view out of the windshield is blinded by snow. The white flakes stick to the glass—hundreds of them. Eastman marvels in the realization that each flake is unique. *Kind of like the cells in each human. No two people are exactly alike.*

Eastman is jolted from his thoughts. What feels like a gun is being pressed hard against the back of his head. Terror and uncertainty course through his veins.

"What the hell!" he exclaims as he reflexively jumps up in his seat and bangs his knee hard on the steering wheel.

"Shit!" Eastman exclaims and rubs his knee.

"Don't move!" a deep male voice commands as he shoves the gun harder against Eastman's head.

Adrenalin rushes through Eastman's body and his bowels churn in his gut.

"What do you want? Do you want money? I have money in my wallet inside my coat," he manages to say.

"You think money can get you out of this, Dr. Eastman?"

God, this is personal. The asshole knows me, Eastman tries to calm himself by taking a deep breath in through his nose and letting it out through his mouth. His heart beats so fast it sounds loud in his ears. He's certain the creep with the gun can hear it. Panic is an emotion he can ill afford. *People who panic often die. I'm not ready to die.* His mind races to thoughts about Noah, his work, and Kathryn. Thinking about Kathryn somehow gives him a bit of courage. What does he have on hand to fight back with? He sees the lighter. He sees his keys. *Both could be potential weapons, but not when a guy has a gun to your head.* He remembers that the car itself is a weapon. *It's running. I can punch it into drive and hit the gas and crash into something. However, I might be dead before I can get it into drive. The other option is to listen to what the man with the gun has to say and hope that the asshole isn't intent on killing him.* Eastman opts for listening.

"You like killing babies, doc?"

Killing babies? He thinks I'm an abortionist. Eastman knew of too many physicians who had performed abortions and had been killed by lunatics like this one. Eastman had protested at abortion clinics in his youth but would never kill anyone over the issue. It didn't make sense to do so. *If you are pro-life, then why would you take a life?* However, people who are extremists didn't view the situation that way.

"Who do you think I am?"

"Real funny, Dr. Eastman. I know you make babies and I know you also kill 'em."

"That's not who I am," Eastman says in a measured voice that sounds surprisingly steady to his ears. Again, he reminds himself to control his panic. He remembers reading somewhere that you have a better chance of surviving a terrible event if you can focus your mind on the situation at hand and find a solution.

The man responds by giving Eastman a hard smack with his gloved hand over his right ear. *Fuck-it hurts like a son of a bitch;* Eastman tries hard not to react.

"Don't fuck with me."

"The last thing I want to do is fuck with you. Just tell me what it is you want."

"I'm gonna tell you something and if you're smart—and I think you're pretty smart—you will listen."

"Certainly," Eastman replies.

The car is uncomfortably warm and the windows are steaming up. Eastman notes a trickle of sweat roll down his back.

"I'm here to give you a message from God."

"From God?"

"Yes, Dr. Eastman, God. I know you must believe in God because you work hard at imitating him. Now, imitation is the highest form of flattery. However, if you read your Bible, you would know that mortal man cannot be God. In fact, you can consider me a messenger of God."

"What is it that God wants to tell me?" he asks feeling outraged and impatient that this nut job is holding him hostage in a car that is baking him.

"God wants you to stop and repent. You need to cease your evil doing immediately!" He drives home his point by hitting Eastman hard in the head with the gun. The pain radiates through Eastman's head, down his neck and into his back. Eastman feels nauseated.

Son of a bitch. I'm going to kill this fucker! Eastman screams in his head.

"Do you hear me?" the man leans forward and Eastman can feel the warmth of the man's breath on his ear. He was so close Eastman can smell the man's pungent breath odor. Was it salami he smells? Eastman chuckles at the thought of the man eating a salami sandwich before attacking him.

The man clips him again with the gun barrel. "Do you think this is funny?"

Eastman's hands fly up to his head in a reflexive gesture - protecting him from another blow. He doesn't chance turning around though. He realizes the guy is unhinged and it wouldn't take much for him to pull the trigger.

"Put your hands down!"

Eastman detects an accent. Midwest? He isn't sure. He listens more carefully as he drops his hands back down into his lap and let's his adrenalin drop too.

"Good. I knew that you weren't stupid. Disrespectful, yes. I want you to give this message to your friends at the LAB. You leave that little boy alone. God made him. Not you!"

Oh God, Noah. I'll need to contact the Gaynors immediately. Eastman wonders if someone isn't already doing this, someone who might be terrifying and possibly hurting them, too. Does this guy work alone or is he part of some extremist organization?

"Are you the only messenger of God?" Eastman asks.

"Of course not, Doctor Eastman. If you read your bible you'd know that there are many messengers."

So he isn't working alone. Or perhaps he's literally referring to the bible, Eastman considers.

"Which messenger of God are you?"

The man with the gun smirks and says, "You can call me Joseph."

Now how am I supposed to interpret that? Literally? Metaphorically? Recalling the Old Testament, Joseph was the son of Jacob. His brothers were jealous of him because he was his father's favorite and he was beaten and sold into slavery. He followed symbols God showed him and ultimately became a powerful man. Under duress this is the best Eastman canrecall of Joseph. So this man saw himself as someone on a mission? Eastman remembered that in the story Joseph had suffered greatly, but he ultimately had courage and was blessed by God. *Maybe the name the gunman gave him has nothing to do with the Bible. Maybe it was just the guy's name,* Eastman thinks as sweat drips down his skin.

"I'm going to leave. You're gonna to count to a hundred. If you turn around before you reach a hundred I will have to shoot you. Understand?"

"Yes."

"One other thing, Doctor Eastman. If you continue with your evil ways, I will come back and kill you. Now start counting. Slowly. Let me hear you."

"One . . . two . . . three . . ." Eastman begins in a quivering tone.

The night air rushes in behind the man as he leaves the car. Eastman is grateful for the coolness of the air and for the departure. He risks retaliation by lifting his eyes to the outside driver side mirror. He sees that Joseph is wearing a cap, dark coat, jeans, gloves, and some kind of work boots.

Joseph kicks the door shut without turning around as he tucks the gun into the back of his pants under his coat. Eastman hears the crunch of Joseph's boots on the snow as he hurries down the street. He doesn't move with the ease of a young man. Eastman thinks he's probably in his forties or fifties. He makes a mental note of this for the police report, along with the name Joseph. Soon his anxiety subsides as he watches the man move out of sight.

Eastman considers driving after him and running him down, but what would that accomplish? Joseph would probably be forced to shoot at him. Eastman knows that he wouldn't be able to run him over. It isn't in him. He feels cowardly and relieved. He hates himself for both. He wishes he had been able to do something to disarm this mad man. Now he's free. But is the man acting alone? Are there others? Eastman speeds off, fishtailing on the slippery road. When he gets the car under control, he grabs his cell and says, "Call Kathryn."

Westchester, New York
Same Night

A groggy Kathryn answers her cell on the third ring. She always keeps it next to her bed in case something happened at the LAB that she needs to respond to immediately. Kathryn glances at the clock. *It's 3 a.m. Three a.m. phone calls usually mean trouble*, she thinks.

The staff was taking turns sitting with the blastocyst of Noah at the LAB. Tonight the job has fallen to Anderson. But it isn't Anderson on the phone.

"James? Is something wrong?" She asks holding the phone tightly and pressing it against her ear.

"Look, can I come over?" Eastman asks breathing heavy and fast into the phone.

"Sure. Is there a problem with the blastocyst?" Kathryn asks sitting up in bed and now wide-awake.

"I'll explain when I get there. Please don't open the door to anyone but me or the police.

"The police? What's going on?" Kathryn demands with concern in her voice.

"Just please do as I say. I'll be there in fifteen minutes."

"If you're trying to scare the shit out of me you're doing a good job."

Eastman punches off the line with Kathryn and calls the police. He asks them to meet him at Kathryn's house and gives them her address. He places a third call to the LAB and speaks to the guard on duty. He tells him what has happened, to inform Dr. Anderson, and to stay on high alert.

His next call was going to be to the Gaynors when he notices a text on his cell. It was from the Gaynors. *Serendipity*, Eastman thinks as he looks up from the text message just in time to see that he is drifting into oncoming traffic!

He tosses his phone onto the seat next to him and quickly corrects his steering. He skids slightly as car next to him blasts its horn. Eastman silently scolds himself for looking at the text while driving.

It takes another thirty long minutes of driving before he finally pulls up in front of Kathryn's house. Twice as long as he told Kathryn despite the fact that he's been flying down the freeway in poor weather conditions and on slick roads. Eastman is concerned Kathryn might be the next target.

He's relieved to note that a police car is parked out front, and he can see the lights on in Kathryn's house shining like a safe beacon through the front window. Yes, she was the lighthouse in his storm. As he puts the car in park in her driveway and kills the engine he remembers the text from the Gaynors. Reaching around into the back seat he retrieves his phone. He reads the text. *Possible exposure to ricin or some other toxic substance. Susan, Noah and I at hospital getting checked out. White powdery substance came in threatening letter. Elliot.*

"Shit!" Eastman exclaims as he exits his car and heads up to Kathryn's door. He hears a dog barking and then Kathryn opens the door before he can knock.

"What the hell is going on James? I've been chatting with the police for at least fifteen minutes now, and I have no idea what's happened to you!"

Eastman brushes past her as he walks inside.

A police officer who looks as if he has a standing date lifting weights every day gets up from his seat on Kathryn's sofa and extends a hand to Eastman. Eastman takes it and shakes it.

"Dr. Eastman, this is Officer Tobey," Kathryn says as she closes the door.

"Officer." Eastman acknowledges the cop.

"It seems we have a serious threat," Eastman says.

"To the LAB?" Kathryn asks.

"To everyone involved with cloning Noah."

"I think you need to start at the beginning," the officer says motioning for everyone to take a seat.

Santa Rosa, California
Same Night

Fortunately, Susan had grabbed Noah from Elliot's arms before he passed out on their bed. The EMTs waiting outside to take them to the hospital were called upstairs by Detective Hannis. They went into full rescue mode, placing an IV in Elliot's arm, hooking him up to a heart monitor, and performing other medical intervention methods.

Suddenly Susan is confronted by a bedroom of strangers asking her medical questions about her husband while she tries to comfort her frightened son. Noah burrows his face into her chest as she rubs his soft blond head and tries to focus on what is being requested of her.

"Elliot is prone to panic attacks. This could be one. Right?" Susan inquires of the EMT's. Elliot probably would recoil in embarrassment hearing her admit this if he was conscious. He never liked to admit that the stress of some situations caused him to collapse at times, but then again—*what if it is ricin?*

Westchester, New York
Same Night

The policeman had spent an hour and a half taking Eastman's statement and then left. Before leaving the officer informed Eastman that the New York City Police Department would have to be the division making the formal investigation, since the incident took place there.

Recanting the encounter had made Eastman feel unnerved. Until now he had spared Kathryn the horrific details, and he knew that he had caused her some anxiety. 'Joseph' might be the kind of lunatic who stops at nothing all in the name of God.

Eastman's adrenalin surge had worn off. He feels bone tired. He is also thinking about what had happened earlier tonight at the Gaynors'. He's anxious to hear from them. All of this is difficult for him to wrap his brain around. It is hard enough to just focus on his work. Now he had the weight of the world on his shoulders with concern for everyone's safety. Eastman glances at his phone. It is now midnight in New York, which means it's still only 9 p.m. in California. He needs to call the Gaynors and talk to them. He punches in the numbers for Susan's phone. He's dismayed to discover it goes straight to voicemail. He tries Elliot's. Same response.

"When do you speak with the FBI?" Kathryn asks.

"Tomorrow, sometime. As the officer told us, they'll want to go through the car," Eastman replies and places the phone back into the pocket of his slacks.

"Sorry your car had to be towed and impounded by the police."

"That reminds me. I'll need to call a cab to take me home," Eastman says.

Kathryn hears the fatigue rippling through his voice. "I can take you back, or you are more than welcome to stay here."

"No. I'm not going to put you out," Eastman says decisively. "It's late and we are both tired."

"You're not putting me out. I'd really like it if you spent the night, if you didn't mind. I'm feeling a bit unnerved by the whole thing too, and would rather not be alone tonight."

Eastman is touched by Kathryn's vulnerability and sees it as a direct contradiction to the assertive woman with whom he had developed a working relationship in The LAB. He finds himself wanting to protect her. He wants nothing more than to hold her close and wrap his arms tightly around her. This is a fantasy, though. Since the kiss, nothing has happened to further a more intimate relationship. The kiss—he finds himself remembering it numerous times during the day. It had been tender and left Eastman with a sense of longing. He is here now not because he didn't want to be alone, but because he cares deeply about her.

"Absolutely, Kathryn."

"Good. I keep vodka in the freezer for nights like this one."

The joke isn't lost on Eastman as he follows her into the kitchen.

"Oh, have you had other nights like this one?" he asks with a bit of a smile.

Kathryn takes the slender glasses from the cupboard and sets them down on the black granite countertop. She pulls a frosty bottle of Grey Goose from her freezer.

"Wow. You can't fit much in there, can you?" Eastman says as he peers inside the tiny space and closes the door.

"Not in the retro models. It holds what I need."

She's so close that he feels her warm breath on his neck. She turns, still holding the bottle and her body brushes up against his. A shot of electricity pulses through his blood.

"On the rocks or straight up" Kathryn replies holding the bottle.

"Straight," Eastman replies and Kathryn pours.

Eastman picks up his glass. "Thanks for this. Thanks for everything," he says toasting her.

The two drink the vodka. It feels warm going down his throat.

"Want another?" Kathryn asks, looking into his eyes.

Eastman holds her gaze as his lips part into a gentle smile and he hopes she can read his mind.

Santa Rosa, California
Same Night

After being thoroughly examined in a special quarantine room at Santa Rosa Memorial Hospital, Susan, Noah, and Elliot were moved to a family style hospital room. Susan was hopeful that they would soon find out what it was they were exposed to. Noah was sacked out in a hospital crib. Susan was amazed by the fact that toddlers had the ability to sleep soundly anywhere. *It's that trust thing*, she thinks as she looks over to Elliot who is also sound asleep and snoring lightly. *The sedative the nurse gave him is doing its job*, she thinks.

As Susan crawls into her bed she mentally reviews what has been said. The FBI had explained everything to them before they were checked into their room. They had informed them that airborne ricin was a significant threat. *Significant threat.*

It had been three hours since they were exposed. Susan hopes it's just chalk or powder. *But wouldn't they know that by now?*

Some jerk just messing with us.

Officer Hannis had told her that their case is being explored as a hate crime. Did someone really hate them for pursuing therapeutic cloning? There were millions of people in similar situations. All they are doing is seeking a cure for their loved one. She and Elliot aren't hurting anyone in their quest to help their son. *Life is hard enough for them without all of this other drama.* Susan thinks just as she drifts off to sleep.

Somewhere in the recess of her mind she hears her cell phone. She allows it to go to voicemail. Next she hear Elliot's phone ring too. Suddenly she doesn't care. *I'm too exhausted to talk to anyone.*

Westchester, New York
Same Night, Late

Anderson sits at his desk attempting to concentrate on his book in the *Lonesome Dove* series. Babysitting a blastocyst afforded him some time to immerse himself in other things he had been putting off. Reading the series was one of them. Anderson's mind wanders back to the text he had received earlier in the evening, from Eastman, letting him know that there was an incident tonight with someone who was upset with the LAB's work. Anderson is eager to hear the whole story. He is no stranger to this sort of thing. There had been security breaches, mostly by animal rights activists, at the research facility where he had been employed in Texas prior to joining the LAB. It seemed to go with the type of the work he did. Setting down his book he thinks back to this time.

Even though he is a supporter of the ethical and humane treatment of animals, many activists didn't agree with his desire to pursue the cloning of animals. He wanted to understand and study the process, learning everything he could because he ultimately believed that there could be cures for disease. Once the process was fully understood in animals, it could better be used in humans. He felt that if the general population viewed the therapeutic cloning of animals favorably, and saw the positive effects it had on animal medicine it would be a natural step to move into human medicine. Weren't drug trials almost always conducted on animals first? Often those medicines, after being safely used on animals for a number of years, were made available for human use. Many times, animals were provided with better cancer treatment, as well as other types of treatments for diseases than were available to humans. It was much easier to get FDA approval for drugs used on animals than for drugs used for people. However, the LAB had begun moving forward in therapeutic human cloning, and Anderson had been asked to provide his insight and expertise. He didn't want to miss the opportunity to be a part of something he thought would change the world in a positive way. He knew there was a frightening side to this work. He and his colleagues were exposed to the same dangers facing physicians who performed abortions on patients in women's healthcare clinics. He realized his work could be deadly. So far, the LAB had been fortunate. There hadn't been any serious threats. But Eastman publishing their efforts seems to have changed all that.

Anderson decides to send Eastman another text message.

"Would really like to talk to you. Contact me when able."

Then he picks up the landline and calls the front desk.

"How are things tonight?"

"Dead as a tomb," Landon Burke the red-headed security guard who looks too young to serve in his position—but in reality has already served two tours of duty in the military—replies to Dr. Anderson.

Anderson glances thoughtfully back at his book, pushes it aside, and gets up to check on the blastocyst. *Maybe something's happening there*, he thinks as he makes his way over to the room where the ball of hope, as Eastman refers to it, is doing its thing.

Santa Rosa, California
Same Night, Late

The incessant playing of Ozzy Osborne's "Miracle Man," coming from Susan's cell phone jolts her out of her sleep and Susan remembers that the ring tone is set for a real miracle man—Dr. Eastman.

Elliot and Noah are asleep and merely stir to the Ozzy Osborne tune. Susan reaches for her phone and clicks it on.

"Hello," she replies in a sleepy voice.

"Susan? I'm sorry for calling so late," Dr. Eastman replies.

"It's fine."

"How are you all doing? Are you still at the hospital?"

She fills Eastman in on the day's events, which unfortunately have the side effect of waking Elliot. He turns on the lamp on the nightstand that divides their beds and listens to Susan's side of the conversation for a while.

"Is that Dr. Eastman?"

Susan nods yes. "Dr. Eastman, Elliot's awake now too. Can I place you on speaker?"

"Of course."

Susan hits the speaker button and instantaneously Dr. Eastman's voice fills the room, "I'm sorry for your troubles, Elliot. I do have some good news though. As

I was telling Susan, the blastocyst has progressed to more than a one-hundred-cell division and is still dividing. We have considerable hopes for more growth."

"That's wonderful news!" Elliot exclaims.

Then Eastman informs them of the man with the gun and his concerns for their safety. Susan feels chills spread throughout her body just as Noah awakes and pulls himself up in his crib. Susan notices that his diaper is full and hanging around his knees. She gets out of bed and retrieves the diaper bag next to Elliot.

"I have to change Noah, go ahead and take the phone off speaker in case he cries," Susan whispers to Elliot.

As Susan changes Noah's diaper she listens to Elliot tell Dr. Eastman that they will know within the next few hours if they were exposed to ricin, and that they most likely would be going home today if they weren't. Then Elliot falls silent listening to Dr. Eastman.

"You seriously think we will need bodyguards?"

Susan spins around toward Elliot in surprise. "Put him back on speaker." She hands Noah a room temperature bottle of milk she had packed in the diaper bag and lays him back down in his crib as Elliot does as she instructs.

"That's for Will Rubin to assess. He's one of the best security guys in the business. Hopefully, these happenings are just scare tactics. However, it would be foolish not to acknowledge the seriousness of the threats."

"If we are being targeted, won't we get FBI protection?" Elliot asks.

"I would think so. However, I still want you to meet with Will. There are extra precautions you should take even with FBI protection," Eastman advises.

Westchester, New York
Same Night, Late

Walking out of the guestroom Eastman discovers Kathryn awake on the sofa in the living room. She's watching what appears to be a Jimmy Stewart film on her big screen television. Lying at Kathryn's feet is one of the biggest dogs Eastman has ever seen.

"Where have you been keeping him?"

Kathryn looks up simultaneously hitting the mute button on the television, and explains, "He was in my room when you arrived. Didn't you hear him bark?"

"Yeah, but I didn't know it was your dog. I thought it was the neighbors. Hey dog," Eastman says as he greeted the hairy beast.

"His name is Doogie," Kathryn says with a smile.

"Doogie? What kind of name is that for a dog?"

"I grew up watching *Doogie Howser*.

Doogie Howser?

"You know—the same guy who plays on *How I Met Your Mother*.

Eastman was lost. He rarely had time to watch TV. "What kind of dog is Doogie?"

Kathryn leans down and scratch's Doogie's head. "He's a Great Dane and he's my best friend."

"Well, that makes me a little jealous, but I'll get over it."

"I just spoke with the Gaynors. They had a bit of a scare tonight too."

"What happened?"

"They were exposed to a powdery white substance someone had mailed to them in an envelope."

"Are they all right?"

"So far so good. They're at the hospital awaiting test results."

"That's scary. Do you think it's the same guy who attacked you?"

"Possibly. We don't know for sure. It's concerning though."

Kathryn wraps her arms around herself and rubs her forearms as a shiver runs through her body.

"I don't want to abandon you, but I should go to the LAB and check on things."

"I'll go with you."

"Are you sure?"

"Of course."

"I didn't want to leave you alone."

"Oh, I'm never alone."

"I know—you have Doogie."

"We can take my car," Kathryn offers, getting up and walking to the door. Doogie follows her. She grabs the dog leash off the coat rack and clips it to his collar.

"We're taking Doogie?"

"Unless you object."

"No. Will he be fine in the car?"

"He'll be fine in the LAB. "

"Well, there's a first time for everything."

"You don't mind bringing a dog to the LAB?"

"I just never thought about it. I'm sure it's fine"

Kathryn, Eastman, and Doogie make their way out the front door and get into her car that's parked next to Eastman's on the driveway. Eastman looks into the backseat admiring the dog's ability to stretch himself from one end of the car to the other. "Any smaller of a backseat and Doogie would have to run alongside the car," he remarks.

Minutes later, the three of them are driving to the LAB. Since there was no traffic on the road this late at night or—to be precise—very early in the morning, they make good time. Soon they arrive at their destination. The front of the building is deliberately nondescript. There are no signs announcing the LAB. Eastman liked the fact that it looked like millions of other office buildings. "The parking lot is closed so park on the street directly across from the building," Eastman tells Kathryn.

After parking and crossing the street the trio make their way to the front door. With a quick swipe of his plastic key card Eastman watches as the light turns from red to green allowing them to enter the building.

Kathryn, Eastman, and Doogie walk up to the security desk where the first line of defense, Landon Burke, greets them with a smile.

With one huge leap up, Doogie places his two large front paws on the top of the security desk, easily balancing on his back legs. Burke seems unfazed as he pets the dog's head. "Whoa, you're one big boy!"

"Doogie, get down," Kathryn admonishes, yanking on the leash and moving him to a sitting position.

"I guess he likes you."

"Dr. MacMurray, Dr. Eastman, the police were here earlier tonight. They spoke to Dr. Anderson. "

"Do you know what they wanted?" Eastman inquires.

"No. They didn't say. Other than that, it's been quiet all evening. Dr. Anderson told me not to let anyone in who doesn't work here and who I personally don't know. So I know something is up. He explained that there was an incident earlier this evening, but that's all he told me."

"Glad you have things under control. Is Dr. Anderson still in the LAB?"

"Yes, Sir. He and a few other employees stayed late."

"Thank you, Burke."

"Sir?"

"Burke?"

"Just how bad was this incident?"

"Apparently, there is someone, or some ones, who are not happy about the work we are doing here—particularly with the creation of the blastocyst. They are against human cloning and have become aggressive in their demands to stop it. I'm also going to order another security guard to work with you in the evenings. I will sit down with you tomorrow night and go over all of this in detail. Can you arrive 30 minutes before your shift?"

"Yes, Sir."

Eastman thinks that the eager-to-please young guard might salute him. Although, appreciative of Burkes respectful attitude and enthusiasm, he resolves to hire another, more seasoned guard, an ex-cop, to work with Burke. He'll also have to discuss protocol with the FBI. In light of everything that's happened, Eastman's concern now extends to the possibility of a bomb or a drive-by shooting. He feels like a fish out of water in dealing with it. The truth is he doesn't know how to proceed. Part of him wants to believe that tonight's incidents are just scare tactics. However, he knows how quickly things can escalate. It isn't just about him. It's about his colleagues and a family with a little boy. How ironic and awful it would be to have Noah harmed while pursuing a quest to save him Eastman thinks and then pushes thought from his mind. He'll rely on the professionals to guide him. He believes he must stay focused on his own quest, which is to harvest Noah's pure, cloned stem cells so that research on a cure could begin. All of these thoughts run through his head as he, Kathryn, and the dog hurry down the hall to find Anderson. They discover him in his office. Upon seeing the trio, Anderson puts down his book and looks up at them. An odd expression crosses his face.

"I think this is the first time I've seen a dog in the LAB," Anderson remarks with a bemused look upon his face.

"His name's Doogie," Kathryn fondly replies and ruffles Doogie's fur.

"Can I give him some of my turkey sandwich?"

"I think Doogie would like that."

Doogie gobbles the treat given to him by Anderson and eagerly looks to him for more.

"I've been trying to reach you, James."

"How's the blastocyst doing?"

"I'll give you an update if you let me in on what the hell's been going on and why you're here at three a.m.," Anderson says with a bit of an edge to his voice.

"Fair enough. Let's go into the room where the blastocyst is kept, I want to check on it and I'll tell you everything that I know."

They follow Eastman down the hall to a door with a security camera mounted above. Eastman slips his plastic card into the door scanner. The door easily opens and Kathryn tethers the dog's leash to a table leg inside. Inside the windowless room the three of them are crowded by a lab bench in front of the table, a stool, microscopes, a small refrigerator, and a specialized hood to keep materials sterile. Sitting on the middle of the center island was an incubator. Inside the incubator is the clone of Noah.

"You can check for yourself, Kathryn, but what I think I'm seeing that the blastocyst has now formed the embryoblast and has become an embryo. As of tonight I've noticed it growing into a trophoblast, which will soon form the placenta. The trophoblast looks very good and is surrounding the inner cell mass and a fluid-filled blastocyst cavity," Anderson reports.

"I'll be damned!" Eastman exults.

"Before you call for a parade, let me take a look," suggests Kathryn.

As much as he likes her, Kathryn's type "A" ways sometimes irritates Eastman and members of the team. Perhaps she should've just accepted Alan's report. However, she is excellent at her job and respected by all, so it makes sense she'd want to confirm. Examining the blastocyst, Kathryn replies to Anderson, "You are correct in your determination, Alan. I'd say we are within days of harvesting the stem cells."

Eastman and Anderson high-five each other. "Now tell me what the hell's going on?" Anderson reminds Eastman. Before Eastman launches into a recap of the evening's events, he suggests that they move to the conference room after Kathryn returns Noah's clone to the incubator. Finally, the three of them, plus the dog, return to the hall outside of the tiny room. Eastman makes certain the door locks behind them.

"May I?" Anderson asks Kathryn as he reaches for the leash. .Kathryn hands him Doogie's leash. Doogie gives a little growl."Doogie!" Kathryn admonishes. "I'm sorry; he's usually pretty mellow."

"Doogie's a smart dog. He must sense that Alan's a veterinarian," Eastman chuckles.

"Ah, yes, I love animals and they hate me."

Kathryn smiles and affectionately touches her dog's head and he turns and licks her hand. "You be nice to Dr. Anderson; he's my friend."

Love me, love my dog, Eastman thinks as he witnesses the bond between the two.

They make their way to the conference room and take seats around the conference table with Doogie lying at Kathryn's feet. .Eastman finishes filling Anderson in on the assault with the gun, the Gaynors' possible ricin exposure, and the fact that the FBI is investigating.

"Holy shit!" Anderson exclaims.

"That about sums it up. Kind of makes you want to lock our clone of Noah in an impenetrable vault to protect it," Kathryn says.

"Did you two come here together?" Anderson asks Kathryn. .The look that passes between Kathryn and Eastman answers Anderson's question.

"I was in Kathryn's area when I was attacked. I met the police at her house. My car was impounded as evidence so Kathryn kindly offered to give me a ride here."

Anderson arches an inquisitive brow.

Realizing Alan suspects that there's more to the story, Eastman decides to move on to the next item on his agenda. "I'm going to call a meeting to discuss safety protocol tomorrow night. I'll send out an email and text message to the team before I leave. We will meet at 9 p.m."

"Sounds good. I have one question, though. You and I are still going to speak at the Stem Cell Research and Therapeutics Conference in Boston - right?" Anderson asks.

"That's right, it's this weekend. Let me give it some thought, but I don't see us not doing it, since we're one of the main speakers."

"I don't know if it's wise to go public at the conference with the progress we've made. I mean, if someone who is a nut job, and may be linked to an entire network of potentially dangerous nut jobs, finds out we are advancing in our work, then that may make all of us, including Noah and his family, extremely vulnerable," Anderson points out.

"Alan's right, James. As much as we need to—and want to—keep people informed about the progress here, we also have to consider the risks involved. I don't want to jeopardize our work. We are making history here and we have an amazing opportunity to pursue avenues that could change the world." Kathryn reminds.

Eastman realizes that changing the world requires an abundance of energy, more energy than he has tonight. "Let's all get some sleep and we will discuss any announcements that might be made later today," Eastman says.

Westchester, New York

"It's four a.m."

"I'm starting to get a second wind," Kathryn beams from the entryway of her living room. Eastman looks as if he could fall over where they're standing.

"Just kidding. Let's go to bed," Kathryn says releasing Doogie's leash.

"If I don't, I think I might just fall asleep standing up," Eastman replies.

"Are you coming?" Kathryn inquires as she heads on down the hall toward her bedroom.

"Doogie and I are going to check the premises and then we'll meet you there."

Doogie follows Eastman around the house as he checks all of the doors and windows making certain they are locked. Eastman doesn't know if the lunatic knows where Kathryn lives, but this madman seems to show up in places he never anticipates.

"All's quiet on the Eastern front," Eastman remarks to Kathryn with a smile as he enters the bedroom. He notices she's standing with her back to him and kicking off her shoes. Despite his fatigue his heart races and a second wind kicks in. He feels almost as nervous as he was his very first time. He wants this to be right in so many ways. He not only desperately wants this woman but also knows he is falling in love with her.

Kathryn has her back to him as she undresses. He watches as she pulls the sweater she is wearing over her head, unhooks her bra and slips out of her pants and lace thong. Eastman admires her beauty—from the top of her head down to her painted red toenails. Her porcelain white skin is accentuated by the dark red hair that falls from her shoulders, slightly curling at the ends at the middle of her back. A lovely birthmark is stamped on the right side of her ribcage. It almost looks to Eastman like a small heart. She turns toward him as he unbuckles his pants. Her small breasts— firm and round. Her stomach flat and her hips gently curved out and around, accentuating her shapely slender legs makes Eastman get a bit hard. Kathryn blushes when she sees him staring at her and the bulge in his pants. He quickly drops his pants and unbuttons his shirt. She folds back the bedspread as he tosses his shirt onto the floor. Together they climb into bed. The covers are crisp and cool and smell fresh to Eastman. Kathryn wiggles down until they come up just under her chin. Eastman smiles playfully as he looks down at her. He can hardly believe his incredible good luck. She's everything and more than he could ever hope to have, a best friend, a colleague, and now a lover. She snuggles up to him. It feels so natural and right to Eastman, as if it has always been this way. He kisses her and then slides down next to her. They make love urgently, playfully, and skillfully. Finally they lay together damp, exhausted, and happy, turning onto his back, more relaxed and sexually satisfied than he can recall, he pulls Kathryn next to him and gently holds her close. "I've never known another woman like you. On some level I've wanted this for a very long time, but I wouldn't allow myself to even go there."

"Why not?"

"Because we work together."

Kathryn kisses his shoulder, yawns lazily, and asks, "Yes, there's that."

"There's so much I want to know about you, Kathryn."

"And I you."

"Did you always know you'd be a scientist?"

"As far back as I can remember I was creating different concoctions of things. We had this playhouse in the back yard that our neighbors had given my family when their kids got too old for it. I turned it into a laboratory."

"So the scientist emerged early in life. What sort of things did you concoct?"

"Weird stuff."

"What was the strangest?"

"I took our dog's fur and mixed it with tree roots and water, then buried it in the dirt to see if I could get the dog's DNA into the tree. At least, that's what my mom told me. I don't really remember."

"How old were you?"

"My mom told me I was six. I can tell you she wasn't too happy about my experiments. Although she never forbade me from playing scientist, she taught me to put more trust and faith into our religious studies."

"Six! Wow, you must've been some kind of genius to even come up with the idea back then."

"Hardly, I was your just better than average student. I do remember taking a firecracker, when I was nine, and mixing the powder with some chemicals I found in the house and placed it into a plastic tube, then closed off the ends with tin foil."

"That could have been dangerous."

"It was. Sometimes my experiments blew up."

"You must've had a guardian angel watching over you if you didn't get hurt."

"But I did get hurt. When my dad found out he spanked me on the butt and dismantled my laboratory. I feel blessed to still have my eyes and fingers. I think God was watching out for me."

"So you believe in God?" Kathryn thoughtfully inquires.

"Don't you?" he asks looking deeply into her eyes.

"I'm not sure. I mean, I do like to think that there is a higher power. If we were to refer to God as life, I would say God is in every living thing."

"Bios and zoë."

"The Greek words that mean mortal life and immortal life," Kathryn replies.

"The immortal renewal of life, zoë. It lives on in us through many generations-the force of life that brings about the origin of species. It's the kind of immortality that is given to us through our off-spring."

"You mean our DNA? Well, that's kind of beautiful. I never knew biology could be so romantic," Kathryn says and snuggles closer to him.

"It is, when you really stop and think about it."

"Oh, I love it when you speak Greek," Kathryn teases and gives him a quick kiss. "Tell me more, James."

"It's kind of incredible when you really consider our lineage—where we come from. We each carry the DNA of our parents' within us, as we do the DNA of their parents before them. I believe that it's what Jesus meant when he says, 'I am the Life.'"

"With the birth of each human being, our family's ancestral lineage is renewed. I knew the Greek words and their meanings, but I never really thought of it like that."

"The first time I recall really beginning to understand the concept of birth and death was when I was about thirteen. My mom and I were watching a movie called *Houseboat*. Have you seen it?"

"No. I like old movies but don't recall that one James."

"It was a touching film. It starred Sophia Loren and Cary Grant. My mom shared her love of films with me by letting me stay up late with her and watching. It was before we could record things."

"It was a treat to be able to get to do that."

"Anyway, in this film, Cary Grant's wife had died and left him with three children. His oldest son, who was a preteen, was bitter and angry over the death of his mother. As a result, he and his father had a tumultuous relationship. Grant's character wanted to repair the relationship with his son, so he took on the challenge of raising his kids, who were living with their grandparents at the time. Somehow they end up living on this houseboat with Sophia Loren as the nanny."

Kathryn arches a brow at the mention of the sultry movie star. "That must've been interesting,"

"That part may have been lost on me as a boy. I do remember that the father explained the death of the mother to his son using a pitcher of water on the deck of the boat. He told his son that the pitcher was a container, much like our bodies. The water inside the pitcher could be likened to our souls. He poured the water onto the deck and asks the son if it was still water. The boy says yes. Then they watched as it flowed off of the boat deck into the lake. The father explained that the water was now part of the lake and discussed how it would be drawn up into the clouds and fall back to the Earth as rain, which nurtured all living things. His son suddenly understood the meaning of a soul and remarked to his father that his mother was still a part of all things that lived. Grant said, 'Exactly. A kind of beautiful immortality.'

"That's kind of how I look at life, we are connected, all one," Kathryn remarks.

"Exactly. There's an immortal force that connects me to my mom and her to her mom."

"You're saying in a sense there is no death?"

"There's death, but there's also immortality."

Kathryn is silent and appears to Eastman as if she is pondering this statement.

"I didn't realize when I was watching the film with my mom that I would soon be the boy in the movie searching for meaning in my own mom's death."

"That must've been incredibly difficult to lose your mom, especially when you were so young."

"I wanted to believe that my mother was with God. I needed to believe that she was in heaven and at peace. I was also angry with God for taking her."

"I can understand that. Why would God take your mom away? At least that's how I would think as a kid—a kid needs her more than God does, right?"

Eastman nodded at the long-ago memory and the feelings that still lay heavy on his heart.

"Is that what led you to putting your faith in science?"

"Yes and no. It was a bit more complicated for me."

"Do you still believe the faith you were taught? I mean, aren't the two incongruent, a scientist and a creationist?"

"There are people who are both."

Eastman notices the sun peeking through the crack in the curtains. It must be almost dawn, he thinks as a yawn escapes him. Then he notices the confused look that crosses over Kathryn's face, like a shadow as the sun moves behind a cloud.

"I'm no longer a creationist. I no longer view the death of my mother as God's will, but as the result of being human."

"All living things die," Kathryn reminds him.

"Yes, and my mom, like anyone else, was susceptible to a deadly disease and she succumbed to it. I just felt that she should've had more time."

"This is what led you to pursuing the work we do?"

"I think being a scientist was always in my DNA. However, her death changed many things for me. I had believed that the world began through evolution and that people were put here by God."

"Yeah, I remember being taught that as a kid too. But I didn't believe it. We were taught one thing at church and another in school. I just never discussed it with my parents or our priest. I thought everything we were taught in church had to do with our spiritual and moral growth, and everything that had to do with science was what we learned in school."

"That's an interesting way of compartmentalizing it. My school and my church both took a creationist view. Evolution was a foreign idea—one that wasn't readily accepted. I remember the day I actually discovered that what I had been taught and believed in was impossible."

"When did you learn that creationism wasn't true?"

"Well, I wasn't a kid. I was in college. My early college courses were based on the belief that the theory of evolution was incorrect and that creationism was the ultimate explanation for all that existed in our universe."

"It's hard to believe that someone as intelligent as you once believed in creationism and that a college actually taught it."

There was a touch of condescending truth in Kathryn's reply that stung Eastman, he winces and falls silent.

"I'm sorry. That came out rudely; I didn't mean any disrespect. It's just hard to wrap my brain around the fact that a brilliant scientist could ever embrace these ideas as the ultimate truth."

"A brilliant scientist, huh?" Eastman teases and tickles Kathryn. She wriggles in his arms. "I'll accept that. On some level I was always questioning this idea. My later college years changed my thinking, and my beliefs about creationism flew out the window. The deeper my knowledge grew, the more my questioning did also. It was my ultimate desire to defend the Bible, but I found myself aligning more and more with everyday scientists who pursued knowledge for the sake of understanding. Contrary to what I'd been taught, I discovered that average scientists weren't out to undermine Christianity and prove that creationism was wrong. They were people who gathered knowledge about fossil studies that supported the theory of evolution."

"I can't imagine how difficult this must have been for you. It sounds like a crisis of faith. Science to me is the obvious choice, but when it flies in the face of religion, most people denounce science and not their faith."

"I did keep a flicker of hope alive that somehow what my faith had taught me would be proven to be the ultimate truth. My final hope in proving the Bible correct hinged on a student who graduated from our college and was sent by our church to work on his doctorate. He was studying the human fossil record at the University of Wisconsin. He was going to provide us with definitive proof that what we had been taught was completely accurate and that the theory of evolution was wrong. That there is a creator. We were very excited and proud of him," Eastman says.

"In the face of science that almost sounds, well, delusional."

"Yes. The creationism theory that we all believed was disproven by one of our own. What he found was that six million year old rocks contained evidence of primates but no hominids. In six hundred thousand years old fossils, there were human-like remains of members of the genus Homo but not modern man. He gave us all proof of the progression of human evolution. He had concluded, along with many other revered scientists that man had evolved over millions of years."

"That must've been surprising to those who sponsored his research to prove the theory of evolution wrong."

"It was. He started out his research motivated by his passion to discover the truth of a creator. He believed in the concept of creationism and dismissed the theory of evolution with all of his being, just as I had. As we all had."

"You were surprised?"

"Surprised? That's an understatement. I felt betrayed by those whom I had trusted within the Christian community and by my academic institution. I felt disheartened having been emotionally committed to something that was a lie."

"So God didn't create man, but he may have created the universe in which man evolved."

Eastman ponders Kathryn's comment and kisses the top of her head.

"I did cling to a miniscule hope that possibly the theory of evolution was wrong. At that point in my life I wanted to make certain this student was absolutely right so I went to speak with him privately. He told me that he felt like he had disappointed us. However, the evidence was too compelling to not believe the truth. As a scientist he said he couldn't turn his back on what he had learned."

"That took courage," Kathryn states with admiration.

"Yes it did. But not everyone saw it that way."

"Some believers will hold onto the theory of creationism even though it's proven wrong, James."

"Sadly, for this student his findings and admission came at a price."

"A price?"

"He was ostracized from the very church and college community that had sent him to prove that their teachings were the correct teachings."

"Given the narrow-mindedness of the community, I would say that in the end, that wasn't a bad thing," Kathryn says with a note of sarcasm to her voice.

"It did hurt him terribly and me too. He was hoping to get them to see what he saw and to make an immediate change."

"And that was?"

"That the truth would be incorporated into the college's religious teachings," Eastman says as he pulls the covers up to their shoulders to ward off a chill in the room.

"A hard truth is often a bitter pill to swallow. Many would rather live in denial than face it."

And some would rather kill or be killed, Eastman thinks.

Eastman's mind wanders as Kathryn lets out a yawn and falls asleep in his arms soon after. What he didn't share with her, that he'd like to someday, is his belief in never having to die. Perhaps it was foolish. However, his research proved that old cells can be made new again. It is the elusive fountain of youth he has been chasing most of his adult life—a realization that there could be immortal life here on earth. That was a conversation for another time.

He looks down on the beautiful woman whose sound asleep and brushes back a soft strand of hair that falls across her cheek. As he holds her, his last thoughts before drifting off to sleep are that he's a lucky man.

Sometimes when you least expect it, you discover the most amazing gift. It was a gift he hopes will last forever.

Westchester, New York

Eastman looks at the clock and sees the big orange numbers 10:19 a.m. Doogie, who had ended up sleeping at the foot of the bed he and Kathryn shared last night, and Kathryn were missing from the bedroom. *How had he slept so late and why didn't Kathryn wake him?* Eastman quickly jumps out of bed. He pulls on his trousers and journeys barefoot out of the bedroom and into the hall to find his companions. Relieved to smell coffee and bacon wafting toward him, he hurries into the kitchen and notices Doogie lying under the kitchen table with his chin resting on his front paws. He looks up to see a radiant Kathryn, freshly showered and dressed in jeans and a green top smiling at Eastman from where she is standing at the stove. Using a pair of tongs she turns the sizzling bacon in the frying pan. Eastman's mouth waters and his stomach growls. The room feels toasty and homey. It had been a long time since anyone has made him breakfast.

"Good morning! Coffee's over there," Kathryn's cheerful voice was as lovely as the birds he sometimes hears outside his bedroom window in the morning.

"Well, good morning."

Kathryn gestures with the tongs she's using to turn bacon in the frying pan, to the counter opposite the stove.

Eastman smiles as he's reminded of a long-ago commercial he had watched on TV when he was just a boy: The woman in it was cooking, dancing and singing, "I can bring home the bacon, fry it up in a pan, and never, never let you forget you're a man."

"Why didn't you wake me?" Eastman asks as he pours himself a cup of delicious-smelling java.

"You needed the sleep."

"What can I do to help you?"

"Sit down and drink your coffee. You can keep me company."

Eastman takes a seat at the table and reaches under it to pat Doogie. "I see you already have someone keeping you company."

"Naw. He's just waiting for the bacon," Kathryn remarks as she uses the tongs to place the fried bacon onto a plate lined with a paper towel.

"Me and Doogie both," Eastman replies, anticipating the food.

Kathryn places the bacon and eggs, all cooked to perfection in Eastman's estimation, in front of him on the table. The bacon tasted even better than it smelled, Eastman realizes after taking a bite.

"You are a woman of many talents, Dr. MacMurray. Cooking is definitely one of them. Thanks so much for making me breakfast. I didn't realize how hungry I was."

Kathryn makes herself a plate and sits down next to Eastman. She slips Doggie a slice of bacon under the table. He eagerly takes it from her hand and licks her fingers.

"Thank you. I could say the same of you except I have yet to taste your cooking."

"I owe you. I'll take you to dinner at your favorite place."

"Don't you cook?"

"Nothing you'd want to eat. I've been known to grill a tasty steak. However, I fear that I'm out of practice. It's been a while."

"Well, I'll take my chances," Kathryn says and takes a bite of egg.

"There's something I've been meaning to discuss with you. I've decided that I'm taking Anderson to Boston. I think we have an obligation to attend the conference. I'd like you to come. However, I need you at the LAB to prepare for the stem cell harvest," Eastman says.

Kathryn sets down her fork and thoughtfully replies, "Are you sure that going to Boston is in all of our best interests?"

"We must continue as if there are no threats."

"But we all know that isn't true. There are very real threats. You had a gun held to your head."

"I know, but we can't allow fear to get in the way of our progress. I don't mean that lightly, either. I think we need to take some serious precautions. How would you feel about having a bodyguard?"

"What? Are you serious? Why do I need a bodyguard? I wasn't threatened."

"Not directly."

"Well, then, everyone who works at the LAB should have a bodyguard," Kathryn replies evenly as she lifts her coffee mug to her lips.

"I just don't know if the person who attacked me knows that we are involved or what your role is at the LAB."

"Is that what we are? Involved?"

"Whatever you want to call it," he says with a shrug.

Kathryn looks at him intently and he wishes he could read her mind. *Did I just say the wrong thing? It's been so long. Please don't let me screw this up.*

"Kathryn, I have deep feelings for you. I'm not used to caring so much about another person. I don't want anything bad to happen to you."

Kathryn starts to reply, setting her mug down on the table, "I…"

Eastman interrupts her by placing a finger to her lips. "Please don't say anything right now. I'm going to grab a quick shower and then we've got to get to the LAB in time for the meeting." Eastman stands up and kisses the top of her head.

"Leave the dishes. I'll do them after my shower."

"You're a man who doesn't cook but who is willing to do the dishes? You've definitely won my heart."

So Kathryn shares my feelings, Eastman realizes with a smile and his heart skips a happy beat.

Santa Rosa, California

After being released from the hospital, the Gaynors and Will Rubin, the bodyguard Eastman recommended for Susan and Noah, explore the inside and outside of the house. After every nook and cranny was explored, the five of them sat down in the living room. Noah soon tired of being restrained, and Elliot enjoyed helping him build a block tower and knocking it down.

"My recommendations include upgrading the security system," Will offers.

"Upgrade how? I thought we already had one of the best?" Susan inquires.

"It's good, but there is more you can do. Motion-detecting lights, and lights that cannot easily be broken would be my outside recommendations."

"That sounds reasonable," Elliot agrees.

"I think that Noah should be relocated to your bedroom for a while."

"Elliot? I'm okay with that. Are you?"

"Not really, but I understand," Elliot replies just as Noah knocks over another tower; this time the blocks land in Elliot's lap.

"Uh oh," Noah says and everyone laughs.

"I think we could all use a little something to eat," Susan says and headed off to the kitchen.

"I have a friend whom I'd like to recommend as a bodyguard for you, Elliot," Rubin says.

"Why do I need a bodyguard?"

"You are involved in what amounts to a high-profile experiment involving your son. Some people are rabidly opposed and have been making threats."

"Yes, but do you really think that someone would actually make a real attempt on our lives?"

Susan returns carrying a tray of cheese, crackers, and sodas, which she sets down in front of the two men.

"Thank you," Rubin says as he helps himself to a wedge of cheese and answers Elliot's question. "I do. I think what just happened to you was close enough. It's a warning that should be taken seriously. It wasn't ricin - this time."

"Do you think it'll happen again?" Susan inquires in concerned tone.

"It could. The FBI will help to keep you safe, but they cannot be with you twenty-four seven. The very nature of what you are all involved in makes you all unwilling high-profile celebrities."

"I never really thought about it like that," Susan says and visibly shudders as a quick set of chills run up her spine.

"I think it's wise for you to be here for Susan and Noah. However, I don't need or want a bodyguard. I've already drawn enough negative attention to myself at work, Rubin."

Susan looks at him with angst. Elliot's refusal to have a body-guard is distressing, she thinks, as she takes a seat next to Will on the sofa.

"I think you should at least think about it, Elliot," Susan says as she reaches for her drink.

"Thanks for the snacks," Will says through a mouthful of chewed cracker and cheese.

Noah toddles over to Susan, and she hands him a cracker. He shoves it into his mouth and puts out a hand for more.

"You eat that one first," Susan instructs.

"I have a bag in the car. I'm going to get it and then get settled into your guestroom."

"Elliot, can you help Rubin with fresh linens and towels?"

"Sure. Will, meet me upstairs after you get your bag. The guest room is down the hall and on the right."

As Susan picks up the cracker crumbs Noah has dropped onto the carpet, she wonders what else might be in store for them.

Butlerville, Indiana

Joe Smith misses Gwen. He is also tired of doing Gwen's cooking and cleaning. He had enough to do running the farm with only one farmhand. He is tired and is reclining on the bed the two of them had once shared. He glanced over at the framed wedding photo sitting on their oak dresser. The thick cover of dust is a reminder of just how long it'd been since she had last cleaned. She told him she'd return if he got treatment. However, he hasn't met those terms and he wouldn't because there was nothing wrong with him. He believed that soon she'd understand his higher purpose and see it as a gift rather than a pervasive darkness inside of him. The darkness, he believed, was a side effect of the anger and rage that pulsed through his veins in anticipation of having to eradicate the world of a demon. It was the demon that was doing unspeakable things to a helpless little boy.

He now knows that God wants him to kill all who are possessed by this demon. He flashed on Eastman's face and knew he had to extinguish the light from his eyes and plunge his dark soul into the bowels of hell. Once he did this he hoped that God would return Gwen to him. He needed her to take care of him and to understand the fact that he has been chosen by God to serve him in one of the highest capacities. His pulse quickened as he thought more about ridding the world of the evil monster. As he thought of strangling the man, he became aware that he had a hard on. This usually happened to him when he had such thoughts. As he slides his hand inside of his jeans, he wishes Gwen was here to take care of it for him. For now, he'll just have to take care of it himself.

He had killed a man by strangling him to death once before. It was a long time ago, when he was in Vietnam. It took a long time for the enemy soldier to die. He remembered the power he felt as he squeezed tight and watched the soldier's pleading eyes go from shining brown to dull black and then his body going limp in his hands. He'd like to kill Eastman this way. The more he thought about choking the life out of Eastman, the closer he came to climaxing. Soon it was Eastman's death and his orgasmic release all at once in his mind. After it was all over, Smith did something he hasn't done in many years. He weeps.

Santa Rosa, California

"Are you the new butler?" Kim jokingly asks.

"I'm Will Rubin and you are Kim, Susan's sister. I recognize you from some of the framed photos in the house," he says extending a hand. Kim accepts the handshake.

"Come on in," Will offers and ushers her through the open door.

"Susan's upstairs, I'll get her for you," Will says as he locks dead bolt lock behind her.

Kim re-reads the headline of the magazine she had bought at the store and can't wait to show Susan.

Before Will can even call for Susan, she's already on her way down the stairs.

A barefoot Susan, dressed in jeans and a pale blue sweater, slides her hand down the stair rail and her heart squeezes upon seeing her sister. Kim has lost at least fifteen pounds, pounds she can ill afford to lose. She looks small in her favorite jean jacket. Kim's hair has thinned and her face is placid. Dark circles ring her hollow eyes—*the mask of grief,* Susan thinks as she swallows a lump that's formed in her throat.

"Kim, you're up early. What brings you over?" Susan injects a cheerful demeanor into her voice as she descends the last two steps. She nods to will at the bottom of the stairs.

"Hey Susan," Kim's voice is riddled with agitation.

"What's wrong?"

"This morning I ventured out early. I couldn't sleep. You know, it's been, well, difficult. I dropped Grace off at swim practice at the high school—Jake usually does it, but I told him I would. I just couldn't stand being in the house another minute. I mean, it's hard."

"It's okay," Susan says touching her sister's arm and leads her to the sofa.

"Will you excuse us?" Susan asks.

"If you don't mind. I'd like to hear what is so upsetting to Kim."

Kim and Susan take a seat on the living room sofa and Will takes the matching upholstered chair directly across from them.

"I stopped off at the grocery store. I got a few things we needed, and I was standing in the checkout line, and . . . "

"Kim, what happened to upset you?" Susan gently asks. Perhaps it was something that reminded her of Josh. There were so many reminders everywhere. Every time she's gone out with her sister they would have to leave wherever they were. Often it was upon a family with a boy the same age as Josh - a terrible reminder that Josh is no longer with them. Susan longs to take her sister's pain away.

"Susan, I'm trying to tell you that this is what's upsetting me," Kim says, and she holds the magazine toward her sister's face.

Susan sees the photo of Noah and then takes the magazine from Kim and reads the headline.

"What the hell?"

"What is it?" Will inquires a Susan scans the magazine.

"Shit!" Susan states.

"What's going?" Elliot inquires as he enters the room through the kitchen holding a cup of tea.

Susan holds up the *World News* magazine article to show Will and Elliot; the face on the cover is a blown-up picture of Noah. The caption beneath it read, "Parents Clone Dying Son in Effort to Replace Him."

"What the hell?" Elliot angrily swears as he stares at it.

"I was completely shocked too. How in the world did they get a close-up photo of him?" Kim inquires.

"Do you mind?" Will asks taking the magazine from Susan. "Unfortunately it's not hard. This one was probably taken with a telephoto lens."

"What are we going to do? How do we keep Noah safe?" Susan asks.

"It's out there now in a not-so-positive way. We knew it would just be a matter of time before the tabloids picked up the story," Will explains.

"This story makes Noah sound like a freak and us like Frankenstein's creators. The entire country will see this," Elliot says furiously.

"Are you more worried about what people will think?" Susan asks Elliot.

"Of course not. I'm frightened for the repercussions this might have for Noah—for us all."

"People think we are doing this to *replace our son*," Susan's voice rises and then falls. "Noah isn't even sick yet. We're trying to save his life! They don't understand."

"What do you expect? It's a rag mag., the type that exploits people. They get sales from being sensationalistic," Kim says and gently touches Susan's arm.

"Look, I know neither of you wants to hear this right now, but at some point you might need to think about going into hiding," Will tells them.

"Hiding?" Elliot questions.

"We don't need to hide. We need to set the record straight. We need to get an interview with *People Magazine* or go on television with Barbara Walters or Oprah," Susan says.

"Before you talk about a PR campaign to get the truth out, we need to consider your son's safety. This magazine coverage is a game changer."

"I hope you're wrong about that, Will," Susan remarks.

"I hope I am too. But it's my job to know better."

Butlerville, Indiana

"Shoot it in the head, for Christ's sake!" Joe's father commanded. "Put it out of its misery." Smith was only twelve years old and mesmerized as he had watched the buck writhe and scream in pain.

Joe was lost in an almost mystical trance recalling the long ago memory. Standing there with his father, he watched the buck struggling to survive. The buck's chest rose and fell in labored breath that misted in the cold air. Joe enjoyed watching the buck do its death dance. He hadn't wanted it to end.

Joe's father had hustled up alongside him and smacked him hard on the back startling his son. "Shoot it in the head. Now!"

Joe took aim and hit the buck in the head. The blast from the gunshot reverberated through Joe's body and unsteadied him on his feet but he held his ground. His adrenalin coursed through his veins as he watched the bucks body go limp, then it twitched and fell still. He dropped his gun and walked up to the buck. When he looked deep into the deer's eyes, he saw a glassy, dark look that seemed endless. There was no light just deadness. The next thing he realized was that his cock was hard. He was glad he was wearing a coat so his daddy couldn't see.

"We don't allow living things to suffer, son," his daddy had admonished him. Joe recalls thinking that maybe there was something different about him - the thing that made him like the killing? It was obvious his daddy didn't see it that way. Joe had wondered why? The death dance was the most beautiful thing he'd ever seen. He wanted it to go on forever.

It was almost evening as Joe approaches his house. Sometimes when he walks his fields he replays this scene from a long ago experience over and over. It was a fond memory. As he approaches his farm house, his thoughts turn to his work at hand - God's work. He says a prayer of thanks for the Internet. He would never have been able to execute many aspects of the terror he hoped to inflict on those godless people who were cloning an innocent little boy had he not been able to research ricin from the privacy of his own home. Also, the Internet had made it easier to find the address where the Gaynors lived. In the end he had decided on scaring the Gaynors instead of actually placing ricin into an envelope and mailing it to them. Besides, he didn't really want to go to the trouble of hurting anyone with ricin. It might lead back to him somehow before he has the opportunity to finish his work. He didn't care about the parents. His hesitation was with the little boy. He couldn't be certain that the boy wouldn't be exposed to the toxin. He knew God wanted him to save Noah. Then another thought had crossed his mind. Perhaps God wanted Joe to be Noah's father? Noah would be the son he never had. Could it be? Was this God's plan?

Getting to Eastman had taken some doing, but he had pulled it off. He just hopes that what he has done will be enough to stop him. He'll be watching, waiting, listening. If he didn't take his message seriously, he'll ask God for another sign. God would direct him. He didn't expect anything from God in return, though. After all, it was a privilege to do God's work. Smith thought about how God sees him as special. He is chosen. But will he be rewarded with the boy? This thought excites him. He also believes it will make Gwen happy too. He kicks a stone and watches it bounce across the dirt on the final path leading up to the back door of his house and thinks of how Gwen has always wanted a child. When he looks up and across the fields into the woods, he sees a deer. The deer seems to be looking straight into his eyes. It occurs to Joe that maybe it is a good time to go hunting. Maybe God wants him to practice his shooting. Besides, he also can use some meat. He'll leave early tomorrow morning.

Washington, D.C.

Senator Levine (D., NY) knows quite well that the wheels of "progress" in Washington turn slowly. However, he isn't going to allow them to gather any speed. In fact, he wants to stick in a monkey wrench and grind them to a halt. There is no way he is going to allow a bill that restricts therapeutic cloning to be passed. He is completely against the Respect Human Life bill. His sister suffers from multiple sclerosis. He knows that stem cell therapy holds the key to a possible cure for MS and many other diseases. This is a down right miracle. Hell, how many people on Capitol Hill have loved ones with debilitating diseases that need cures? How many members of Congress have contended with their own health crises that might be aided by this effort? He also believes that the whole issue of cloning should be left up to each individual state. It isn't a federal matter. His state had voted to support therapeutic cloning and promising research is taking place there. As far as he is concerned the Respect Human Life name should be given to Senator Matthew's sponsored legislation in support of therapeutic cloning as it held the key to providing longer, better quality lives for people who have disease.

The Senator ponders all of these thoughts as he finishes the last of his whole wheat bagel with whipped cream cheese for breakfast. Unable to find a napkin, he wipes his fingers on the inside of his shirt he untucks and then re-tucks.

His ultimate hope resides in Dr. Eastman's and the LAB's work. Levine truly believes that his friend will soon unlock the door to curing many diseases. The problem is that many of his constituents didn't understand the difference between reproductive cloning and therapeutic cloning. Currently there are several states that are pursuing therapeutic cloning.

Anyway, he'd organize a Congressional briefing and have the brainiac scientist explain the miraculous qualities this type of science held for so many people. Levine often wonders if any of them ever read anything? Just in case they didn't, he'd have the best and brightest explain it to them.

Levine has made up his mind. He will ask his aides to organize a briefing. The timing is right. He'll also call his old college roommate from Harvard and let him know that he needed to be the star player at a Congressional briefing. It wouldn't hurt to have a couple of ethicists on-hand, too. He hopes Eastman and some of his team members would be on-board with his plan.

Levine brushes aside a stack of papers and folders on his desk and finds a place to put up his feet. He leans back in the black leather recliner and places a call to Eastman's cell.

Eastman is sitting at his desk writing up some notes and picks up on the second ring.

"Hey, Jamie boy!" Eastman recognizes the voice immediately. He had a deep affection for his friend, but hated being called Jamie. Most people refer to him as Eastman or, in the case of his family and close friends - James.

"Well, if it isn't Paulie! How are things on the hill?"

"That depends. How are things at the LAB?"

"We've got some things cooking. Why do you ask?"

"You've been causing quite a stir in things that matter around here on the hill. The powers that be have been keeping a close eye on you, sir."

"Ah yes, those powers. Last I remember, my old friend was one of those powers," Eastman says with a chuckle.

"Let me get to the point. There is going to be a Congressional hearing on human cloning up here, and I need a star witness—one who's interested in continuing the pursuit of therapeutic cloning and stem cell research," Levine explains.

"When do you want me to speak?"

"Next month."

"Wow, that's like time warp speed by Washington standards."

"Well, there are some people who are feeling a bit threatened about your latest scientific endeavors. I just want to make sure that the wrong shit doesn't get spun and that the accurate information gets put out there."

"I can do that. You want me to bring up some of my team?"

"I want your team, a couple of ethicists, and I want the Gaynors too."

Eastman pauses considering this last request. Protecting Noah and his family is and remains a priority.

"Jamie boy, you there?"

"Yeah. Why do you want the Gaynors?"

"I want a human face on this thing. I want people to see that we aren't just talking in numbers; millions of people with diseases could benefit from your work. I want our message to have a face," Levine says sitting straight up in his chair and planting his feet firmly on the floor underneath it.

"And you want that face to be Noah's?"

"I was thinking the parents, but the boy, a little boy now that will be compelling."

"Don't you have others you could bring in to testify?"

"Yeah, there are others. One of my aide's sisters has cerebral palsy. There are lots of people we could trot out but none directly involved with what you are pursuing," Levine replies.

"I've got to talk this over with them. Things have gotten a bit heated around here, and I don't want to do anything to jeopardize their safety."

"You mean you've gotten threats?"

"We all have. Ever since Noah's face appeared on the cover of that magazine and an ill-informed story followed in print."

"Holy crap. I should've figured on that. Do you know where the threats are coming from?" Levine asks planting both feet on the floor and leans forward in his chair.

"So far, we only know of one man."

"You can reassure the Gaynors that if they do decide to testify that security won't be a problem. Also, all the more reason for them to be at the hearing."

"I understand, set-the-record-straight sort of thing. If the boy becomes the face of the cause, though, I'm afraid he could be in a lot of danger."

"Not *if*. He is the face. I mean, it's already gotten there and in not so good of a way. You can't hide that shit forever."

"True. My priority is keeping them safe."

"I thought it was saving the boy."

Eastman was silent for a moment as he thought about their exchange.

"Jamie?"

"Let me contact them. I'll get back to you."

"Sounds good. Make it sooner rather than later, OK?"

As he ends his phone conversation with Eastman, Levine looks up to see his assistant standing there with her iPhone and a Starbucks coffee cup. "It's time for your first meeting, Senator."

Levine nods to his aide and says his goodbye to Eastman, "Another day at the saw mill. We'll talk later."

His young aide looks perplexed. "Never mind. It's a saying before your time. I just hope this one isn't a snoozer. I need a nap today."

Levine's aide hands him his double espresso mocha. "Here, this may help you to stay awake."

"You don't miss a beat."

Westchester, New York
The LAB

The timing for the hearing couldn't have been worse, Eastman realizes as he prepares for the stem cell harvest from Noah's clone. He doesn't want to divide his attention between his work and political issues that may ultimately affect his work. He leans forward in his desk chair and rubs his face hard with his hands as he considers the fact that the bill that is most likely to pass the House will be brought to the Senate for a final vote, and this will determine whether or not the federal government will have the authority to tell the states that they can no longer pursue any type of cloning, not just reproductive cloning (which no one was currently pursuing in the United States), but therapeutic cloning as well. Eastman leans back in his chair and considers the fact that it is important that members of Congress get to hear what he and his team has to say. *How to approach?* This can be boiled down into the plight of one real family—a family whose only agenda is to save the life of their son.

Putting his feet up on his desk and leaning back in his office chair, Eastman presses the Gaynor's home phone number on his cell phone. As it rings, he wonders how many people still had land lines in their homes. Probably not many.

"Elliot? This is James Eastman."

"Hey, I'm glad you called. I'm hoping for an update on the hearing," Elliot replies.

"That's what I'm calling about. I want to give you a heads up that I sent an email a few minutes ago. It briefs you and Susan on what to expect, when you'll speak, and what types of questions you might be asked."

"Great. Thanks. I'll look for it."

"Susan and I talked it over and we want to inform you that we will be bringing Noah to the hearing."

"Are you sure? I'm concerned for his safety."

"We feel he's safer with us. Besides, he has his own personal bodyguard—Will."

"How's that going?"

"It's been different having someone else in the house. However, he's great, and it's given me some piece of mind while I'm at work knowing he's here."

"I'm glad to hear it. Will's a good friend, but more importantly he's good at what he does."

"Will we be able to meet with you prior to the hearing?"

"Yes, we'll meet in the morning an hour before the hearing."

"When does the stem harvesting take place?"

"Soon after. I have a conference in Boston after the hearing, and then I'll return to the LAB where we'll perform the procedure," Eastman says putting his feet back on the floor and leaning forward in his chair. "I reserved two rooms at the Key Bridge Marriot Hotel under the name Davies. If anyone asks, your son's name is Reed."

"Thanks, but why Davies?"

"It was my mom's maiden name. I thought it was best to keep a low profile."

"I'm praying that all goes well."

"You and me both."

Santa Rosa, California
The Next Night

Susan has been up most of the night. She finds it impossible to sleep. She hasn't wanted to wake Elliot or Noah, so she quietly slips into her white silk robe and heads downstairs to the kitchen. A cup of warm cocoa and a little television might help to slow her racing mind. She can't stop thinking about the possibility of going into hiding. How can they afford it? There's no witness protection program for them. Elliot wouldn't be able to work. She wouldn't be able to work, at least not at their current occupations. It wasn't as if they had enough savings to live off for years. They had depleted a lot of their savings to assist in the cloning process. The travel and healthcare costs were minuscule compared to what the LAB had paid, but all the same it was quite a large sum for a family with a young child. Susan didn't want to even consider leaving her house. She loved their house. She loved looking out the back kitchen door to the yard filled with toys. This was her dream, and slowly it was becoming a nightmare. Would she be able to see and talk to her sister and her friends? If they left, could they rent out their house? Would the people living here be safe? She had a million questions and no answers—and now they were going to have to attend the Congressional hearing and attempt to sway Congress to support their cause. It felt like a Herculean task.

Susan feels her chest tighten and her stomach turn as she pours the milk into a coffee mug and then places it into the microwave. While it is heating, she gets out the cocoa from the cupboard. The more she thinks about the entire situation, the more resolved she becomes to stay put. But what if that means something bad might happen to Noah? Why would someone actually want to hurt a little boy?

What she needs is a "mind dump" or mental dump onto paper as her sister called it. Susan decides that she's going to write down all of her questions, concerns and fears, and go through them with Will in the morning. She also believes it will help her to get back to sleep. One thing is for certain: If she had to do it over again, she would. She truly believes this affords Noah the best chance for a long, happy, life. Dr. Eastman has informed them that they are assembling the team to harvest the stem cells very soon. After that, they can start working on a genetic modification of the ALD gene. This is huge. This is the hope that she needs to hang on to in order to save Noah. It is more than hope, though. It is reality. It is really, really, happening. Susan's worries change to excitement. Oh, why can't the rest of the world rejoice with them? This isn't just for Noah. The far-reaching implications of this are for everyone who suffers from disease. How many lives will be saved through this research? Surely the person or persons who hated them and want them to stop have family or friends who might need this miracle of science.

Susan retrieves the pen from the junk drawer next to the back door, the microwave dings, jolting Susan from her thoughts and signaling that her milk is ready. Just then she hears a crunching sound outside the door. She freezes; clutching the pen she cautiously approaches the window in the door. As she presses her face against the glass for a better look, a man's face peers back from the other side. Susan lets out an ear piercing scream and the man darts away.

Will takes the stairs to the kitchen three at a time as he pushes past Elliot who has started down the stairs just ahead of him. Susan's screams have elicited a full-court-press response from the two men in the house. Will lands in the kitchen just a few seconds ahead of Elliot, wearing only his boxers and wielding a gun. Susan doesn't know which she's more shocked by the guy outside or her wild-eyed bodyguard in his skivvies packing heat.

"Someone was staring at me through the window. It was hard to see because it's so dark out," Susan breathlessly explains to Will.

Will nods and hurries out the back door, "You guys stay in the kitchen," he instructs over his shoulder.

"Where's Noah?"

"I checked him first. He's sleeping," Elliot replies.

"Elliot, you mean my screams didn't wake him?"

"I guess it's true what they say about kids sleeping through almost anything."

Susan snuggles closer to Elliot as he wraps his arms tightly around her in a big bear hug. He feels warm and good, she thinks, as he pulls her face into his chest and strokes the back of her hair.

"It's okay now."

"I know. It just really scared me."

"It scares me too. I am feeling more uncertain about my ability to keep you and Noah safe."

"We have Will," Susan reminds him just as the bodyguard returns through the kitchen door.

Elliot feels a stab of jealously. He views it as his ultimate duty as husband, and father, to be the protector. Susan now sees Will as her protector and Eastman as Noah's savior. Well, that might be an exaggeration. However, Elliot is feeling more and more emasculated these days.

"I didn't see anyone. I did see shoe prints in the dirt. I think we need to report this to the police," Will says.

"Well then, we better get dressed."

"Take your time. I'll contact them and then answer the door when they arrive."

"Um, don't you think you might want to put on some—pants?" Susan reminds Will.

Will looks down at his bare legs.

"Let's all go up and get dressed."

Washington, D.C.
Two Days Later

Early on an overcast morning, the Gaynors and Eastman arrive on Capitol Hill. First, the bodyguards, including Will Rubin, step out of the limo. After scanning the immediate area for potential threats and determining it is safe, the bodyguards assist the Gaynors, Eastman, and two of his staff members from the limo and onto the sidewalk. They are immediately surrounded by the D.C. police, reporters with still cameras, and news cameras covering their every move. Susan protectively hugs her son as they are hurried up the Capitol steps by the bodyguards and police. She pauses when she reaches the second to last row of steps and takes in the view along with Elliot, Dr. Eastman, and Kathryn McMurray. As far as the eye can see, there are hundreds, maybe thousands, of people. Many are chanting and cheering so loudly that Susan presses Noah's head against her cheek. Rubin is saying something to her, but she can't quite make out the words as it is too loud to hear. He grabs her arm and moves her and Noah quickly up the last steps towards the buildings doors. Rubin is moving Susan so quickly she trips. Elliot, who is one step behind, steadies her and Noah and keeps them from falling. The reporters follow, shoving microphones in their faces and shouting questions above the noise. A person yells out "Noah's Mom!" Susan and Elliot turn around and take another look at the sea of people lining the street. A man gives her a thumbs-up. Further down, many others are holding signs. Some read, "Don't mess with Mother Nature!" "Go Home!" "Accept your son's fate!" "You can't replace your son!" Others are encouraging: "May God be with you and this miracle of science!" "We Love You, Noah!" "Please fight for a cure!"

Susan is speechless. Until now, she has had no real idea that their fight to save their son would be a fight that would involve much of the nation. She wonders if there are more people supporting therapeutic cloning than opposing it? It is hard to gage by the crowd. She also wonders if people know the whole story and understand the difference between reproductive and therapeutic cloning. *If you are going to oppose something, then you should fully understand what it is you are opposing*, she thinks. She'll makes certain she says this to the men and women who will soon be hearing their story. Their story matters. Not just to them, but too many people. Susan believes with all of her heart that God is with her on this. Elliot grabs her hand just as they are practically shoved through the doors of the Capitol by their bodyguards. Susan holds Elliot's hand and silently prays for strength as she holds onto their son.

Her heart squeezes as she considers the fact that Noah has become a poster child for this cause. She never wanted this for him. A normal life is all she and Elliot ever wanted, and still wanted for Noah. However, she realizes that his plight represents the plight of millions of sick people and their loved ones. She kisses the top of his head and notices that he's regressed to sucking his thumb. He is comforting himself. It was a frightening and confusing time. Susan realizes that if she could suck her thumb she would too and smiles down at her little boy.

From the hallway where they are now passing through additional security, Susan can see that the doors to the room where the hearing will take place are wide open. Inside the room is a raised, mahogany dais where the members of Congress will soon sit. Susan can see some of the members taking their seats. Portraits of the President and Vice President hang on the wall in back of the dais. Blue carpeting stretches throughout the room, accentuated by red and gold tones in the drapes. The U.S. flag hangs directly behind the members of Congress. Susan can't help but be reminded of the Fourth of July and Memorial Day. Unlike the holidays, none of this is fun though. Bile rises in her throat and she grimaces as she swallows it back down. She is scared, excited, and nervous and her internal organs are now reflecting this.

After going through security, the party enters the room and is directed to a row of tables in front of the dais where invited experts are already seated. Long cables snake along the floor like black and gray pythons hooked up to microphones on the tables. The hearing is being recorded and filmed by CSPAN and most of the major networks.

"Snakes mama," Noah says delighted.

"They do look like snakes but they are called cables," Susan replies, glad that her little boy isn't afraid of snakes.

"Kay-balls," Noah repeats.

"Yes, they're for the cameras," Susan tells him pointing to one of the cameras.

Noah lays his head back down on her shoulder and pops his thumb back into his mouth.

Susan thinks back to Eastman's earlier briefing on what to expect, or at least, on what might be expected. He had referred to the bipartisan Congressional hearing as a briefing on human cloning advancement, called by Senator Paul Levine (D., NY.) and Senator Ed Levesque, (R., VA.). Both senators were advocates of using cloned stems cells for medical research.

Susan and Elliot were made aware of the fact that the rest of the senators remain divided over the two different approaches to human cloning. The Gaynors themselves are in favor of banning reproductive cloning. However, what concerns them the most is the bill S. 245, introduced by Senator Rick Morales (R., KS) and Kathleen Sullivan (D., LA), along with twenty-seven other senators supported. This bill will ban the procedure known as "somatic cell nuclear transfer" to create human embryos for any purpose. If this bill passes, the pursuit of therapeutic cloning could be illegal in the United States. It is a significant concern to the Gaynors and millions of others who support this type of research. The bill has now been approved twice by the House. Another bill that has passed the House but not the Senate is S.303. This bill will allow for human embryo research through cloning while making it illegal to allow the live birth of cloned humans. Senator Paul McGuire (D., ND) and Senator Quinton Hughes (R., UT) have co-sponsored the bill. The fight for, and against, human cloning is truly a bipartisan effort in a Congress that is too often polarized. Alliances were being formed across party lines in the case of therapeutic human cloning. This topic truly made for strange bedfellows. Eastman hopes for at least one senator, who is well-educated about cloning and understands the difference between therapeutic or somatic cell nuclear transfer (SCNT) and reproductive cloning that will help to make their case.

In addition, the galleries of supporters of S.303 include a number of scientific and patient advocacy groups who oppose bill S. 245, claiming that it will block potentially promising medical research. The galleries of detractors who are present include the Catholic Bishops' Conference, pro-life groups, and others opposed to human cloning. If the bill is to pass, S. 303 would authorize human cloning itself, not prohibit the actions (implantation and gestation) needed to allow a cloned human to develop and be born.

Eastman had warned the Gaynors that this Congressional debate will proceed along similar lines of the abortion debate. Some members of the President's Council on Bioethics and some members of Congress did favor some funding of research involving "spare" embryos from fertility clinics, but they vehemently opposed the creation of human embryos solely to destroy them in research. Even some members of the House who support a "pro-choice" position on abortion had voted for the House-approved cloning ban. Interestingly enough, these included Republican, Democrat, and independent members. By the same token, some pro-life legislation supporters in the Senate oppose S.303. In the past, Senator Hughes had argued that human embryos had no moral status as human beings unless they had resided in a mother's womb, and also that humans arising from the cloning procedure might not have the legal status of human beings even if they were born.

Susan recalls this entire discussion as they take their seats at the table. Susan pushes Noah's diaper bag behind her chair. She can't remember ever seeing a congressional hearing with a diaper bag close on hand. This thought makes her smile. Noah sits in her lap still sucking his thumb. She realizes he's still feeling overwhelmed. She's feeling overwhelmed too. Her training as a lawyer takes over and she's all business - except for the toddler in her lap. She smiles at the thought. Eastman had told both her and Elliot that this fight is a kind of perfect storm: It involves ethics, morals, the human condition, finances, politics, and religion. It has all of the makings of a feature film or best-selling novel. However, this isn't a fictional story. It is the true story of two parents' fight to save their child's life, and the story of everyone who suffers from a currently incurable disease or loves someone who does.

The Gaynors and Eastman are not the only speakers scheduled for this morning. There are to be arguments presented by special interest groups both for and against this type of scientific research.

As Eastman takes his seat he thinks about the ethical questions posed to Congress and the legislative attempts to regulate, through federal law, the patenting of cloned human embryos has failed. Biotechnology firms want to be able to patent their cloned human embryos. Genetic material from patients with certain diseases might be used to mass produce cloned embryos as "models" for those diseases—to be marketed and researched in the same way that marketing of genetically tailored laboratory mice are already being done. This would pave the way to making them commercially viable. So far, the U.S. Patent and Trademark Office had denied these applications citing the Thirteenth Amendment's ban on owning human beings.

Potentially, therapeutic human cloning could be a multi-billion dollar industry. However, Eastman is not driven by the money. It is a cause for him. Children shouldn't die from disease. Children shouldn't lose their parents to disease. He would remind anyone who would listen. It is as simple as that. Everyone is entitled to a full lifespan in his view. What a full lifespan is varied. If his work was successful it would be a very, very long one which posed its own ethical and moral dilemmas.

Eastman wants to be able to patent the process, but not necessarily the product. Also, he knows that there is a huge misconception regarding what constitutes a human being. Eastman wouldn't be doing what he was doing if he believes in any way, shape, or form that the harvesting of cloned embryonic stem cells at the blastocyst stage was the same as conducting research using a fetus. A blastocyst isn't, and never will be, a human being. He has discussed this with the Gaynors and is fully prepared to speak on it today if asked.

Eastman's thoughts are interrupted as he and Dr. MacMurray, the Gaynors, and ethicist Gerald Brown are welcomed by the committee. After introductions are exchanged, Dr. Eastman is asked to address the committee chair, Senator Paul Levine.

"Dr. Eastman please tell us about what you and the LAB are currently working on that directly affects this hearing."

"Certainly."

Eastman provides a brief overview, citing when the LAB had been founded, what work they have done, the scientific breakthroughs they have achieved, and their hopes for the future."

"How did you become interested in this work?" Senator Levine inquires.

Dr. Eastman tells his own story of his plight, watching his mother die from breast cancer when he was only 15 years old.

"I think many of us here can relate to your story on a personal level as breast cancer is one of the most diagnosed diseases in the United States," Levine responds.

"Cancer is a disease that will one day be treated through therapeutic cloning in a much less invasive way with a longer life expectancy," Eastman replies.

"Please explain, briefly," Levine instructs.

"There is some evidence, but not a mainstream therapy, that by cloning a cancer patients own immune cells we can cure the disease. In other cancer cases we have been able to slow the disease."

Susan scans the audience and wonders how many of these people suffer with diseases that therapeutic cloning might cure? How many people in the room have life-threatening food allergies and heart problems, cancer, diabetes, cystic fibrosis, or multiple sclerosis? Even if they personally haven't experienced any of these, how many of them have close friends or family members who have?

"Mrs. Gaynor, would you like to speak?" Senator Levine asks.

Susan shifts the weight from her now sleeping toddler in her lap.

"From there is just fine. No need to stand," Levine offers.

"Thank you. My name is Susan Gaynor. Sleeping in my lap is my son Noah who has ALD. Dr. Eastman informed you the particulars of this disease earlier in the hearing so I won't waste precious time going over the disease. I just want to say in regard to therapeutic human cloning we see it as a viable cure for our son's disease. We'd also like to remind the distinguished members of this hearing that this isn't a fight for only our son; this is a fight for everyone. Politics is about people, religion is about people, medical and research is about people. This cause affects every single person in this room and beyond."

"Dr. Eastman, please explain to us why adult stem cells are not preferred in treatment applications," Senator Levine inquires.

"Adult stem cells can be found in mature cells and in some organs. For example, bone marrow cells are a type of adult stem cells that have been used in transplants for more than forty years. But because adult stem cells are taken from parts of the body that already have a purpose, they may be limited as to what they can be turned into," Eastman explains.

Senator Anne Wilcox Brice, who is in support of therapeutic cloning, addressed Kathryn. "Dr. MacMurray, isn't it true that embryonic stem cells are proposed as the preferred choice for stem cell therapy?"

Kathryn replies, "Yes, embryonic stem cells come from four- or five-day-old fertilized eggs and they have the ability to turn into any type of human cell in the body. Since human embryonic stem cells were first discovered in 1998, researchers have been trying to take these unique cells and coax them into becoming cells for every part of the body, which then could be used to repair damage or regenerate tissue."

"There's been a virtual ban on funding this type of research, which has slowed the field down," Brice counters.

"Yes. Because of this, researchers have developed another source of stem cells: skin cells. Scientists have learned how to turn the clock back on skin cells so they're like embryos; skin stem cells have the same "blank slate" properties as embryonic stem cells, but without the controversy. These cells are called "IPS," or induced pluripotent stem cells. There are no approved embryonic stem cell treatments in the United States. However, the Food and Drug Administration has approved two experimental clinical trials in humans using treatments made from human embryonic stem cells. One of these, to repair spinal cord injuries, was stopped due to the high cost of this type of research the other trial to restore vision in people with macular degeneration is still underway. In fact, we've had the first safety trial with it in Great Britain."

"Is there hope," Brice asks, leading the questioning in the direction she favors, "that embryonic stem cells might someday lead to treatments for

Parkinson's disease, diabetes, traumatic spinal cord injury, Duchene muscular dystrophy, and other conditions?"

"Absolutely, however, using cloned embryonic stem cells gives us the best chance at being successful in treating disease."

Senator Levine then asks Eastman to address the differences between therapeutic cloning and reproductive cloning. "Dr. Eastman, please explain the differences between what is referred to as therapeutic cloning and what is referred to as reproductive cloning. Also, please inform us of the importance and significance of therapeutic cloning research."

Eastman clears his throat and takes a drink of water from the glass placed within his reach. He knows he must create a clear sense of understanding in the committee members or he won't be successful in garnering the support he needs, not only for the LAB, but for all of the other researchers throughout the country working in regenerative medicine. "SCNT, or therapeutic cloning, is an alternative method that may be used to create embryonic stem cells. It refers to the removal of the nucleus from a donor, or ideally, a maternal donor's egg. The donated egg contains the donor's genetic material or what we commonly refer to as our DNA. Once the donor's genetic material, or DNA, has been removed from the egg by removing the nucleus, we then take genetic material from the patient and inject it into the unfertilized egg. We can take the patient's DNA from virtually any cell in his body because each one of our cells contains our DNA."

"Correct me if I'm wrong," Senator Brice says, "but as I understand it, the newly reconstituted egg is then stimulated through a specific laboratory technique involving electric currents that coax it into fusion. If successful, the egg is considered to be activated and the egg cell begins dividing. After five to seven days in culture, there is just enough cell division to amount to a ball of cells sitting on the head of straight pin. The embryonic stem cells can then be removed and used to create many more embryonic stem cells in culture. These embryonic stem cell lines are genetically identical to the cell from which the DNA was removed."

Eastman beams; Senator Brice is what he had hoped for. In her he sees a senator who possesses a firm understanding of what it is they are attempting to achieve. He hopes she might be an ally.

"Yes, that's correct," Eastman replies and adds, "Once the embryonic stem cell lines are created, we can begin experimenting on them to find a cure for disease. It's being done now using mice. However, mice are far removed from humans and lack the advantage of allowing us to work with a person's own DNA material."

Senator Levine asks, "Dr. Eastman, perhaps you can explain to me and my esteemed colleagues why there's a need to use embryonic cells at all? I mean, adult stem cells aren't rejected by the immune system, they can produce a variety of body tissues, and they don't involve destroying embryos."

"I'm glad you asked me that, Senator Levine. There are several reasons. Embryonic stem cells are purer cells. Most adult stem cells are rare. They may be difficult or dangerous to harvest from patients. They also have a limited capacity to divide in a laboratory. This means they cannot be grown in large enough quantities to be of therapeutic value. Finally, adult stem cells have not been discovered for all types of tissue. Giving back patients their adult stem cells is not always an ideal therapy."

"Can you give us an example?" Levine asks.

"Let's look at cancer patients. These cells are sometimes damaged by early rounds of chemotherapy or are even contaminated with cancer cells and are difficult to purify. Furthermore, in *all* cases, stem cells are seriously limited through the very nature of cellular aging, unlike cloned embryonic stem cells. Newer stem cells can divide many, many more times than older stem cells. After adult stem cells divide a certain number of times, they burn themselves out. There is a limited lifespan for them. Human embryonic stem cells can go on dividing indefinitely, producing unlimited quantities of cells. Not so for the cells derived from adult bone marrow."

Senator Levine, still trying to help Eastman along without being too abstract asks, "Break it down for us. Simplify the science, please."

"A forty-or fifty-year-old patient who had received a stem cell transplant using adult stem cells might essentially have the immune system of a seventy- or eighty-year-old. These cells were older at the time of use and aged more quickly. However, using cloned embryonic stem cells, this would not be the case. The use of embryonic stem cells is like going back in time, a sort of fountain of youth, if you will, and allows us to take the cell from the beginning stages of development. It's younger, often healthier, and more viable than an aged cell."

Senator John Dukesbury speaks up. "I just don't understand here, Dr. Eastman. If you grow clones to use for therapeutic research an' all, I mean takin' an ol' kidney or liver when needed, or one of them—these stem cell things you talkin' about, well, where in the hell are you gonna keep 'em? In a closet somewhere?"

There is a ripple of laughter that reverberates throughout the room. Eastman suddenly realizes the mentality of some of the people they are up against.

"Senator Dukesbury, you misunderstood, sir. You are referring to reproductive cloning with the goal of creating a human being. We have no desire to do this. In fact, we are opposed to reproductive cloning," Eastman explains.

Senator Liz Reed (D., MN) says, "There is both a light and a dark side to science. I'm sure you all recall that the Swedish inventor Alfred Nobel, for whom the Nobel Peace Prize was named, didn't want the scientific technology he provided us with to be used to harm people. Nobel tightly controlled the patent on dynamite he had for many years until others found a way around the patent and used it for military purposes. While you speak of the benefits of therapeutic cloning, we also have to look at how this scientific technology can be pursued in ways that ultimately cause harm to humanity."

Senator Jack Parish (D., NJ), whose state currently has the most supportive laws allowing therapeutic cloning, addresses the senator who has just spoken. "You are correct. I believe it's the great philosopher Sting who says, 'I've never seen a miracle of science that didn't go from a blessing to a curse.'

Another chuckle goes through the audience and Senator Parish continues. "The down side to pursuing therapeutic cloning is the fact that this knowledge could be used to create a human being. This knowledge will one day be out there and there is nothing— nothing at all— that we can do to stop the acquisition of knowledge. However, I do believe that this is an opportunity to witness the best humanity has to offer. I ask you, do we close the door, out of fear, on pursuing scientific knowledge that can ultimately save us, too?"

Dr. Eastman jumps in. "Sir, if I may?" Senator Levine nods to him. "Taking old, broken-down and diseased cells and making them young again is the result of knowledge that has been given to us. If we possess the knowledge, then we have the duty to help

Senator Kathleen Sullivan (D., LA) speaks up with concern. "We have a duty, as Senator Reed touched upon, to enact laws to prevent pursuing aspects of this science that we never intended."

"The knowledge is there for both therapeutic and reproductive uses of human cloning," Eastman replies. "I believe the common ground here is that none of us want to see the pursuit of reproductive cloning. However, therapeutic cloning can afford us the ability to save lives. We can control how far cloned human cells divide and choose to go no further than needed. This is often prior to embryonic development. It is before the ball of cells edivide into a placenta and an embryo. This is an early, early stage of development. Even earlier than the frozen embryos donated from in vitro-fertilization procedures that we're already using for stem cell research. I believe this new type of research, using the very early stage cloned cells, to be ethically and morally responsible. We are on the very brink of discovering how to apply this knowledge to save or improve the lives of millions of people who suffer from all sorts of diseases. Diseases such as heart disease, Parkinson's, diabetes, and some types of cancers, just to name a few.

"But is it morally and ethically correct? Can we stop at therapeutic cloning without venturing further into reproductive cloning?" Senator Reed asks.

"It's the ultimate test of our character as human beings. I believe that laws can be enacted that will prevent reproductive cloning in the United States."

Senator Albert Hanson (R., MI) jumps in. "I understand and believe that pursuing scientific knowledge helps us to survive. I'm a cancer survivor myself. Without the advent of stem cell transplant therapy, I might not be here today. What I don't understand is that if we can get stem cells from people, why do we need to pursue cloning? I mean, what about cord blood banking after the birth of a human baby? It can be used therapeutically if needed later on in life too. It's a rich source of young stem cells that haven't aged. It can be stored and used to help treat many types of disease."

"Good points," Eastman replies. "Cord blood contains hematopoietic stem cells, progenitor cells which can form platelets, red and white blood cells. Cord blood cells are currently used to treat blood- and immune-system-related genetic diseases, cancers, and blood disorders. It's one of the most hopeful areas of regenerative medicine that is currently practiced. However, we can do better because with cord blood banking we are limited in what we can do. One of the greatest disadvantages is the limited amount of hematopoietic cells from individual donations of umbilical cord blood as a source of hematopoietic stem cells for clinical transplantation. Another area we need to consider is genetic makeup. Unfortunately, abnormal cells may be transferred. There can also be an increase in mortality associated with transplantation because the rate of thrombocytes and myeloid engraftments are much lower than what has been discovered in comparably matched bone marrow, resulting in failure of the engraftment."

Eastman paused and looks deeply into the faces of the Congressional panel. Few were following what he was saying. While he was making salient points, he realizes he needs to state it in a way that most people will comprehend.

"In regenerative medicine, or therapeutic human cloning, the goal is to cure disease in people through stem cell therapy using a patient's own cloned stem cells. This type of procedure isn't as limited as other types of procedures currently available and being practiced," Eastman says.

"Such as the use of stem cells in cord blood banking," Senator Hanson asks.

"Yes. Again, the stem cells we can get from therapeutic cloning are much better for fighting against many types of disease because of the compatibility factor to the person we are giving them to. Through therapeutic cloning research, we are also able to do gene therapy, something that can have a tremendous effect on eradicating diseases that we are currently unable to cure."

"Basically less risk and more therapeutic potential," Senator Reed says.

"Absolutely," Eastman replies.

"Okay, good. However, we're back to the same question. Is this ethical, is it moral, or is it wrong, Dr. Eastman?" Senator Reed asks.

Eastman states firmly, "I think it's unethical, and if I may add, it's morally wrong *not* to pursue scientific knowledge that can cure disease and ultimately ensure the survival of the human race." Eastman paused, sips his water and then adds, "We fear that which we do not understand. Throughout time, we have feared a loss of control over that which is human. Maybe because we have never been able to scientifically, politically, or even religiously define what exactly it means to be human. There's an element of the unknown, a soul, something that can't be measured or seen, but we somehow know exists. Man has feared technology since the advent of machines. Things that possessed human attributes were considered to be demonic. Throughout history, we have both embraced and denounced machines and feared that they might one day replace us. We feared the scientific technology of test tube babies and denounced this procedure until it was understood that the use of this technology is a way for people experiencing infertility to have a family. The fear that is with us in this room today is the fear that clones might replace people. But the point that is missed here is the fact that the purpose of therapeutic cloning is not to grow human beings, but in fact, to save the lives of people that already exist."

Gerald Brown, sitting on Eastman's right side, clears his throat and taps Eastman on the arm. "If you don't mind, I'd like to answer this question as an ethicist."

"Senator Levine, Chairperson, may Dr. Brown address the committee?" Eastman awkwardly inquires.

"Of course. We'd all like to hear from Dr. Brown," Levine replies.

Addressing the committee Brown says, "Therapeutic cloning involves using embryos that have not implanted in the uterus. There's no way for them to grow or to develop beyond a certain stage. They haven't yet committed to becoming a human being. ethicists such as myself, who study embryology, are very comfortable with the idea of pre therefore, -implanted embryos being discarded in the same way that sperm is if a pregnancy is not the ultimate desire."

"We don't even know if any of this is safe. There are so many things that could go wrong. So many avenues left open for discussion. Where is the assurance?" Senator Hanson inquires.

"There are no absolutes," Eastman responds. "None of us at the LAB deal in absolutes. The assurances are that given support, oversight, and understanding, we can achieve the very best outcome possible. Please don't close down an avenue of research that might be of value in the future treatment of human disease. Time, science, and medical practice will be the ultimate proofs of whether these strategies are going to benefit mankind."

Kathryn MacMurray jumped in, quickly introducing herself and stating, "I don't think you all understand what an amazing breakthrough this is. I mean, the idea that you can take a person of any age, take their skin cell, and give them back their own cells—ones that are now young! If this research is allowed to proceed, by the time we grow old, this will be a routine procedure. A patient can get a skin cell removed at the doctor's office and they'll receive a new organ and be healed. It's not science fiction. This is very real, and we believe very doable. In fact, as many of you know, they are currently doing this in Japan. They have grown the first human liver."

Senator Hanson looks doubtful. "It's my understanding that it's not a properly functioning human liver."

"True. But it's a significant start," Kathryn retorts.

Senator Quinton Matthews (R., UT), who had helped to draft the Matthews-Lovett Bill that would allow for therapeutic cloning and stem cell research—a bill that had died a few years earlier in the Senate—was a well-known right-to-life advocate. He had sat silently listening until now. "At the core of my support for regenerative medical research is my belief that human life requires a mother's womb. Under the Matthews-Lovett Bill, the egg, with the nucleus removed, is never fertilized with sperm, so there is no chance of birth, ever. Furthermore, I do not consider human life to be viable until it attaches to the womb and actually has a chance of survival."

In a booming voice, Senator Dukesbury challenges Matthews' comment. "All human embryos should have a chance to be brought to term." With a sweeping gesture of his arm, he addresses his young, petite, Congressional aide, Carrie Baker, who stands in the back of the room by the main doors. "Bring them on out here, Ms. Baker, so we can all see what children who started from frozen embryos look like. Children many of you contend should not be born."

Right on cue, Baker leads a dozen children ranging in age from six to twelve years old down through the main door of the room down the aisle to stand in front of the dais. Baker lines the children up so they are facing the audience. They are very close to where the Gaynors, Eastman, Gerald, and Kathryn sit. Noah is awake and eating a small pile of goldfish crackers Susan has placed before him on the table. He smiles at a six-year-old girl who is carrying a small teddy bear. She looks very uncomfortable, but she smiles back at Noah. He points to her bear. She walks over and hands the bear to him. Noah gives it a hug and hands it back to the girl. "Thank you," Susan says to the cute pigtailed girl dressed in a lady bug shirt as she walks back to line.

Dukesbury speaks into the microphone, and his voice made Susan jump a little. "Now, take a good look at these beautiful children. They were conceived through IVF or in-vitro fertilization. They were once embryos just like the ones you now want to destroy to create stem cell cultures!"

If this hasn't been shocking enough, to Susan Gaynor's horror, and to the shock of many others in the room, Senator Dukesbury asks a pretty six-year-old girl, "Now, you are happy being a little girl, aren't you, honey?"

Baker, standing next to the girl, nudges her and spoke softly in her ear just after the Senator asks her the question. The little girl answered awkwardly, "Yes, Sir," in a very soft voice.

"What's your name?" Dukesbury asks.

She jumps a little and looks as if she might cry. Susan wonders where the girls' parents are? She looks around and sees that there is no adult coming to her rescue. Susan hands Noah to Elliot, and walks over to the little girl with it.

When the nervous child fails to speak, Baker speaks for her. "Her name is Everly Wade."

Susan places an arm around the little girl who buries her face into Susan's skirt.

"I'm sure little Everly here is happy to be a little girl and not a dead embryo used in some ungodly experiment," Dukesbury says.

Susan and Elliot, as well as many others, recoil at the senator's words.

Senate majority Leader Ely Walker (R., OH) has had enough of Dukesbury's tasteless and thoughtless theatrics. "I think that we are done. Let's all thank these children."

Tentative applause rippled throughout the auditorium. Senator Walker addresses the children. "Thank you very much for coming today. You may exit the stage now."

Susan hugs Everly goodbye and takes her seat.

Carrie Baker looks up at Senator Dukesbury. He nods to her as she leads the children back up the aisle and out the door to the sound of applause.

Theatrics aside, the Senate majority leader Walker states in an impassioned and thunderous voice, "For God's sake we're not talking about what do with embryos. We are talking about whether or not therapeutic, not reproductive, cloning should be permitted as a viable and plausible use of regenerative medicine in this country."

"May I address the panel?" Susan inquires.

"Yes, you may," Senator Levine replies.

"You have the luxury of time to argue, debate, and politicize what many of us believe is our right to medical and technological advancements. We don't have this time. My son, Noah, does not. Nor do millions of people listening to this hearing. I implore you to not stop us from trying to save our son's life or the lives of many whom you love. One of the greatest minds on Earth, Albert Einstein, was once asked what was man's meaning and purpose in life, or why we are here. He replied that he didn't definitively know why. However, he believed that we were here for the sake of others whose countless souls we are connected to by a bond of empathy. I ask you not only to have empathy for our son, Noah, but also to have empathy for all of those whom you love and care for who are suffering with different diseases. Our nation needs this type of medical advancement. We need to be able to pursue the technology so we can help each other."

The audience responds by mostly applauding Susan's comments.

"I and the rest of the committee members would like to thank Mr. and Mrs. Gaynor, Noah, Drs. Eastman, MacMurray, and Brown for joining us here today. This is extended to the rest of the honored guests. I think we can all say that we have learned a lot from this proceeding. With no further ado I will adjourn this meeting," states Senate Majority Leader Walker.

As Eastman, Kathryn, the Gaynors, and the rest of their group walk up the aisle the paparazzi are in full force, and cameras snap in their faces. A reporter shoves a microphone in front of the Gaynors, demanding, "What did you hope to accomplish with today's hearing?"

"Understanding," Elliot thoughtfully replies, and as the reporter is about to ask the next question, Elliot says, "No more questions please." The party keeps moving down the steps. A picketer shouts, "You can't replace your son!" Elliot protectively escorts Susan, who is holding Noah tightly against her chest once again, out the doors and down the steps to the waiting limo. Will flanks them from behind, acutely aware of the need for their safety at all times along with the rest of the bodyguards and LAB members.

Standing in the crowd just across the sidewalk, and directly across from their limo, is a man in a gray zipped-up hoodie. He is also wearing a black wool beanie pulled down tight over his head. He has his hands deep in his front pockets. He briefly stares at the Gaynors and Dr. Eastman. Then he puts his head down, turns and walks away. He didn't need to see any more. He knew they aren't going to stop. It is now up to him to stop them. Sadly, Joe Smith realizes that some people would have to die.

Westchester, New York
Next Day

Kathryn had just returned from walking Doogie when she sees Eastman standing on her front porch balancing a large pizza box and a six-pack of Sam Adams.

"Hey, James, sorry we're late. Doogie decided he wants to take me for a longer than usual walk tonight," Kathryn says as she hurries to unlock and open the door.

"No worries. I was just concerned that something might've happened."

"Really, you need to stop doing that. I'm fine. I have my trusty companion here, and I've lived on my own for many years now."

"Yeah, but this is the first time we've had some nut threatening us and our work."

"The nut threatened you. Not me. I understand your concern," Kathryn gently says as they move inside the house toward the coffee table.

"Is it okay if I set it down here?" Eastman asks.

"Absolutely, but I warn you. Doogie will make a bee line for that pizza box once I unleash him," Kathryn says, unleashing Doogie and setting the leash by the door. Once free, Doogie trots over to the pizza box and sniffs it with his nose.

"Can I give him a piece?"

"Not unless you want to clean up what will happen later - it ain't gonna be pretty."

"I'll pass."

"Doogie, that's not for you. Come with me," she instructs the dog and he follows her into the kitchen.

"I'm going to feed the Doogie dog food. Make yourself at home."

As she feeds the dog, Eastman takes a seat on the sofa and pops the top off a Sam Adams.

"Come on Kathryn, pizza's getting cold."

"I'm done," Kathryn says entering the living room.

She takes a seat next to Eastman on the sofa and he hands her a slice of double cheese with pepperoni.

"Hmmm this looks good!"

Eastman is tired from the trip back from D.C. last night. He expects that Kathryn is too. He's glad to be spending the evening together before he has to leave for Boston tomorrow.

"Mmm, my favorite. Thank you."

As she chews a big bite of pizza, Eastman takes a pull on his beer.

I have something I want to tell you."

"Oh?" Kathryn manages around a mouth full of cheese and dough.

"I'm placing you in charge of the LAB when Alan and I leave for the conference tomorrow. I need you to get everything in place for the harvesting of the cells."

"No problem. I was kind of expecting to be," Kathryn replies as she picks up a bottle of beer Eastman's opened for her.

Eastman glances at her with a mixture of appreciation and longing.

"I wish you could go with us. However, I need you to be here keeping a close eye on our project."

"I will. I'll be fine, James. Please don't worry."

Eastman leans in and kisses her before she had a chance to sip her beer. "I'm going to miss you. Anything you want me to bring you back from Boston?"

"Like what? A cream pie?" Kathryn jokingly asks.

"Your wish is my command," he replies with a smile.

"Ha, ha. Actually, if you do make it over to Faneuil Hall I'd love one of their brownies."

"Actually, we are speaking there."

"I thought the event was at the Hyatt Hotel?"

"It is, but Anderson and I have been assigned to speak at the Hall."

"That's different."

"I think it has to do with getting the attendees to patronize the place. You know - they make deals with tourism boards when setting up conferences."

"Is anyone else speaking there?"

"I believe so. Now any special kind of brownie you desire?"

"I like them all. Surprise me."

"As you wish."

"Well, then, there is something else I wish, but it's before you go," Kathryn says and kisses him playfully on the lips.

Boston, Massachusetts

The Hyatt is quite nice but Faneuil Hall is one of Eastman's favorite places to visit in Boston. The Stem Cell Research Conference has arranged for a special tour of the Hall for the conference attendees. Eastman reads this in the packet of information given to him at check in. Unfortunately, Eastman wouldn't be able to go on the tour because it was to be held just before he and Anderson are to give their talk. In any event, he knows he'll be downstairs getting one of the infamous brownies in the Quincy Marketplace food court to take home to Kathryn just prior to his talk.

Eastman and Anderson board the elevator from the lobby after checking into both the hotel and conference. The elevator is crowded, filled with other conference attendees wearing badges. A man dressed in jeans and cowboy boots squeezes in next to the two. For a brief second Eastman thinks he might know him. But just as quickly as the thought comes, Eastman dismisses it.

"Eleventh floor," Anderson says to an older gentleman who is kindly pressing the floor buttons for all who have boarded.

"Let's run through our slides again once we get settled." Anderson looks at his watch. "We have some time."

"Sounds like a plan," Eastman replies, running his thumb over the smooth edge of the plastic room key.

"We could go down to the restaurant or we could order room service after we're done."

"Either's good for me. Perhaps getting a bite out might be good. They're lots of good places in the area."

"I'd like to check out the conference room at Faneuil Hall to get a feel for it," Anderson says.

"Maybe we can get in there tomorrow while everyone is touring," Eastman replies.

"That reminds me. Would you mind coming back to the hotel after we speak, grabbing my bag, and checking out?"

"Sure, why? You're not planning on coming back to the hotel?"

"I'm hoping to meet briefly with Dr. Takabe after our presentation. I'll be cutting it close and will meet you at the airport."

"Sure. Have you arranged a meeting?"

"Not yet. I'm going to leave him a message at the front desk."

"So you're hopeful."

"Oh yeah."

"Well, if it works out you can fill me in on the plane ride home."

"I'll have nothing better to do," Eastman offers with a smile. The elevator doors open and the two, along with the man wearing the cowboy boots and a young woman pulling a dark blue suitcase half her size, step into the hall. Eastman notices the man following them to their room. As he slides the plastic hotel key into the door, he turns to see the man moving down the hall just as Anderson pushes the door open for Eastman.

"Know that guy?"

"I thought I might."

Boston, Massachusetts
Late Afternoon, Next Day

Eastman attends one of the last afternoon conferences at the Hyatt Hotel. There is only one other presentation scheduled at Faneuil Hall besides his and Andersons. It's Dr. Takabe's. It was to be held just before his in a separate conference room. Eastman is hoping to catch some of it before he and Anderson began theirs.

While Eastman settles into the seat of one of the Hyatt's luxurious conference rooms, waiting for the guest speaker to present, he falls deep into thought. He thinks it's clever how the offsite venue of the hall was purposely done by the conference in conjunction with Boston Tourism. It's one way to get the attendees to visit the hall, Eastman smiles. He'd have to take a page out their book and come up with some creative ways to raise capital. A tour of the LAB? He thinks and smiles. I wonder how much we could charge? Well that wasn't going to happen now. The last thing he or anyone wanted was a parade of people through there with Noah's clone under guard.

He thinks about how unfortunate it is that Dr. Takabe is presenting at Faneuil Hall just before he and Anderson are to give their presentation. It probably won't be possible to set up for their presentation and listen to Takabes too. Dr. Takabe and his team had come from Japan and were well on their way to growing a human liver, something that had never been done before. The tissue was underdeveloped and lacked bile ducts. The hepatocytes didn't form neat plates, not like in a real liver. However, the tissue did have blood vessels that proved functional when it was transplanted under the skin of a mouse. Genetic tests showed that the tissue expressed many of the genes that are expressed in a real liver. They also noted that when the tissue was transferred to the mouse, the liver was able to metabolize some drugs that human livers metabolize but mouse livers cannot. Basically, Dr. Takabe's team claimed that their work was "the first report demonstrating the creation of a human functional organ with vascular networks from pluripotent stem cells—resulting only after hundreds of trials." Eastman assumes that this had cost big, big bucks. It was Japan, though, not the United States, helping to foot the bill. It seems that Japan didn't have the same religious and political hindrances against therapeutic cloning as the United States. If anything, scientists like Takebe were revered and their work was financially supported by the government. Researchers were also working on printing organs with 3D printers both in Japan and in the U.S. This would one day be a profitable business, if not ultimately a much needed one. It was an exciting time in both science and medicine.

Eastman reminds himself to leave a message for Dr. Takabe with the concierge asking him if he had a few minutes to meet after he and Anderson finished with their portion of the conference. After all it was the very last conference of the night. Maybe they could grab a quick beer or some Sake. He wasn't sure what Takabe drank. Just then, Eastman's thoughts were abruptly interrupted. "Good afternoon, I'm Dr. Charles Weir."

Faneuil Hall
Early Evening

Built in 1742, Faneuil Hall had served all of these years as a marketplace and meeting hall. The ground floor contains shops and eating establishments. The second floor was known as the Great Hall. Historic speeches were made here. The upper floors contained a museum and armory of the Ancient and Honorable Artillery Company of Massachusetts. It also included three long granite buildings called North Market, South Market, and Quincy Market. It operated as an indoor/outdoor mall and food court. The food court was impressive as it contained many different types of foods and was located under the impressive old dome in the center of the structure. This was where Eastman is headed to get the brownies he is craving. A sparkling glimpse of metal caught his eye on the top of the building. Eastman saw the gilded grasshopper weathervane. The grasshopper has been there for more than two centuries, and for some reason it never ceases to make him smile. Getting out of the cab, Eastman says to Anderson, "I'll meet you in the conference room after I run a little errand in the food court."

Anderson's brow arches, "The food court?"

"Yeah, I am going to get one of their world-renowned brownies. Would you like one?"

"Chocolate with walnuts. Thanks!" Anderson says carrying their laptops and briefcases as he hurries into the building with Eastman close behind.

The place was crowded and warm. Eastman can smell the brownies and other edibles. His mouth begins to water. As he weaves in and out of the crowd of people carrying purses, briefcases, and packages he knows he will order the chocolate fudge brownie with walnuts for himself too. However, he doesn't have a clue as to what Kathryn might like.

Eastman is next in line. "Half a dozen of the fudge brownies with walnuts," he tells the clerk. After signing the receipt and tucking his card back into his wallet, he grabs his brownie package and hurries up the escalator to the second floor, hoping Kathryn likes walnuts. There were a million little things he didn't know about her but hopefully there would be time to discover them. The escalator is crowded, but most of the people didn't get off with him on the second floor. They headed on up to the third floor where there were more exciting things, like a museum.

Westchester, New York

Kathryn is working late at the LAB. She feels compelled to get a leg up on the preparation that's needed to be complete before the stem cell harvest. She wonders how many live stem cells they would have to use for research. She has harvested fetal stem cells before. They had been leftover, frozen embryos from IVF (in vitro fertilization) procedures that had been donated for medical and scientific purposes where she had worked prior to joining the team at the LAB. She and Eastman share many views about their work, but viewing embryos as human life wasn't one of them. Still, she respects Eastman and the LAB's decision not to use them. This was the first time that she would be harvesting stem cells from a live cloned human blastocyst. She is running on adrenalin and feels mildly anxious.

As exciting as this procedure is, its historic significance is an oppressive responsibility. Kathryn feels the weight of the world on her shoulders. She needs to successfully execute the procedure. She is also acutely aware of how the success of this procedure will ultimately open the door to an entire new era of medicine. There will be both blessings and curses in this new era. She has thought about this many times. However, today she needs to focus on the task at hand and her focus needs to be laser sharp.

This is the first viable human clone in the world, as far as she and anyone else knows' for certain. It was like handling a rare jewel. Excitement shot through her body at the thought. Other scientists had claimed to have gotten this far with therapeutic cloning. Others even claimed to have succeeded at reproductive cloning—stating they had created the world's first cloned human being. None of it was true, though. At least, it couldn't be scientifically proven. She and the LAB were the first. She hopes everything with the harvest goes well. She'll see to it. She touches her locket that hangs around her neck for good luck and lets her mind wander over the miraculous feat she is about to undertake with the team.

Harvesting the stems cells was only the first step.

Faneuil Hall
Evening

With their presentation complete, having finally finished greeting the audience members who approach them afterwards, Anderson is powering off the laptop when he steals a glance at his watch. "Hey, James, it's getting late and we have a plane to catch."

Just as Eastman is about to reply, his cell phone signals a text message. He didn't recognize the number. It read, *Dr. Eastman, I'd like to meet with you in your conference room in 20 minutes - Takabe.*

Eastman is excited. He got the meeting he had hoped for before leaving Boston. There were a few very important considerations he wanted to discuss regarding the next phase of the stem cell harvesting procedure.

"Alan, I just got a text from Dr. Takabe. He said he will make it work to meet here."

"Now?"

"Yeah. Are you still willing to check out of the hotel and meet me at the airport?"

"Sure. No problem. But will you make the flight?" he inquires, placing the laptop in his briefcase and glancing at his watch.

Eastman thought for a moment. If Takebe didn't show for another 20 minutes, this would severely cut into the time he'd have to make the flight. Obviously they wouldn't be going for drinks.

Alan looks up to see the frown lines burrowed deep into Eastman's forehead as he was thinking.

"Don't miss the plane. We've got a big day tomorrow," Anderson reminds.

"I'm not planning on it. But if I do, I'll be on the one right behind you."

"Then you'll owe me the extra bag fee," Anderson warns.

Although he said it in jest, everyone who knew Anderson knew he was tight with his money.

"I won't forget, and hey, I can always pay you in brownies," Eastman teases as he waves the bag.

"I suggest you give me one now. You know, I'll need the extra energy having to lug your bag around!"

Eastman tosses him a brownie. "Either way, I'll text you and let you know which flight I'm on."

Anderson nods as he has mouth full of brownie while leaving the conference room carrying his laptop and brief case.

Arlington, Virginia
Same Night

Will Rubin is moving quickly. He left Eastman a voice message on Eastman's cell letting him know that they are moving from the Key Bridge Marriott to the Four Seasons Hotel, and they would meet him at the LAB for the stem cell procedure with Noah's clone. The Gaynors had been spotted by paparazzi in the hotel lobby. There had been a small scene. Well, not so small, but Rubin had swiftly and quietly intervened moving the boy and his parents away from the paparazzi.

The unwanted attention caused people in the hotel lobby to speculate who the parents and little boy are.

Fortunately for the Gaynors and Rubin, the hotel guests had them pegged as a celebrity couple they couldn't quite name. A young woman in the lobby carrying a backpack and dressed in faded jeans with her brown hair swept back in a ponytail, approached Susan and asks her who she was. Susan replies icily, "No one." The young woman looks stung and huffs off in the direction of the front desk. Elliot protectively places his arm around Susan and pulls her and Noah, who was cradled in Susan's arms, close and moves toward the front doors. Rubin is on his cell phone securing transportation. He tells the Gaynors that he has checked out and that they would spend the night at the Four Seasons and then fly to New York to meet with Eastman prior to departing JFK. He makes certain that no one else was within earshot when he fills them in on their new itinerary. The Gaynors and Rubin pile into the private car with tinted windows as the driver places their luggage into the trunk. Elliot carefully secures Noah into his car seat. As they pull away Elliot notices a couple more guys with cameras getting out of a car in front of the hotel. He hopes that they haven't seen them.

Rubin leans back into the front seat next to the driver allowing him to relax a bit and says, "We got out of there just in time."

"That was too close, Will. Can we be certain this won't happen again?" Elliot inquired from the back seat where he, Susan and Noah sit.

"No."

Susan shoots a concerned glance at Elliot as a sleeping Noah lay in her lap. It always amazed Susan how babies and toddlers could fall asleep almost anywhere. Maybe it was a coping mechanism? It was one she wishes she had.

"How much longer before we arrive at the Hilton?" Rubin asks the cab driver?

"About ten minutes," the cabby says with an Indian accent.

"But I thought we were," Elliot never got to finish his question as Rubin raises a finger to his lips signaling Elliot to be quiet.

The part of the plan that Rubin hadn't filled them in on was a series of boarding private cars at a couple of different hotels just in case they are being tailed. He also didn't want the cab driver to know where they were staying."

"Can you step on it?" Rubin asks the cabby as he pressed a hundred dollar bill into the cabbie's right hand.

The cabby looks at the bill and then speeds up. He skillfully weaves in and out of traffic. Susan braces herself for a wild ride, or possibly two, and places a protective hand on Noah's car seat. Elliot looks out the back window to see if he can tell if anyone is following them. He sees a greenish gray Pontiac G6 following them into the other lane, but the car doesn't appear to be keeping pace with them. Elliot just hopes that his family will soon be safely tucked into their room at the hotel - whichever one that was now going to be?

Boston, Massachusetts
Same Night

Eastman awakes to the faces of a fireman, two police officers, and a paramedic. Confused, frightened, and angry, he wonders how badly he's hurt. "What the hell?"

"Stay down," the paramedic warns.

"Do you remember what happened to you?" the older officer with a gray mustache asks him.

"Yeah, I presented at a conference here tonight," Eastman replies.

"How long ago was that?"

"Um, I'm not sure. I was meeting someone after."

"Who were you meeting?"

"Dr. Takabe."

"Where is Dr. Takabe?"

"He never showed. It was Joseph. Joseph appeared from inside the bookcase." The cops exchange doubtful glances.

"I'll check it out, Jim," The younger cop says to the older one.

"You just lay back down. It looks like you had quite a blow to the head. Do you know who did it?" the older cop named Jim asks Eastman.

"Joseph hit me," Eastman replies, easing back down to the floor.

"Okay, okay, now who is this Joseph character?"

"He's a guy who wants me to stop the work I'm doing."

Shining a light into his eyes, the paramedic remarks, "possible concussion."

As the paramedics were transporting Eastman out of the conference room on a stretcher, the younger cop approaches the older one. "See anything?" Jim asks.

"No. The bookcase is tightly anchored to the wall."

"That was some knock on the head the guy got. If it was me I'd be seeing things too."

"Are we going to follow up with him at the hospital?" the younger cop inquires.

"Yeah. Something happened in here and hopefully, he will be making more sense once the docs start working on him."

As the paramedic team roll Eastman into an elevator and take him down to the ground level where an ambulance is waiting, the paramedic replies, "A janitor heard moaning from inside here. He was the one to first discover you. Then he alerted security."

"Please thank him for me."

Eastman feels the bump up into the ambulance. His whole body is sore. It feels as if he were skiing over a big mogul. Eastman started to think about the last time he had skied. *Where had it been? Breckenridge, Colorado? It didn't matter. He was just gliding over the snow and why were people yelling at him?*

"Dr. Eastman, I need you to keep talking to me. Is there anyone we should notify?" the paramedic attending him asks. Then someone says something to the paramedic.

Eastman thinks of Anderson. Shit. He is going to miss his flight. He told Anderson he'd text him.

"Yes. My colleague Dr. Anderson. I'm supposed to catch a flight with him - or was."

"Do you have his contact info?"

"Not on me - well yes, in my cell phone."

"Eastman reaches around to find his phone."

"You just lie still, we can take care of this when we arrive at the hospital," the paramedic tells him.

"The police are going to meet us at the hospital. They will want a statement," says the other paramedic as the doors to the ambulance close.

Eastman weakly raises his head to tell them to contact Alan right away, that he may be in danger, and then vomits all over himself.

The paramedic assists in cleaning him up and helping him not to choke or aspirate on his own fluids.

The ambulance pulls out into the street and heads towards the hospital as Eastman slips back into unconsciousness.

Boston, Massachusetts
One hour earlier

Sitting on board the plane in the Logan International Airport, Anderson wonders, *Where the hell is James?* Anderson reminds himself that Eastman had said that he'd catch the next flight home if he missed this one. But he was going to text him and tell him that. Anderson decided to send him a quick text before he turns off his phone. However, Eastman must've had the same idea as one from him appeared almost simultaneously. *Missed flight. Will be on next. Moving meeting time at LAB tomorrow morning to 7 a.m.*

This didn't make sense. Eastman would be taking a later flight home and moved up the meeting time by three hours? Confused, Anderson texted back: I *guess you plan on sleeping on plane? Don't understand the change in time but will see you at 7 a.m. I'll bring your suitcase to the LAB. You owe me.*

Westchester, New York
Late Same Night

Unfortunately for Dr. MacMurray, she had left her voicemail on voice-activated when leaving her phone to go to the ladies room. She often left the voice-activation mode on when working if she was busy using her hands and needed to reply to a text by speaking. Fortunately, there was only one other person working in the section of the LAB where she is tonight. Savannah is a young intern, fresh out of Stanford's graduate school, and she is assisting Dr. MacMurray with some final preparations that need to be completed before tomorrow morning.

The voice seems to come out of nowhere. It sounds like the Siri voice on her iPhone. Savannah jumps a little when she hears it. *Message from James. Moving meeting from 10 a.m. to 7 a.m. be on time.*

James? That was Dr. Eastman. Crap. Now they'd all have to be there three hours earlier. She isn't going to get much sleep if any and she certainly wasn't going to get it with her boyfriend. She'll also need to inform Dr. MacMurray when she returns. It was going to be awkward telling her that she had listened to her text message. But hey, Dr. MacMurray is the one who left it on voice activate, Savannah thinks.

Faneuil Hall
Two Hours Earlier

Joe Smith had been gone before the janitor could catch a glimpse of him. He had heard the guy coming but had already planned his escape accordingly.

He left Eastman's crumpled body lying on the floor, careful to note that he was still breathing, and walked quickly over to the bookcase. He slid in behind it and pulled hard on the heavy thing, getting it to close behind him.

A secret passage behind a bookcase is almost a cliché, he thinks, as he slides sideways back through the open passage and pulls the heavy bookcase door closed. He has made his exit just in time, as he can hear muffled voices in the room. He allows himself to listen for a minute. He doesn't want to chance being discovered. However, he doesn't expect anyone to know about the passageway. But you never knew. If the janitor has worked there a while and knows about the history of the building, he just might relay this info to the cops. But he doubted it.

Smith was pleased as punch about how things have worked out, he smiles as he begins descending the narrow, musty, stone steps. He hadn't been certain how he might get Eastman alone. He saw an opportunity when he overheard him leaving a message for Dr. Takabe with the concierge. It paid to follow Eastman around the hotel. Sending Eastman a text message pretending to be Dr. Takabe and asking him to meet was easy. He worded the message carefully just in case Takabe had gotten a hold of him too. He wanted him to think he would make it work out to meet him after all even if Takabe had declined in the first place. The rest of the plan had fallen into place. Thank you, smartphone! Smith could research almost anything from this little device. It was easier tracking Eastman than it was a deer.

The hidden passageway inside the conference room Smith discovered sounded too good to be true. The Lord worked in mysterious ways. He didn't question, just accepted his good fortune. Of course, God helped those who helped themselves. According to the info he found on the Internet, the secret passage was to have been built so that people who needed protecting could be removed privately and quickly. He imagined that many political figures, as well as high-ranking military personnel of long ago, would've been in need of a quick escape when discussions at the hall went wrong.

Smith had checked it out earlier in the day before the conference was to be held there. He had looked around the room, taking inventory. He had a vague idea of where the passage might be located. It was then he noticed a life-size, gold-framed sketch of Abraham Lincoln that hung on the wall next to the staircase that took visitors to the mezzanine. This was the sketch he had read about. He removed the sketch. It was awkwardly tall and heavy. Smith gently leaned it against the same wall, two feet to the left from where it hung. He ran his hands over the cold, smooth wall. Nothing. No seams, no passage. Disappointment settled into his heart. Not willing to give up he moved his hand to the right of the where the painting hung and followed them up to the bookcase next to it. It was then that he felt the seams of the bookcase. He could feel a small draft was coming through the seam? Could the bookcase be the passage? It almost seems cliché' he thinks. Smith attempts to pull the bookcase away from the wall but it doesn't budge. He had expected to find the passageway behind the sketch of Lincoln as he had researched. I guess they were a little off in their estimate? Maybe it had been sealed for good? Smith had been thinking up plan B, tracing his fingers down the seam when he feels a stronger draft coming from the lower left corner of one of the bottom of the bookcase. He jams his hunting knife into the place where he feels the stronger draft. The knife goes in clean and smooth. He moves the knife up and then thrusts it down, creating a small opening. Smith closes his knife and sticks it back into the front pocket of his jeans. He grabs tightly onto the corner of bookcase/door and pulls hard. It opens! Only a couple of inches, but it is enough for Smith to see that he has discovered the secret passage.

Unfortunately, there hadn't been time to walk all the way through the passageway early to check it out. It was reported to exit into the basement. He had to believe that this was the case. It would be a good place to hide and surprise Eastman. All of these thoughts replayed through Smith's head as he climbs inside the bookcase.

With the meeting completed with Eastman, Smith now would make his escape through it too, he thinks as he tucks Eastman's wallet with identification, cell phone, and a small plastic white card into his jacket pocket. Anyone discovering Eastman wouldn't know who he was. This would give Smith more time. He doubted that Eastman would be coming to anytime soon. He had given him quite the hit on the head with the gun handle. It had felt good to hurt the son of a bitch. Smith smiles at the thought.

As he quickly descends deeper down the staircase into the bowels of the historic building, he is careful to walk stooped over so he won't smack his head on the stone ceiling. People back then were a lot shorter. He almost coughs from the stale air, but suppresses it for fear he might be heard. A sense of claustrophobia overcomes him. He fights to focus on his escape. A cobweb strokes his face and he recoils, recalling snakes in trees in the jungle. The memory makes him break out into a cold sweat. He was having a flashback. He works hard to control his mind and his fears. *There are no snakes in here*, he tells himself. There might be spiders though. He doesn't much care for them either. However, they didn't make his flesh crawl like snakes did during his time in the military. He had been assigned to Panama. One place he'll never return. He hurries, and on the final turn he can hear the noise of what sounds like a heavy furnace. He also sees a dim flicker of light. As he descends the last five steps, he soon smacks into a solid wooden door that abruptly stands in front of the last step down. The light from the basement is shining through a thin crack in the door. Smith prays the door at the bottom of the stairs isn't locked. This is something he didn't have time to check earlier. He pulls down on the heavy metal handle. It moves, unwillingly, but all the same, it moves. It also squeaks. However, when he pushes against the door it doesn't budge.

"Shit," Smith angrily swears.

He pushes harder with his shoulder leaning his full body weight into the effort. He doesn't want to make noise and draw attention to himself if there is a maintenance worker in the basement. He has no choice but to hit it as hard as he can. He gives it one full shoulder slam, and he feels it budge. Something on the other side makes a crashing sound.

"Damn it!"

No time to worry if someone else is down here with him or if anyone has heard. He shoves himself into the door. It opens and he hurries through the open door. Unfortunately, he trips over boxes and falls onto a pile of crates that had been stacked against the door. He scrambles to his feet. "Damn it!" he says as he realizes that he is making a lot of noise. He stands still, quietly listening to see if he's been discovered. He thinks about what his next move might be. A few seconds pass. Smith doesn't' hear anyone coming. He is safe for now. No one else is down here with him. *God's shielding me.*

He looks around the basement. It's vast and filled with boxes belonging too many of the different proprietors of the Faneuil Hall shops. There are old pipes and cobwebs running in different directions above the ceiling. The floor is worn and has patchy concrete from many years of wear. Although he didn't come in this way, Smith's research had shown that there is a delivery elevator and ladder that could be accessed above ground on the sidewalk nearest the street. He also knows that it will be located next to the old boiler and coal shoot. He moves in the general direction of where he thinks it might be. He is aware of time and is feeling mildly panicky when he finally sees the old coal shoot.

Next to it is a ladder leading up to the ancient cellar door. He thinks they would have come up with a more modern delivery method. Maybe there was another one. He wasn't sure. However, he'd take this one. As he climbs the ladder, he hopes that he can open the old cellar door that will lead to the sidewalk. He sends up a silent prayer.

God was with him. It was open. *They must have been expecting a delivery, or just had one*, Smith thinks as he hurries onto the street. The air was crisp. He inhaled deeply. The fresh air felt good in his lungs and helps him to focus.

Since he had already gotten rid of his own cellphone, in case he was caught, he made the first call from Eastman's phone as he is walking away from Faneuil Hall. He prays that time was on his side. He needs to orchestrate this just right so he can successfully complete God's mission.

"I didn't recognize the number. You're damn lucky I answered," Smith's friend says.

"Do you have the package?" Smith inquires.

"Yeah. Meet me outside the Starbucks located one block north of the LAB on Broadway."

"I'll text you from this phone when I'm 30 minutes away."

"Sounds good."

Smith hails a Yellow Cab and quickly folds himself into the back seat after it comes to a stop at the curb. "The train station."

"Cold as a witch's tit out tonight."

"I didn't notice," Smith replies coolly. "There's a hundred bucks in it for you if you get me there faster."

"You got it."

As the cab speeds through the dark streets, Smith anticipates that he'll arrive in time to board the next train to New York City. According to his smartphone, Amtrak's Acela Express would take approximately five and a half hours to get to Westchester. He liked the trains. They went fast, were mostly on time, and unlike airplanes, there was no real security he had to pass through. He could also purchase a ticket with cash and remain anonymous.

Soon they pull up in front of the station. Smith pays the fare in cash and tips the cabby one hundred dollars, as promised.

It wasn't long before he is comfortably on board hunkered down next to a window seat. There is nothing to see—just dark, as they zip past the countryside. Smith looks through Eastman's phone. He had sent the first text message to Dr. Anderson as he doesn't want him to get suspicious. He sent a similar text message to everyone who had received Eastman's earlier text telling them to meet at ten a.m. Eastman had sent it out as a group message. Smith texts- as Eastman, *Moving meeting from 10 a.m. to 7 a.m. be on time.* He couldn't believe his good luck. He carefully read through Eastman's text messages. There were only two. One to someone telling them he'd be bringing them a surprise. Well, this person would get a surprise all right if she/he worked for the LAB; Smith considers and gives a little chuckle. The other was one sent, actually from Eastman's cell to Dr. Takabe informing him that he was looking forward to the meeting. Well, how nice, Smith thought again, and smiles. He saw that there were a few voicemail messages for him as well. He attempted to retrieve the voicemail messages but discovered that they were password protected. Damn! How he wishes he could access these as well. He got up from his seat and went inside the bathroom. He had to pee. Afterwards he pulls the Sim card and battery from the phone and tossed them into the bathroom trash, burying them deep under a pile of damp paper towels. He wants to get rid of the phone before Eastman discovers it is missing and calls the police.

As he washes his hands and face, Smith hopes that he has hurt Eastman just badly enough to keep him in Boston for a while, but not badly enough to kill him. Smith's mission is to seek out and to destroy the clone along with as many of the scientists who are a part of this abomination as possible. The only one he didn't want to destroy right away is Eastman. He wants Eastman to experience the loss and to be held accountable before the world as an example of what will happen if anyone is to ever pursue this evil doing again.

As he exits the bathroom, Smith wonders how long it will be before Eastman will be able to contact any of them. He hopes the knock on the head with the butt of his gun would put Eastman out long enough for him to do his job. It is now after ten p.m. He figures he will have just enough time to get back to New York, meet his friend at Starbucks to pick up the package and take the bomb to the LAB. His plan was tight, but did leave room for error.

As he takes his seat, he pulls the coveted item out of his pocket and looks carefully. "Damn good luck," he says to himself as he gazes on the white plastic card with Eastman's picture on it. It is a key card, most likely to the LAB, as it had no other identifying marks on it. This was gold. Another tight smile appears on his lips as he sucks in air and whistled through his teeth. The key probably gives access to all areas of the LAB, including the place the clone is kept. Eastman will have that kind of clearance. Getting in shouldn't be too difficult. He looks out the window into the darkness that streams past him. Smith is too keyed up to rest. However, he thinks he should force himself to do so. He still has a lot of work ahead of him. He also doesn't want to draw any attention to himself by having to engage in conversation with another passenger. It's better to look as if he is asleep and soon he was.

New York, New York
Same Night

The Jet Blue #3814 flight to John F. Kennedy Airport has been uneventful, except for the fact that Eastman isn't onboard and the fact that Anderson's anxiety is mounting. None of it adds up. It feels wrong. Why didn't James answer either of the two text messages he had sent him after departing the plane? The logical answer would be that he was in the air and his phone was on airplane mode. But why in the hell choose to move the meeting up three hours? They are both tired from the conference and needed to be alert and well-rested before they began the stem cell procedure. Perhaps there is something going on with the blastocyst? Kathryn will have the answer, Anderson thinks as he is waiting for his and Eastman's bags from the carousel. He will give her a quick call and get some answers before leaving the airport.

Boston, Massachusetts
Same Night

Eastman floats in and out of consciousness at Massachusetts General Hospital. At some point he remembers being taken for a CT scan. The attending ER physician informs him that he has a concussion and leaves. Eastman recalls asking the ER Nurse for his cell phone earlier, and the nurse telling him that she'll look for it. That is the last thing he recalls before he goes out again. He is now conscious and fully aware of his surroundings. Eastman has no idea how long he's been out. He sees the IV taped to the top of his left hand and the oxygen clip on his right index finger. Despite the tubes and needles, he tries to sit up in the bed. A thunderous explosion of pain in his head overtakes him and he carefully lies back down. A wave of nausea rolls over his stomach and up into his throat. He is able to swallow it down. Within seconds, a nurse is by his side. He wonders if he is being given anything for the pain.

"You need to stay down and take it easy. You had quite a blow to your head," she explains as she gently but firmly eases him back down into the bed.

"I need my cell phone," Eastman tells her. "It's urgent that I contact my colleagues and tell them where I am."

"The nurse on duty before me told me that she looked for your phone, and it is not with your belongings. She doesn't believe you had it on you when you were brought in," she informs him with all the authority of the chief of medicine. "The doctor will be in to speak with you shortly."

Eastman realizes that he has either lost his cell phone on the way to the hospital or, worse, Joseph has it. "Can you please get the bag with my personal items in it? I need to see them right away."

The nurse dutifully extracted a bag of items from the cupboard and gently empties the contents of the bag onto the table at the end of the bed. She carefully holds up the objects so he can see them without having to sit up. It is an effort to focus on his belongings. He feels disoriented. Eastman sees his wallet, a tube of Carmex, and the hotel key card. Wait. Where was the key card to the LAB?

"Is there a plastic key card with my things?"

"There's one for the Hyatt."

"No. This would be white with a photo of me on it."

"I'm sorry. It isn't here."

The sudden realization that the key card is missing, the very real likelihood that Joseph has it jolts Eastman into coherency and then into action.

"What time is it?" Eastman demands feeling a ripple of fear reverberate through his body.

"It's six thirty."

"Not at night?"

"No, in the morning," the nurse replies,

"I need to make a call."

"If you need to use the phone, there's one by the table. Just push nine first. Actually, I can help you call out," she says moving the phone closer to him.

"Thanks," Eastman replies.

The problem was that he didn't have anyone's number. Trying to remember everyone's numbers made his head hurt worse. He's relieved when he remembers the main number for the LAB. The guard at the desk will have Kathryn's and Anderson's numbers. Damn smart phones. It is too easy to just enter numbers and forget about them. Thank God he can recall the LAB's number and punches it into the phone. *This will save a little time.*

The guard picks up on the second ring. He motions to the nurse for a pen and paper.

Westchester, New York
Early Morning

It is a hazy morning as Smith's tires crunched against the gravel as he pulls his truck to a stop outside the Starbucks on Broadway. He looks at his watch. It's 6:30 a.m. on the dot. He can see through the windows that Starbucks is open and already has several customers inside. He turns off the engine, checks the clock on the dashboard, and lets his thoughts wander as he waits. The train ride went smoothly as did picking up his truck from where he had left it parked near the train station. Now he is free to focus on the final part of his plan. He thinks about how he will soon be killing Eastman *after* he endures the pain of losing his precious lab, clone, and colleagues. Smith has also thought of including the Gaynors in his plan. He wonders if they are still on the East Coast. This plan would have to wait for another time. He doesn't want to take a chance on hurting the boy. However, he does want to take him away from those monsters that are his parents. What kind of parent clones their own child, their flesh and blood? He feels the boy would be better off with new parents. Maybe he can be the boy's father. That could be Plan B. The thought excites Smith. He realizes he needs to stay focused on Plan A for now though. He'll do away with the clone and the people who have made it. Then he'll find a way to take the boy from the parents. He is certain God will want this.

Smith mentally takes inventory of the stash of items packed in the truck. He has Eastman's key card. *I'll bet the farm that this is the key that will give me access to the LAB. It will not only get me inside the building, but also access to the room where the clone is.*

Smith anticipates that such a coveted entity, as a clone, would be kept under lock and key. It will also be kept under constant surveillance. He will have to be careful. He wants to make certain he destroys it. That is the most important part of his mission. He must destroy this abomination. Smith thinks that if he happens to kill some of the monster-makers along with the clone, even better. He knows the bomb he will place will cause significant damage and start a fire. Mass destruction should be achieved rapidly.

Smith retrieves his gun from under his seat and tucks it into the belt of his pants. He is able to hide it nicely under the white lab coat he is wearing. It amazes Smith how far you can get wearing a white lab coat like the one he has picked up at a medical supply store near where his friend who had made the bomb lives. If you look and act with authority, then you aren't often stopped and questioned. If for some reason this doesn't work he will grab one of the key players at the LAB and force him to open the door to the clone. He'll place and activate the bomb in a closet or cupboard. This way, it will go unnoticed. He reminds himself that he will have exactly fifteen minutes to get in and out before it explodes.

He is jolted from his thoughts by a knock on the passenger side window. He sees his friend, the bomb maker, holding a small box. Smith smiles at his friend. He leans across the seats and opens the passenger side door. His friend is a stout man with gray hair who still wears his old army jacket. His friend climbs up into the cab of the truck and closes the door. He sets the box on the seat next to Smith.

"It works just like I told you," the bomb maker informs.

Smith nods. He can hardly contain his excitement and the adrenalin rush that is coursing through his veins.

"So, you got any questions?"

"No," Smith replies and hands his friend the envelope filled with cash.

He clasps his friends shoulder. "It's good to see you again."

"Godspeed," his friend says, stashing his payment inside his jacket and nervously climbs back out of the cab. He scans the area for cops and seeing none starts walking towards his own car.

Smith places the bomb in his briefcase. Even though he is certain he will go unnoticed wearing a lab coat, ID tags, and carrying a brief case, carrying an extra package is likely to draw attention. As he starts the engine to his truck he realizes that moving past the guard's desk will take a little finessing, but if luck is on his side, and he hopes it is, the guard will leave his post after Smith calls him to say that there is a suspicious package at the back delivery area. He almost forgot about them until he started the car engine and a couple of them start to meow. Smith had gone to pick up some Crown Royal when he saw the kid with the box. He will place the box with the kittens he had picked up earlier at the grocery store at the LAB's back door. This should keep the guard off balance for a few minutes as he makes his way inside the building.

He had gotten the little flea-ridden fuzz balls from a kid outside the grocery store near the Starbucks. It was a score. He needed something nonthreatening to leave outside of the LAB. If they are nervous at all, then the guards and people at the LAB might be disarmed by the arrival of kittens. I mean, who didn't love kittens and puppies? Smith anticipates that the guard will go outside thinking that he might be on the verge of discovering something like a bomb, and lo and behold, he would find a box of meek little mewing kitties. They were too young to crawl out of the box, but too old to be bottle-fed. Smith had placed a saucer of water and some wet canned kitten food inside. *Even kittens deserved a last meal*, he thinks. As Smith puts the truck in reverse and looks out the back window his gaze drops to the box of kittens. A tenacious little orange one with his eyes at half-mast has stood up and walked over to the food. Smith watches him eat, licking at the food with his tiny pink tongue. He feels a bit guilty when he realizes that this little guy will have to burn with the rest of the facility and people inside. This guy seems to have spunk. Something Smith appreciates.

New York, New York
Sunday Morning

It is after midnight when Anderson sees Kathryn's number came up on his cell. "Thanks for calling me back," he tells her.

"Of course."

"Is everything okay with the blastocyst? Are we all set for the procedure?"

"Yes, Alan, everything is fine," Kathryn replies.

"Have you heard from James?"

"I got a text message telling me that we are all to meet at the LAB at seven a.m. tomorrow morning, which of course is now today. Do you know why James moved it up? I tried texting him—asking him—but he didn't reply."

"I'm not sure. Somehow it doesn't seem right."

"Well, maybe he has a compelling reason to move up the procedure. Why didn't he come back with you?"

"He was meeting with Dr. Takabe. He said he'd be on the next flight if he missed the one with me," Anderson explains as he raised his arm to hail a cab.

"Well, he should be arriving in an hour or so, right?"

"If he made the flight."

"Why wouldn't he? What's going on, Alan?"

"I'm not sure. Do you know if Zorvelli got a text to meet at seven too?"

"The last time I saw him was around nine p.m. He said he was going home to get some sleep and that I should too."

"We need to get in contact with him."

"It's kind of late. I don't want to wake him especially if we're all meeting so early."

"Wake him up. We need to figure this out. Let's keep trying James too."

"Do you think something happened to him?" Kathryn asks with hesitancy and fear in her voice and asks, "Should we call the police?"

"No, no. It's way too soon for anything like that. Besides, everything is most likely okay."

"I sure hope you're right."

"Let's talk to Zorvelli. If James is on the later flight, he should be landing in an hour. Let's wait and see if he responds to our message then."

"I don't think you'd be asking me all of this if you didn't think something was amiss."

Anderson silently agrees. "I'll call you if I hear anything. You do the same." Anderson presses "end call" just as the cab pulls to the curb.

Westchester, New York
Sunday Morning

Charlie Baylor isn't the nervous type. He finds working as a guard to his liking. He is laid back and enjoys the quiet of the night shift, even though it can be a bit boring. He isn't allowed to be distracted. No radio, iPod, playing on his phone, watching television, or napping. He was told to remain vigilant and alert. Not that this was so different from the way things were normally - but he knew something more was up. Eastman was adamant about no sleeping on the job. The best that he could do for a nap was to spend time lost in his thoughts. Sometimes he'd take notes. He has an idea that one day he'll write a television series or a novel. He isn't as interested in what type of work is being done at the LAB as he is in the people who work there. This last week had been intern season when young graduate students study with the more seasoned scientists. Charlie likes the interns. The majority of them make the most of their time there by staying late in order to accommodate their daytime class schedules. It makes it a lot less lonely for him at night. In fact, there is a variety of activity around the LAB now since the clone happened. What did the white coats refer to it as? A blastocyst! Charlie didn't really understand it. He knows that it is a big deal though. He also knows that something really important and life changing is happening because of it. Dr. Eastman called only a few minutes ago and explained that there might be something going on that needs his vigilant attention. He hadn't explained what that might be though. He warns Charlie to be on the alert for anything out of the ordinary. Then he has asked him to look up Dr. Zorvelli's and Dr.

MacMurray's phone numbers. That was strange. Why didn't he have them in his cell phone? Charlie didn't ask questions. He just did what he is told.

The warning Dr. Eastman has given Charlie makes him a little jumpy. He watches the door and doesn't leave his post. He calls the other night guard, Burke, on his cell and relays the warning from Dr. Eastman. Burke passes along the information to the guard stationed outside the room where the blastocyst is kept. The guard looking after the blastocyst is an older, seasoned guy, who has worked as a cop for many years. The hairs on the back of his neck stand up as he's informed of the higher alert

Charlie Baylor feels good about having informed the rest of the security team. He was used to taking orders but liked giving them even better. He had served as a Marine, but after being discharged, he hadn't been sure what he wanted to do. The job at the LAB suited him. It was quiet at night, and he preferred this to any loud ruckus. Dr. Eastman had requested that he take over Burke's duties at the front desk and Burke be moved to his position in the back. Charlie considered this an indication in increased confidence of him, as it put him on the first line of attack. He was licensed to carry a gun. Eastman requested that he have it on him at all times now. There were cameras throughout the building and cameras focusing on the outside of the building. Key cards had to be used to gain access to almost every room in the building and to the building itself. Identification tags were also worn. It was locked down pretty tight. Still, Charlie Baylor has an uneasy feeling. It was the kind of gut alarm bell he had experienced when he was on active duty.

He looks up at the camera monitors and sees something unusual. It is a guy in a pullover, wearing a baseball cap and jeans, carrying a medium-sized cardboard box. He was setting a box down by the back door of the building.

Charlie calls Burke on his handheld radio. Burke tells him he will check it out. When Charlie looks back at the monitor, he notices that the guy dropping off the box was now out of sight.

He calls Burke back.

"Don't touch the box," he warns Burke.

"Then how will I know what's in it?"

"Just look around it, see if you can see inside it or hear anything without touching it."

"Got it," Burke says.

Just then, Dr. Zorvelli enters through the front door with a few interns.

Zorvelli gives a nod to Charlie. "We have a seven a.m. meeting with Dr. Eastman. Has he arrived?"

"No sir, I haven't seen him yet."

Charlie is just about to ask one of the interns to check in at the desk because he hasn't seen him before. He also looks a bit too old to be interning. However, the slender man in the white lab coat carrying a briefcase flashes his badge along with the others and appears as if he is familiar with the routine. Charlie guesses that this is someone who was reinventing himself, as his instructor at the junior college had said when talking about people having more than one career. Before he can ask the intern for a closer look at his badge, Charlie is distracted by Burke radioing him. "Hey, I got something here," he says as Charlie's adrenalin shoots through the roof.

"What is it?" Charlie asks excitedly as the interns follow Dr. Zorvelli down the hall.

"It's pretty dangerous all right," Burke says flatly.

"Is it a bomb?" Charlie asks, as beads of sweat brake out on his forehead.

"Don't call the bomb squad. Call Animal Control. We've got half a dozen kittens," Burke says with a laugh.

"Kittens?" Baylor asks confused.

"Yeah, kittens. I guess the jerk that dropped them off thought we were the Humane Society."

"What're you going to do with them?"

"Bring them inside. Maybe one of these docs who have been summoned here this morning will know what do for them.

"Hey, try checking with Dr. Anderson. He's a veterinarian," Baylor suggests.

Westchester, New York
Same Day.

Kathryn is running late. She glances at her phone and sees it's 6:58 a.m. She brings Doogie along in the car. She didn't want to leave him home alone and besides it feels better taking him along. He is almost as good as having a bodyguard. Most people are a bit apprehensive when they first met him due to his enormous size. Kathryn is almost to the LAB. Doogie is lying in the backseat of her Prius. Head touching one door and tail the other on the opposite side of the care. She doesn't like having to park on the street down the road from the LAB. There is a large parking lot adjacent to the building. However, they had started locking it and using a guard ever since people who didn't work there had started parking in it. It was fine during regular working hours, but when they needed to come in early or stay late, she and the others had to park on the street. The LAB couldn't afford to pay for a guard to patrol the parking lot around the clock, and it was impossible to have the staff open and close it as they went in and out.

Kathryn and Doogie were now less than half a block from the LAB. Kathryn didn't know if she is irritated about having to walk a bit of distance or upset that she has to come in so early, or worried after not hearing from Eastman or Anderson. She decides it's the later. Why hadn't she heard anything? She knows in her gut that something is terribly wrong. Something bad might have already happened to James. Ever since that crazy lunatic held a gun to his head and threatened him, she has been worried for his safety. She glances at her watch. It is close to seven. She wishes with all her heart that when she walks into the conference room she sees him sitting at the table. As she looks for a place to park she looks around for James' car. She doesn't see it parked on the street. She pulls her car parallel with the sidewalk in a small open space and puts it into park. Turning off the car engine, Doogie pops up and sticks his head between the two front seats. "We're hear boy," Kathryn tells him as she opens her door. Doogie excitedly jumps into the passenger seat and exits the car right after Kathryn. "You're too big to go climbing around the car," Kathryn admonishes Doogie as she locks the car door. Grabbing Doogie's leash, Katheryn is distracted by the ringing of her phone in her coat pocket. She fishes it out. It is a number she doesn't recognize. Before she can say hello she hears James' voice, "Kathryn?"

"James?" Kathryn's heart leaps into her throat and relief washes over her. "Anderson and I have been trying to get a hold of you! Where are you? Are you all right?"

The rapid-fire questions are mind numbing for Eastman.

"Listen carefully, Kathryn I think you and the rest of the team may be in danger. The police have been dispatched to the LAB."

"Danger?" Kathryn asks in alarm as adrenalin shot through her body. "Where are you?"

"I'm in Boston. I don't have time to go into all of this. I'm trying to contact as many team members as I can. I think that guy who held a gun to my head has my cell phone. Did you get a call or text from it?"

"We all got a text from you - or the guy. You called a seven a.m. meeting at the LAB. We thought this was strange because originally we were going to start at ten."

Eastman feels his blood pressure plummet. He felt a tightness seize his chest. Fear clutches him. He feels an overwhelming responsibility for the safety and well-being of his staff, the Gaynors and the clone. Good God, the clone and Kathryn.

"Kathryn, where are you?"

"I'm on my way into the building. Anderson is on his way too, or maybe he's already there. I don't know. He thought something wasn't right when you didn't show up at the airport. He's been trying to find you."

"Listen to me," Eastman says urgently. "Don't go inside that building. Get away from there. Call everyone and tell them not to come to the meeting. Tell them to evacuate the LAB."

Suddenly, Eastman hears what sounds like a deafening explosion in the background. The call connection ends.

"Kathryn!" Kathryn!" Eastman futilely shouts into the phone.

Westchester, New York.

Joe Smith sprints the few minutes distance from the LAB to where his truck is parked. He isn't sure he will get out alive. It's 7 a.m. now. . He has been careful. He has shed the white coat brief case and the gun inside the building. He knows the building will explode any minute now and all evidence will be destroyed.

Smith had left a letter to his now estranged wife inside his truck just in case he doesn't make it back. It explains why he had done what he had done. He wants her and the rest of the world to know that he will have died a hero. Thankfully, this isn't the case. He's out of breath as he opens the door to his truck and climbs safely back inside the cab. He retrieves the letter from the glove box as he concentrates on catching his breath. His hands are shaking as he lights a match and burns the letter. He lets the ashes fall to the rubber floor mats. Destroying all evidence in case he is pulled over was vital to his freedom. Someday he will tell Gwen everything when she decides to talk to him. He knows that God is proud of him. He wants Gwen to be proud too. He thinks of all of this as he hears the explosion. Time to open the Crown Royal,

How soon would Eastman be hearing the news? Smith smiles and wonders. He uncaps the bottle of Crown Royal he had been saving. He takes a healthy slug of it to steady his nerves. He also toasts the heavens. Smith knows that the people he has just blown up are going to hell. As the amber liquid warms and calms him he thinks back on all that's transpired.

Finding where the clone was kept had taken a little more doing than getting into the building. He had wanted to remain in the shadows, not talking to anyone so he had to be careful to listen. He learned where the clone was kept when he overheard two interns discussing it.

He opened the door and saw the guard. He had been expecting as much. He fingered the safety on the gun in his lab coat pocket.

The guard opened his mouth, possibly to ask him who the hell he was, and that's when Smith shot him. The silencer worked great. Hardly a sound except for the thud the guard's body made when it fell against the door and then onto the ground.

Blood spilled out of the guards head and then his mouth as Smith stepped over him. Smith noticed that his name tag read "Burke."

The door was locked. Smith used Eastman's key card for the first time. He had come in with Dr. Zorvelli and the others, so there had been no need before to try it out.

He wasn't surprised, but perhaps a bit relieved, when it opened the door. He was safely inside the tiny room and he looked around, unsure where the monster would be kept. There were containers with lights and something that looked like a tiny portable refrigerator. *Could it be kept in there?* Smith wondered as he searched the room. Well, he didn't need to see the damn thing. He knew it was in there, somewhere, and that was good enough. He thought it must be bigger though - perhaps the size of the boy.

Smith took the bomb from his brief case and set it carefully on the counter. He had to act fast before anyone saw the guard on the floor.

Smith activated the bomb, allowing himself no more than six minutes to get from the building to the car. He had timed it as best he could.

He left the room and exited the LAB through the back door where the kittens had been placed. For a brief second he felt bad about having to sacrifice them. However, they were dying for a higher purpose. *They'd go to heaven too*, he thinks as he caps the Crown Royal and starts his truck.

Washington, D.C.
Saturday, Night Before

Elliot rubs his face vigorously with his hands as he sits at the desk inside their Four Seasons Hotel room. He is checking his email on his laptop as Susan stands behind him, peering over his shoulder. Noah is still napping on one of the double beds. Elliot reads an email an associate has sent him. "I thought you should know that someone has created a Facebook page for Noah." Elliot clicks on the link embedded in the email. "Noah the First Human Clone." It has one hundred thousand likes! Elliot's face and neck turn the color of beet juice. Susan clutches the back of Elliot's chair digging her nails into the leather. "Are you kidding me?" she says angrily.

"How could someone use our son to create such a horrible page in a huge public forum? This makes me think of parents of bullied children on Facebook," Susan says.

"Look, Susan, this has gotten so far out of hand I don't even know how to pull us back into a normal life. It's like we've turned Noah and our family into some kind of freak show."

"People can think whatever they want, but they're not faced with keeping their child alive. How easy it is to condemn and ridicule us when nothing is at stake for these people." Susan cries.

Elliot turns away from the computer and looks up toward Susan. His eyes meet hers. He notices that her mascara is smeared under her eyes. It reminds Elliot of his high school football days. *They've been drafted into a game in which they had to tackle tough issues, make difficult decisions, and play defense to protect their son. They ventured out to find a cure for their son and in the process they had to contend with a firestorm of political, ethical, religious, and moral issues. It has been the two of them against the world. However, it was now the world against the three of them. Realistically, how long could they live in this kind of pressure cooker? What kind of life will it be for Noah?*

"This page makes us sound like desperate people who will go to any lengths to save our child," Susan says tapping her forefinger against the computer screen for emphasis.

"We are. That much is true." Elliot takes the box of tissues from the desk, and hands a couple to Susan.

"When is enough, enough? When do we say stop, Susan?"

"When we find a cure for Noah!" Susan shouts as she blows her nose into the tissue.

"I don't think that's ever going to happen in his lifetime."

"Don't ask me to give up on our son, Elliot. Ever!"

"I'm not giving up on him. I just want him to have a normal life while he's still with us."

"The normal life ended when we discovered Noah had ALD. Everything changed. It's easy to forget as long as Noah is asymptomatic. However, it's in there. It's in his DNA just waiting to be expressed."

Noah stirs in his sleep.

Elliot places a hand gently on Susan's arm. "I'm sorry. I truly am. All of this publicity is forcing us to go into hiding. I hate it. I don't even know how I will care for you and Noah. I'd do anything for Noah, but I didn't sign up for all of this. Do you understand?"

"We don't always get to choose how we want things to go. No one is forcing you to stay, Elliot. You can go. Remember, though, Noah doesn't have that luxury."

Elliot jumps up angrily and accidentally knocks over the chair he's been sitting in. It falls back onto the floor with a thud.

"For Christ's sake, Susan, I'm not telling you that I'm leaving you and Noah. I'm just telling you that I don't want all of this other bullshit that's happening to us. I can't wrap my brain around it all!" Noah is startled awake, sits up, and rubs his eyes with his little fists.

Susan hurries over to Noah and scoops him up into her arms. She is shaking. Holding Noah gives her as much, if not more, comfort as he receives from her. This is a new side to Elliot, Susan realizes. He rarely raises his voice to her. Susan sits down on the edge of the bed and holds Noah in her lap. She drops her head down onto his and snuggles her toddler.

There is a loud knock at the door. Elliot opens it and finds Will Rubin on the other side.

"I heard commotion from next door, is everything okay?" Rubin inquires.

"Yeah, just peachy," Elliot hastily replies grabbing his jacket and quickly brushing past Rubin as he walks out.

Rubin moves inside the room and walks over to Susan and Noah.

"Can I get you anything?" he tenderly asks Susan seeing her tears.

Susan looks up at him. She smiles through tear-filled eyes. "Sorry, Will. It's been a long, hard day."

Noah reaches up to his mom's face. "Mommy, hungry," he says.

"Okay honey. I'll get you something to eat," Susan replies and nuzzled her face into his neck. Noah let out a giggle.

"Are you hungry too?" Will inquires.

"I think we could all use something to eat."

"The room service menu is on the desk," Susan says, and she puts Noah down on the bed and he takes it as an invitation to bounce.

"I don't feel like going out looking like this," Susan replies.

"I think it's better if we keep a low profile."

She hopes Elliot would return soon.

"Will, I'm thinking we should skip viewing the procedure and head back home."

"Fine by me. How do you think Elliot will feel about it?"

"Relieved. This has been too much stress on us all. There's no real reason to be there. I'm certain Dr. Eastman will call us as soon as he knows anything."

Westchester, New York
Sunday Morning

At 7:05 a.m. according to the big clock on the bank across the street, the blast knocks Kathryn and Doogie back by a good five feet. Kathryn hits her head on the asphalt and loses consciousness. Doogie scrambles to his feet and was by Kathryn's side within seconds. He licks her face, whimpers, licks her face again, and then bites into her coat. He drags her by her coat back away from what is a burning building. He drags her body at least 200 feet back to the car. He sits down next to her, panting and whimpering, and licking her face.

A NYPD cop and his partner, responding to the explosion, pull up alongside Doogie and Kathryn. The older cop driving the car, a seasoned officer, tells his younger, female partner to call for an ambulance as he exits his vehicle and walks quickly around the front to the woman and dog. He carefully approaches the dog. He doesn't want to frighten the dog guarding the woman. He bends slightly at the waist and extends his hand in a friendly gesture. He smiles, displaying a set of white teeth that seem to stretch back to the salt and pepper curls that spring out from beneath his hat. The dog gives a low warning growl.

"Good dog," the cop says in a gentle and reassuring voice. "You are such a good dog!" he praises Doogie. "I just want to help your guardian," he explains, placing his hands palms up in front of the dog.

Doogie recognizes the friendly gesture and wags his tail.

The cop checks the pulse in Kathryn's neck. "She's alive," he shouts over his shoulder to his approaching partner.

"Good. Ambulance in-route, Harry," she informs him.

"Get a blanket from the car," Harry instructs his partner.

"Sure thing."

Harry checks Doogie's collar and notes that it says he belongs to Kathryn McMurray. He is happy to have her name.

"Kathryn McMurray, hang on. Help is on the way," he tells her despite the fact that she cannot hear him.

Boston, Massachusetts
Sunday Morning

Even though Eastman is receiving excellent care, he wants to get the hell out of Massachusetts General Hospital and find Kathryn. He tried calling her back at 7:10 a.m., but her phone went to voicemail. Had he heard an explosion? His mind is reeling. He feels caught between two realities. He is basically stuck hundreds of miles away in a hospital room with an incapacitating head injury and the overwhelming angst he feels in his desire to be with Kathryn. He wants to run all the way to New York to protect her. *Please let her be safe*, he murmurs as the phone in his room rings. Eastman picks up before it rings again.

"Kathryn!"

"No, it's Anderson. I got your message, but I didn't recognize the number. Where the hell are you?"

I'm at Massachusetts General."

"What happened?"

"There's no time to explain. Where are you?"

"I'm on my way to the LAB for the extremely early meeting you called. What the hell is going on?"

Eastman's blood runs cold. *God, please don't let anything happen to Kathryn*, Eastman silently prays but knows in his heart of hearts that something terrible just did. They had been set up. The crazy lunatic who called himself Joseph wanted them all at the LAB at the same time. Something was going down.

"Listen to me. I need you to get ahold of Kathryn. She was walking toward the LAB when I heard an explosion and her phone died," Eastman says and his voice catches in his throat. He swallows the lump that has formed and continues, "Call the police and tell them to get to the LAB. Call everyone you can think of and tell them I didn't call a meeting this morning. Call Will Rubin. Please tell me his number is still in your phone." Eastman is talking a mile a minute, terrified of what might happen.

"I've got it. But who do you want me to call first?"

"Kathryn! Then the police. Shit, just call them all. I believe that guy who wants to kill me has my cell phone! Hurry and when you talk to Will, tell him not to come anywhere near the LAB. Tell him to move the Gaynors to a safe location. But before you do any of it, try Kathryn. Hurry, Alan, please hurry," Eastman pleads and what is left unsaid is *please don't let her be dead*

Eastman looks up to see a nurse enter the room with two formidable-looking strangers.

"I'm on it," Anderson says and clicks off.

A big man in black jeans, a gray T-shirt, and cowboy boots, accompanied by a woman in black jeans and a white turtleneck sweater, also wearing boots, flashes an ID and enters the room.

"Who are you?"

"FBI," says the woman in the turtleneck. "We need to talk to you, Dr. Eastman."

Westchester, New York
Sunday Morning

By 7:15 a.m. Zorvelli was swearing under his breath. He is about ten miles away from the LAB when he drives up to the first veterinary office he can find. It is closed. Nothing, not even the Humane Society, wherever the fuck that was, was open this time of the morning. He is pissed because he is missing the meeting. His time was more important than dealing with kittens. Anderson was the fucking veterinarian. This should be his errand. Why couldn't they just have left the kittens in another room while they had the meeting? He didn't think they could have fleas that would infect the entire lab this young. It was that new intern, the one who says her dad was a vet. She might have had a point. They were very careful not to introduce anything that might contaminate the lab. Why the hell had the guard decided to bring them in? And when Zorvelli suggested that they just put them back outside, that little intern acted like he was suggesting they be put to death.

He must have had his own soft spot, though, not to have pulled seniority and told her to take them out of there. She is from Iowa State and barely knows her way around New York. No, like the patriarchal figure of the LAB he has become, Zorvelli decides to take the damn little mewing things and get some help. In all honesty, he was hooked the minute he laid eyes on them. He didn't know anything about kittens, but someone had guessed their age to be between three and four weeks. They wouldn't survive long without some medical attention. There were two gray ones, a black and white, a calico, and a striped orange one. All were lying curled tightly into a ball. The orange one, however, actually stood up, stretched, opened his eyes, and licked Zorvelli's finger. It was amazing. He could fit the little guy in the palm of his hand. If he found somewhere to take them, he'd tell them he wanted to keep the orange one. *This kitten had moxie, spunk—he is a fighter,* Zorvelli thinks. Aren't there emergency veterinary hospitals that were open all night?

Then he remembers one that is near the eye doctor he occasionally uses. He turns the car around to a chorus of plaintive mews. How could such tiny things make so much noise? He guesses they must be really hungry. They didn't seem to be able to eat the canned cat food left in the box. They most likely need bottles.

"Pipe down. I'm taking you to get some food," Zorvelli says to the kittens as his own stomach grumbles. He could use some breakfast. Maybe he'd be a really nice guy and stop and get some donuts for the LAB and a double espresso for himself when he finishes with this fools' errand. This is his day for good deeds. He just hopes that Eastman isn't pissed that he has left for such a reason. Anyway, he wonders for the eleventh time why Eastman would call such an early meeting after he and Anderson had been in Boston the night before? The meeting had originally been scheduled for ten a.m. Why would he change it to be so early? When Zorvelli called Anderson, he had seemed just as confused. He mentioned that Eastman hadn't shown for his flight. Something was off. He didn't know what, but he halfway felt that there really was no seven a.m. meeting, even though the text had come from Eastman's cell phone number. Even if there was, he and Eastman weren't on the same page. Zorvelli didn't always share Eastman's feelings when Eastman considered something to be urgent. Zorvelli felt that they could wait on some things—like choosing to publish the fact that they had cloned the first human. It was provocative and had caused a lot of backlash and blowback.

He rubbed his pinky finger down the little orange guys back. Oh, who was he kidding? He had no time for pets. He barely had time to shower and shave these days with all of the work at the LAB and the stem cells from the clone being ready to harvest.

Boston, Massachusetts
Sunday Morning

"I'm Mark Grimswald and this is Fran Delano," the agent says to Eastman. "We're here to ask you some questions."

Eastman is hooked back up to IVs and monitors in his hospital room. He needs to get the agents to dispatch law enforcement to the LAB, to Kathryn, to everything that is precious to him Twenty minutes have gone by since he last tried calling Kathryn. It's now 7:30 a.m. Since he couldn't untether himself from the bed and run all the way to New York, he knows that his best chance was to let the FBI do it for him. He takes a deep breath, steadies his nerves, beats down the panic, and says with all of the authority he can muster, "I believe that we have a matter of urgency to contend with. I'm afraid that my friends, my colleagues, and a young boy and his family, are all in grave danger."

Delano moves closer to Eastman's bed. "We know who you are and what you're doing. We also know a bit about what happened in Faneuil Hall today. Work with us. Just slow down and start with how you ended up here and why you believe these people are in danger," Delano says shooting a concerned glance at Grimswald.

Eastman is visibly upset that he needs to waste precious time telling him the entire story. However, he also realizes that they will be more likely to quickly provide aide and support if he cooperates. He tells them about his conversation with Dr. MacMurray and the explosion he heard just before the phone went dead. He sent up a silent prayer that they would begin taking the proper action before it was too late. *Please don't let it be too late*, he prays. "Listen to me. You have to call whoever can put a stop to this madness to get to the LAB right now!"

Westchester, New York

The turmoil, grief and loss of the past two days are reflected in the rain storms that are currently pounding the East Coast.

The destruction from the bomb had been massive and total. Eleven people had died: the three security guards, five scientists, two students, and one firefighter. Noah's clone had been destroyed as well. The explosion and the ensuing fire had destroyed life and property both inside and outside of the LAB - perhaps the reliance of the human spirit or hope. It had left Eastman changed. He left Massachusetts General Hospital and traveled by plane the day after the end (as he began to refer to the loss). He felt that somehow he could have, should have done something more that would have prevented this tragedy.

He felt a deep sense of personal responsibility that never stops rankling inside his soul. Eastman feels as if he has failed so many people who depended on him, the men and women who were injured and who died, all of the research they were about to embark, along with the Gaynors' hope for their son. All of the time and energy they had put into trying to save their son's life, destroyed by one man's personal agenda. At least the police believed that the killer had been working alone. Why hadn't Eastman stopped him in Faneuil Hall when he had had the chance? None of this would have happened had he been able to do something then. The deaths of the guards, the young students, members of his team, the pain their families will continue to endure. Eastman didn't think he could feel lower. Yes, he could. He could if Kathryn had died too. For this much he was thankful. Could she, would she, ever forgive him?

The bombing of the building coincided with the passage of the Respect Human Life Act. It made all cloning unlawful by order of the federal government.

For the first time in a long time, Eastman feels totally powerless and utterly defeated. He was also frustrated and disheartened. He felt robbed of his chance to help millions of people. That was the big picture. The small picture focused on one little boy, Noah Gaynor, whose chance at a long life had been destroyed. Eastman didn't know what to do with all of these feelings. He felt he owed something to the families of those who had died. He also felt responsible for the members of the team who were still alive, and who were looking to him for direction, as well as to Noah and his family. Most of all he felt terrible about what happened to Kathryn.

Westchester, New York

It was Wednesday morning when Kathryn opens her eyes in her room at Westchester Medical Center. Eastman strokes the back of her hand as she lay in her hospital bed. She looks up at him with her beautiful green eyes framed by the thick auburn hair that fanned around her face on her white pillow. "How's my boy?"

"You mean me or Doogie?" Eastman smiles with tears in his eyes.

Kathryn returns his smile and is deeply touched by his tears. "Come on now. I'm a little beat, up but I'm going to be as good as new."

"I'm so sorry, Kathryn, for everything."

Kathryn attempts to sit up. "They told me that Doogie is okay - that's right?"

"He's totally fine. He's been given a daily diet of steak and lots of attention. Anderson is taking care of him. I'm looking forward to taking care of the two of you just as soon as they spring you if you can ever forgive me."

"Ever forgive you?"

"Yes. I'm so very sorry for everything, Kathryn."

"I'm fine. I just want to go home," Kathryn remarks and then more thoughtfully inquires," What do you have to be sorry for?"

"Everything."

"You didn't do this. It was that madman Joseph. At least that's what the police told me. How's Zorvelli? Is he okay?"

"He wasn't anywhere near the LAB when it blew."

"Is there anything left of the LAB of our work?"

"It's gone."

"Gone?"

Eastman swallows hard. Tears well up in his eyes. "It blew up. We, um, we lost several team members and others who worked there."

Kathryn leans back into her pillow and turns her face toward the window. She is silent for what seems to Eastman an eternity. He wishes he didn't have to tell her this on top of everything else.

"Was it really the guy who calls himself Joseph? The one who wanted to kill us?" she asks turning her face back to his.

"We don't know for certain, but the police and FBI believe that he's the one and that he acted alone. However, there is nothing left of the LAB and no one who can testify to the fact that he was even there," Eastman says.

"You're still in danger, then."

"We all are to some extent. The FBI is investigating and protecting all of us. There are two agents outside your door who want to talk to you soon."

"And the Gaynors, Noah?"

"The FBI and Will Rubin are protecting them. They've gone into hiding."

Kathryn is quiet as she processes what Eastman has just told her. Eastman is surprised by her outburst that happens next.

"Screw him! That asshole! And everyone else who doesn't believe in our work! You aren't going to let our team members die in vain, are you? You aren't going to allow that little boy and millions of others who are suffering to be stopped by an ignorant government and a murderer?"

Kathryn's words resonate with him much as if she's slaps him across the face. He realizes she isn't going to tolerate his feelings of deep sadness and guilt.

"Shhh. Just rest."

"Not until you promise, and I mean *promise* me, that you will do everything in your power to find another place for us to begin again. I won't accept anything less from you. I know you. I know you feel bad. I do too. This isn't your fault. None of it is. You need to stop looking as if you need to apologize to everyone."

"Kathryn, my concern right now is for you and your health."

"We got an ass kicking. But I'm not going to lie here and let them win. We are right. What we are doing is right. We have a responsibility to continue to pursue this. I think we owe it to the members of our team who have given their lives to this cause."

Kathryn doesn't unlock her eyes from his. Eastman thinks about her words, but he doesn't share her passion. He is too sad and too pummeled. "It's too soon, Kathryn."

"Do you believe in me?" Kathryn asks as she furrows her brow.

"Of course I do."

"I believe in you. But the greater question is, do you still believe in our work, in what we do?"

"Yes. But, Kathryn this is a nightmare."

Hearing the rain pelt the glass, Eastman glances over to the window. Sheets of water roll down the window again and again. He can relate inside to what he is seeing outside. "It's like I'm drowning inside. It's like everything has been washed away and I have no idea where to go from here."

"We've had a setback."

"More like a beating, Kathryn."

"But it isn't over. Science doesn't stop. Progress doesn't stop just because there are brick walls and roadblocks. Do it for Noah. Build us an Ark, James. Take us in a new direction. We can rise above all of these troubled waters and eventually succeed. I have every, every faith in you."

Kathryn's words reverberate in Eastman's head and most importantly in his heart. He realizes that what he feels for her is reciprocated tenfold. He feels he doesn't deserve it, but at the same time he embraces it, and it makes him feel stronger. But feeling stronger is a far cry from getting up and rebuilding.

"Brick walls and roadblocks? Seriously? We were blown up, Kathryn. People died. The clone died. Our own government doesn't want us pursuing this."

"Yes and its awful. You didn't do this. That insane asshole did. Look, things don't stop because of ignorant and crazy people. They stop because people give up. They quit. I'm not a quitter, James. I don't think you are, either, or I wouldn't have fallen in love with you."

Eastman looks deeply into her eyes and gently brushes her hair back from her face. He can't recall the last time a woman had said she's in love with him. He realizes that he is deeply in love with her; more than that, though, they both are deeply committed to their work and maybe that's what binds them so tightly. They share a passion. It is rare to find someone who understands this kind of commitment.

"Talk to what's left the team. If you can find a place for us, somewhere in this world, then let's get back to work," she says softly.

"Kathryn, do you know what you're asking?"

"Yes I do. We don't let evil win. What we're doing is good. It's right. We don't give up."

In the back of his mind, Eastman can hear his old professor saying, "He got Louise Brown with one fertilized egg that day." Kathryn was the fire in the belly that would be the impetus for moving him out of defeat into action. He doesn't know how or when or where, but he won't abandon his life's work because of this. This was a setback - a huge one. What did his mother always remind, "Take setbacks and turn them into opportunities. That's how you succeed." To call this a setback though seemed trite. He would talk to the team, talk to the Gaynors. But first they must all grieve their losses. *A time to be born, a time to die, a time to mourn, a time to cast away sorrow, a time to every purpose under God's heaven.*

Adelaide, Australia
January, the following year

Eastman holds out much hope, for the support of scientific research in regenerative medicine in the immediate future. He hopes that he and his core team will one day return to the United States to pursue their work. For now, he is happy with his decision to take his team with him, uniting forces with the Australian Centre for Therapeutic Cloning Research and the National Australian Stem Cell Foundation.

He believes that the Australian government and people will continue to look favorably on this type of research. At least that's the hope but like the U.S. anything can change politically, legally. Eastman's reminded of the fact that several years earlier, the Australian Government wasn't in support of therapeutic cloning. Eventually that had all changed. Public opinion had changed, and with it, the political attitude toward cloning had changed too. Like wildlife with displaced habits regenerative medicine often had to find receptive locations to pursue its work.

Eastman smiles as he looks over at the framed photo that hangs on the wall next to the big-screen TV in his office. He recalls another big change in his life. He and Kathryn had married in Bora Bora in a traditional native ceremony. Just to make certain it was all legal; they had been married before a judge in Sydney, Australia too.

Living in Australia had taken some time to adjust to, but truthfully, the new lab isn't a whole lot different from the one they had lost in New York. This is where he and Kathryn now spend the majority of their time. Even Doogie seems to have embraced his new life down under, Eastman reflects.

Queensland, Australia

On the beach seashore in Mission Bay, a five-year-old boy brings his mother a purple starfish he has found in a pool of rocks near the water. His mother explores the creature with all of the marvel and wonder she sees in her son's eyes when he runs up to her with it.

"Oh, how lovely. He's beautiful," she says as she gently touches the precious object in her son's small but capable hands. "We should put him back in the water, though, where he'll be happy."

Noah runs off to place his prize back in the tide pool as his father snaps photographs of his son on his digital camera. Elliot had told Susan that he wants to capture every minute of his son's life, afraid that these special times might end sooner rather than later for they are constantly reminded of how all too fragile life is. Both he and Susan know that the time they have with their son is precious. In a way they both view what has happened to their family as a gift. While he would never wish this on anyone, he realizes that they might not have regarded the time they have together in the way they do now.

It is as much a blessing as it is a loss for them both. Susan loves more deeply, and strangely, she fears less. The worst that could happen, in her eyes, has already occurred. Their son is inflicted with an incurable disease. While they both hold out hope for a cure, however remote the chances are, they have learned to live their lives in the moment and are grateful for every second they have together.

Elliot hands Susan the camera. Noah laughs with delight as they wade into the ocean and another wave sends him floating back up onto the sand. Elliot seems to share in the joy as he's laughing too.

Kathryn's billowy white sundress swirls around her tanned legs in the ocean breeze. Her black sunglasses shade her eyes from the bright sun. Her right hand holds her floppy straw hat squarely on her head as she makes her way through the sand towards Susan.

Susan smiles and greets her with a hug.

"You look positively radiant. Marriage agrees with you."

"Thank you, James sends his greetings," Kathryn beams.

Kathryn informs Susan of the progress that they are making at the lab. The blastocyst has developed to the stage where they can harvest the stem cells. After this, they will begin the work that will ultimately lead to a cure for Noah. Susan is excited, but doesn't let her emotions run too high. This is the exact point at which their lives had been taken in a new direction. She hopes that this time they'll be given the opportunity they were robbed of in what seems almost like a lifetime ago. Kathryn and Susan also discuss the fact that President Longran has received a second term. Susan arches an eyebrow and asks, "Do you think that someday the team from the LAB will relocate back to the United States?"

"Maybe. For now, though, things are going really well here," Kathryn says with a twinkle in her eye. "We'd like you and Elliot to be at the procedure when we harvest the stem cells," and then adds, "for luck."

"Thank you. I'll talk to Elliot about it. I think we'd like that." Susan replies as she watches her husband lift their son up high and then set him back down in the foaming water.

"Noah looks amazing, so vibrant and happy. Are you still following the Lorenzo's oil diet?"

"Yes. So far so good. We're hoping that it will continue to prevent the expression of the disease until Dr. Eastman, and all of you, have a cure for him."

Kathryn squeezes Susan's hand in acknowledgment of this dream. The two women have grown close. They share an unspoken and unique bond that developed out their shared commitment to save Noah. Both of these women are working to give Noah a lifetime full of experiences and realized dreams. One of the most precious things of all that remains in their favor is time. Time is still on their side. No one knows when time would run out, but for now they believe it will be long enough to find a cure.

Australian Stem Cell Centre
The Next Day

"Here we have the clone of a little boy who suffers from ALD. We will begin harvesting the stem cells this week and start working on a cure." Eastman is filled with pride as he says this to a reporter who is touring the lab. "How will you cure his disease?" the reporter inquires.

"This will be achieved through therapeutic cloning-as we have achieved here. Also through gene therapy and embryonic stem cell differentiation. All of this will be used to create a custom-tailored cellular therapy for this genetic disorder," Eastman explains.

"And can you do this to treat other diseases?"

"Absolutely," Eastman replies.

Life doesn't always give one second chances, Eastman thinks. He is grateful beyond words. He's counting on one more little miracle due in about six months. Eastman's life is about to change once again. He and Kathryn will soon have the chance to leave a legacy behind in this world that will be even greater than their work. It will be their child. A million hopes and dreams will follow. Eastman's first hope is that the baby will be healthy.

Acknowledgements

A BOOK IS never written alone. There are those who help you craft it, edit it, and those important people that cheer you on getting you to believe you can actually write and complete it. I was blessed to have an abundance of all over the eleven years it took me to finish this manuscript. What began as story based loosely on the true story of a parent's fight to save their child's life evolved into a deeper understanding of the field of therapeutic cloning. There is so much promise in this type of medicine that will one day help so many people who are diagnosed with many different types of disease. The irony of the fact that my own cancer diagnosis arrived at the time this book was to be published is not lost on me.

The scientists who are working in this rapidly advancing and potentially life-saving field are the true heroes who should also be thanked. In researching this manuscript, I researched valuable information from Advanced Cell Technology, Inc., Geron Corporation, L'Alliance Boviteq, and ViaGen. Also mentioned in the book, Cambrian Genomics.

Thank you to the physicians, surgeons, nurses, staff and technicians at Kaiser Permanente who have worked diligently to help me live a longer life. Especially, Dr. John C. Parker, Dr. John Wright, Dr. Nicolaj Andersen, Dr. Ramey Littell, Dr. Laurel Imhoff, Dr. Ryan Hubbard, and RN Dorella Gil. Very special thanks to the nurses at the Kaiser Santa Rosa infusion center. You are all angels. I'm blessed to have such an amazing team.

Editors Extraordinaire
Don Weise
Marsha Calhoun
Arlene Miller

To my readers who read the manuscript, some who tirelessly listened to numerous revisions and provided valuable feedback:

Mark Ross
Barrett Ross
Jeannette Boudreau Esq.
Deborah Antinori

To my friends and family (children - Tyler, Barrett and Savannah) I love and appreciate you all. Especially Debbie Antinori who cheered me on and helped me to believe that I could make it to the finish line despite all of life's challenges thrown my way.

My husband who continues to love, inspire and believe in me despite my insecurities and uncertainty that this diagnosis has brought to our family.

Life doesn't always move in the direction we expect and that's what makes it so interesting, unpredictable, and precious. Being able to have a longer, good quality of life is a gift. I pray for this gift for the millions of people who are struggling with disease and the surgeons, doctors, nurses, medical and mental health professionals who help them to achieve it. While none of us are guaranteed a lifetime - we all hope for one. My cancer diagnosis is not unique. My own diagnosis has made my life more real and fragile, strangely beautiful and definitely worth fighting for. I'm rooting for us all.

About the Author

Author Bio

CHERI BARTON ROSS, M.A, F.T., is author of *Pet Loss and Children: Establishing a Healthy Foundation* (Routledge, 2005), *Pet Loss and Human Emotion, Second Edition, A Guide to Recovery* (Routledge 2007). She is also an adjunct psychology professor at Santa Rosa Junior College, Santa Rosa, CA, a journalist, editor, and playwright, and founder of the Redwood Empire Veterinary Medical Association Pet Loss Support Group. This is her first fictional novel. She lives in Sonoma County, CA with her husband, children and pets.

Made in the USA
Coppell, TX
10 February 2020